Personality Devel
with Mental Reta

*Personality Developme
culmination of more tha
mental retardation. As a
Zigler emphasizes the ir
understanding the beha
gues that personality, e
influential in the perfor
nonretarded individuals

In addition to summ
mental retardation, *Per
Retardation* integrates tl
the relationship betwe
mance. Empirical work
sionals involved in ide
tarded individuals intc
research with their app
*with Mental Retardatic
mental retardation.

Edward Zigler is Ster
where he is also Direc
Social Policy. He is Hc
Center. Professor Zigle
(with R. M. Hodapp) a
tion and Development
Families and Governn
Kagan and N. W. Hall).

Dianne Bennett-Gates lectures on the Psychology of Special Needs Individuals at Cardiff University, Wales.

Personality Development in Individuals with Mental Retardation

Edited by

Edward Zigler
Yale University

and Dianne Bennett-Gates
Cardiff University

CAMBRIDGE
UNIVERSITY PRESS

PUBLISHED BY THE PRESS SYNDICATE OF THE UNIVERSITY OF CAMBRIDGE
The Pitt Building, Trumpington Street, Cambridge, United Kingdom

CAMBRIDGE UNIVERSITY PRESS
The Edinburgh Building, Cambridge CB2 2RU, UK   www.cup.cam.ac.uk
40 West 20th Street, New York, NY 10011-4211, USA   www.cup.org
10 Stamford Road, Oakleigh, Melbourne 3166, Australia
Ruiz de Alarcón 13, 28014 Madrid, Spain

First published 1999

Printed in the United States of America
Typeface Times Roman 10.5/13   *System* MagnaType™ [AG]

*A catalog record for this book is available from
the British Library.*

Library of Congress Cataloging-in-Publication Data
Personality development in individuals with mental retardation /
edited by Edward Zigler, Dianne Bennett-Gates.
p. cm.
ISBN 0-521-63048-7 (hardcover). – ISBN 0-521-63969-8 (pbk.)
1. Mentally handicapped – Psychology. 2. Personality development.
3. Personality and motivation. I. Zigler, Edward, 1930–   .
II. Bennett-Gates, Dianne.
RC570.2.P47   1999
155.2′5 – dc21   98-46761
                                                         CIP

ISBN 0 521 63048 7 hardback
ISBN 0 521 63963 8 paperback

This book is dedicated to Seymour Sarason,
who saw the humanity in individuals with
mental retardation long before we did.

Contents

Contributors

Dianne Bennett-Gates, Ph.D.
Research Associate
Department of Psychology
Yale University

Jane Bybee, Ph.D.
Department of Psychology
Suffolk University

Donald J. Cohen, M.D.
Irving B. Harris Professor of Child Psychiatry, Pediatrics and Psychology
Director, Yale Child Study Center
Yale University

Elisabeth M. Dykens, Ph.D.
Assistant Professor
Neuropsychiatric Institute
University of California, Los Angeles

Deborah J. Fidler
Graduate School of Education and Information Studies
University of California, Los Angeles

Marion Glick, Ph.D.
Department of Psychology
Yale University

Robert M. Hodapp, Ph.D.
Associate Professor
Graduate School of Education and Information Studies
University of California, Los Angeles

Shulamith Kreitler
Tel Aviv University

Harvey N. Switzky, Ph.D.
Professor
Department of Educational Psychology
Northern Illinois University

John R. Weisz, Ph.D.
Professor of Psychology
Department of Psychology
University of California, Los Angeles

Edward Zigler, Ph.D.
Sterling Professor of Psychology
Director, Yale Bush Center in Child Development and Social Policy
Yale University

Tables

Foreword

Donald J. Cohen

How do boys and girls become the full individuals they are as children, and what shapes the patterns of the personalities they will have as adults? Why do children become outgoing or withdrawn, confident or tentative, exploratory or constrained, hard working or desultory, secure or worried, happy or sad? Why do some feel they can trust their own judgment, while some need to check with others before acting, and then act contrary to what they themselves know? If they are retarded or bright, how does their IQ affect their personality formation?

Professor Edward Zigler has asked these questions with particular reference to children whose lives are influenced by factors that may place them out of the "mainstream." In this book, he and his colleagues focus on the personality development of individuals with mental retardation, but their observations are relevant to all children, and especially those who are at developmental risk. This body of scientific work demonstrates that retarded children are, first and foremost, children, and that their lives can and should be understood within the main framework of developmental psychology.

For almost forty years, Ed Zigler has brought clinical sensitivity and scientific rigor to the study of mental retardation. Like all truly productive and creative investigators, he has been intrigued by a core group of perplexing phenomena to which he has returned over and again with new concepts and methods. Throughout, he has retained the clinician's appreciation for complexity, while forcing himself, his students, and the field to be tough-minded in their research designs, measurement, and analyses.

Zigler's curiosity has proven to be infectious to his devoted graduate students − and their students and several generations of grand-students − and to colleagues who have come in contact with his ideas throughout the world. In literally hundreds of scientific studies, they have explored how children with mental retardation approach intellectual tasks, understand the world, feel about themselves, and relate socially. They have studied how children's experiences at home, school, and in different living situations affect their functioning, and the very complicated ways in which "intelligence" influences competence, performance, and the patterns of functions that constitute personality.

All children and adults try to make sense both of their external worlds and of their inner lives, as best they can. Much of mental life is directed to understanding the life that is being led. Self-reflective activities are memory-making and self-creating. Indeed the need for coherent self-understanding is central to creating a stable self-representation and the continuity of psychological experience. The reflective process starts early in life and ends only when life ends, and it engages the attention of individuals at all levels of intellectual capacity. The sense that individuals with mental retardation can make of their lives – how they may represent themselves and their relations with others – affects their socializing, working, problem solving, and happiness. Their self-understanding is the result of many factors, including their cognitive skills and achievements, and the opportunities to love and to be loved, to belong to a caring family, to feel secure, to reach goals, and to be comforted in times of distress.

The major changes during the past two decades in the educational and living situations of individuals with retardation have vastly altered the types of representations of self and others they are likely to create. Individuals with retardation now have new expectations for themselves and others. As reflected in this book, these advances have led to review and revision of the scientific findings on personality development of individuals with retardation. Their personality development, just like that of any other group of children, reflects not only what they bring into the world but what they find in it.

Research in this area of developmental psychology must confront thorny theoretical issues. Chief among them is what precisely is intelligence, and what is tested by tests of intelligence? Of course, parents know which of their children is really bright, and who is average or somewhat below; teachers can array their students from top to bottom in reading and math; and even in universities we distinguish those colleagues who have achieved a lot on the basis of sweat and hard work from those who with perhaps less effort have earned their professorial distinction with the help of God-given brilliance. We also know that there are bright children who fail in school, and very intelligent adults who do not achieve what was expected of them at the time they graduated as class valedictorians. Between IQ and life, there are uncountable twists of fate.

There are many ways in which these concepts get scientists into trouble. A research industry has developed from translating the intuitive understanding of what it is to be bright or dull to the next steps – specifying precisely what we mean by these terms and relating these concepts to formal tests. How can a batch of verbal, math, puzzle, and picture tasks become the operational definitions of the underlying concept of "Intelligence" or "intelligences," usable across ages, places, and enormous differences in individual experience? The arguments about the meaning and measurement of intelligence are not yet over. Until we know more, there will be continuing debates about fundamental issues, including what sense to make of diagnostic terms such as mental retardation.

One of Zigler's major contributions has been to show that however one understands and measures intelligence, the performance of children is not only a function of how intelligent they are, but also of many other life ingredients. This contribution has been especially important in relation to children with lower levels of intelligence. He has studied, and then has described, the consequences of the tendency to simply lump these children together as "mentally retarded," and then to use this to define their entire range of functioning, as if a life can be reduced to a single number. Unfortunately, such homogenization into a class can become a prophetic determination of opportunities, and thus of outcome.

Zigler has demonstrated that most children with mental retardation progress from one phase of cognitive functioning to the next like other children, and their cognitive apparatus is not structured very differently. They are not developmental "strangers." In fact, they generally think and perform as one would expect, given their level of mental development and their experiences within their families and schools. These ideas, as reviewed in this book, may seem obvious today. Yet, like many scientific ideas whose time has come, they were not always so clear to scientists or policymakers. For many years, Zigler's theoretical and empirical studies on the normal developmental progression of individuals with retardation and on the ways that personality and motivation influence performance were both controversial and easily misunderstood. During this period, some critics contested his ideas of normal phases in developmental progression, while others felt that he downplayed intellectual factors (IQ) and over-emphasized "motivation" as the cause of retardation. And it has taken the concerted work of parents, advocates, and professionals to increasingly translate the basic message of this body of research on motivational factors into individualized, educational, and programmatic opportunities.

Within the academic world, retardation has often been an insular field, separated from the mainlands of developmental psychology, education, pediatrics, and child psychiatry. Thus, researchers and clinicians who study and work with individuals with mental retardation have often been marginalized – as if they were engaged in something apart and "special." One of Zigler's major achievements has been to help bring research on retardation into the broader field of psychology, to show that the concepts of developmental psychology are useful in understanding retardation, and to demonstrate that research from the field of retardation can illuminate issues in psychology. The research in this book is strong evidence of this mutual enrichment.

There are three remarkable contributions from the research program of Ed Zigler and his collaborators to current paradigms in developmental psychology.

- First, the application of the principles of normal development to the study and understanding of individuals with developmental disabilities and disorders has powerfully influenced the emergence of the entire field of developmental psychopathology.
- Second, research on syndromes of mental retardation that are caused by definable organic factors, such as Down syndrome, is at the forefront of research on developmental studies of brain–behavior relations and gene–environment interactions. Today, Fragile X, Prader–Willi, Williams, Angelmans, Smith–Magenis, and hundreds of other genetically defined types of mental retardation provide natural models for unraveling the contributions of genetic endowment to cognitive and personal development. They also provide important clues to understanding the neurobiological and experiential basis for vulnerability to particular forms of psychiatric and behavioral difficulties – such as anxiety disorders, obsessive-compulsive disorder, attentional disorders, communication disorders, and profound disorders of social attachment – in individuals with and without mental retardation.
- Third, the clarification of the long-term consequences of both early experiences and current life situations on cognitive and personality functioning has been a model for studies of life-course and continuities and discontinuities in development.

While this book is in one sense a summary, and will be a locus classicus for an entire field of research, it is also in an important sense a work in progress. The ability to define almost a thousand genetic forms of mental retardation is already shaping the types of studies that can be done and is producing exciting findings. The availability of further genetic research on specific syndromes, as well as on the genetic contributions to the underlying cognitive processes that define intelligence (e.g., attentional mechanisms, cognitive and language processing, perceptual mechanisms, etc.), will allow behavioral and developmental researchers to study gene–environment interactions and individual differences within genetically defined groups. The potential for this research is already visible in this book. There are other methodologies – including studies of genetic epidemiology, neuro-imaging, neuropsychopharmacology, social-cognitive development, and treatment evaluation – that will enrich our understanding of the multiple determinants of children's development, including personality development of children with intellectual abilities across the entire spectrum of IQ. It will be of great interest to see the ways in which some quite fuzzy categories – such as "cultural-familial" retardation – will become disaggregated and reconceptualized with new knowledge. Also, the discovery of multiple genes involved with IQ will clarify Zigler's quite early and highly influential theoretical work on the polygenic nature of IQ and the two types of retardation syndromes. Thus, the broad-gauged research program initiated by Zigler, and now continued by his many students and collaborators, is likely to continue to be a vital tradition within the field of developmental psychology for decades to come.

A review of Zigler's life's work in the scientific study of developmental psychopathology and retardation reveals two other areas to which his work has contributed significantly. First, to a remarkable extent, participation in this research program has shaped the careers of dozens of young scientists; some of them have stayed within this field of research, and others have taken the lessons into other branches of psychology. Second, this research program has not led to dry, academic studies of interest only to other scientists. There are powerful issues of policy that depend on the understanding of the nature of intelligence; the value (and limitations) of categorizing people on the basis of levels of IQ and intelligence; and the various social, personal, cognitive, and personality/motivational factors that influence development from early childhood throughout life. Policymakers turn to authentic research for guidance, and data are among the most powerful instruments in the hands of advocates who are pressing for change. By influencing and defining policy and programs, the findings from this research program have real consequences for real people.

Zigler and his colleagues have brought individuals with retardation into the scientific world of all children and adults. Thus, they have provided firm scientific support for the revolution in social policy concerning individuals with retardation. Their findings have helped to ensure that children with retardation will have opportunities to develop to their fullest capacities. Within the United States, federal legislation on education for individuals with disabilities still awaits the extrapolation of these scientific findings to a national consensus and to law. Yet, programs such as Special Olympics International have already shaped and reflect this underlying concept of the roles of motivational and personality factors. In turn, the benefits of Special Olympics and similar programs for the adaptive functioning and self-esteem of individuals with retardation reinforce Ed Zigler's scientific theories.

In the past, most individuals with retardation functioned below their intellectual level. Today, on the basis of scientific studies, clinicians and educators can advise parents on the types of experiences and opportunities that can help individuals with retardation develop optimally. Parents and teachers can anticipate that some individuals with retardation will reach levels of social and vocational competence well beyond the expectations that can be predicted by their intelligence alone. With suitable help, individuals with retardation will experience the challenges and failures that are part of life, and also develop the capacities and skills to deal with hurt feelings, disappointments, and anxieties. Many will become productive workers and live in their own homes, and some will enter the still relatively uncharted domains of marriage and parenting.

Advances in molecular biology and other research areas are likely to dramatically change the landscape of mental retardation – prenatal diagnosis, molecular therapies, and other treatments are sure to have an increasingly powerful effect on early diagnosis and intervention. As in the past, ethical and policy issues will constantly need to be rethought in the context of new knowledge.

This book does not end with a final answer or a single, breakthrough discovery or cure. Instead, it ends with a challenge to the various fields concerned with individuals with mental retardation to continue the serious, scientific investigation of the many factors that shape the lives of these individuals. There will be decades of thrilling work ahead, as behavioral and biological sciences use new methods to unravel the many interactions between genetic, constitutional, and experiential factors in development – over the course of a life and from one generation to the next. The research in this book describes a major stream of research that has led to the current understanding of the development of individuals with retardation; it also provides a glimpse of the exciting prospects ahead. The pioneering contribution of Edward Zigler to mental retardation – over and above his specific theories and the rich abundance of research findings – has been to foresee the importance of this field for all research on child development and to emphasize that the goal of authentic, clinically engaged research is to help individuals with retardation become whole people living among friends and family in society.

1   The Individual with Mental Retardation as a Whole Person

Edward Zigler

Given the plethora of far from consistent research reports, confusing definitions, opposing theories, and strong views and counterviews in the area of mental retardation, it behooves us to anchor our approach to the subject on some common ground. I think we can all agree that the essential defining feature of mental retardation is lower intelligence than that displayed by the modal member of an appropriate reference group. Stated somewhat differently, I do not believe that anyone would argue with the statement that a 7-year-old retarded child is less intelligent than a 7-year-old child who is not retarded. Unfortunately, when we venture even a short distance from this statement, we immediately find ourselves adrift on a sea of definitional uncertainty. For if we ask the rather basic question of what we mean by intelligence, we encounter considerable disagreement that has only intensified in recent years.

IQ versus Social Adaptation

Many people insist that intelligence refers to nothing more than the quality of the behaviors shown by an individual assessed against some criterion of social adaptation. Others have argued that a clear distinction must be drawn between intelligence and the sheer manifestation of adaptive or socially competent behaviors that are typically labeled "intelligent." Inherent in this latter position is the view that behaviors indicative of social adaptation do not inevitably reflect normal intellectual functioning any more than the relative absence of such behaviors in the criminal, the psychiatric patient, or the social misfit inevitably reflects intellectual subnormality. Thinkers who espouse this latter view, including myself (Zigler, 1987), have argued that the concept of social adaptation is much too vague, and that the behaviors often placed within its rubric frequently stem from nonintellective influences. As a result, we have concluded that the ultimate referents of

1

intelligence cannot be the occurrence or lack of a wide variety of behaviors that are rather subjectively designated as socially competent or adaptive.

However, in seeking some more satisfying definition of intelligence, we too have been rather arbitrary. The basic problem is that definition-making is an arbitrary exercise. This point is easily substantiated by looking at the similarities and differences in the definitions of mental retardation advanced by the American Association on Mental Retardation (1992), the American Psychiatric Association (1994), and Division 33 of the American Psychological Association (Jacobson & Mulick, 1996), as well as the critiques concerning them (e.g., MacMillan, Gresham, & Siperstein, 1993). Obviously, even the professionals cannot agree on a "true" definition of the phenomenon. This proves to me that it is really fruitless to argue whether a definition is true or false. The more appropriate point of contention is whether one definition is more useful than another in respect to organizing our thinking, bringing clarity to areas of confusion, and giving direction to our empirical efforts and treatment practices.

With such criteria in mind, I, along with others, have argued that intelligence is a hypothetical construct having as its ultimate referents the cognitive processes of the individual – for example, thought, memory, concept-formation, and reasoning. Approached in this way, the problem of defining intelligence becomes one with the problem of the nature of cognition and its development. I should note that the attention to development here owes much to Tuddenham (1962), who suggested that a theory of intelligence must provide an explanation of the curve of change in cognitive ability throughout the entire lifespan, must deal with the ontogenesis of the psychological processes that mediate test performance, and must encompass the organization and vicissitudes of these processes from earliest infancy to senescence.

The delineation of cognition and its development as the essential focus of intelligence, and thus of mental retardation, has a certain appeal since it relates so readily to at least one noncontroversial phenomenon that forever differentiates the retarded individual from one of average intellect. Two adults of quite disparate IQs (for example, one of 70 and one of 100) may be employed in the same occupation, be members of the same union, participate in the same type of community and recreational activities, and be successfully married and raising families. In terms of standard social adaptation indices, these two individuals appear to be quite similar. However, when we shift our attention to the development and present manifestation of the formal cognitive characteristics of these two people, we have no difficulty distinguishing between them. They function quite differently on a wide variety of cognitive tasks and on a wide array of psychometric measures that also assess, albeit far from perfectly, basic cognitive processes. The individual of IQ 100 is clearly superior to the individual of IQ 70 in meeting the cognitive demands posed by these tasks. Thus we can state with certainty that in adults at the peak of their intellectual development, the cognitive functioning of the average adult is at a higher level than that of the adult with mental retardation.

If we approach the cognitive differences between these two individuals from a developmental point of view, we observe that the retarded individual progresses through the same sequence of stages of cognitive development as does the individual of average intellect, but at a slower rate. The performance of a child with mental retardation will thus resemble that of a younger, nonretarded child who is at the same developmental level more than that of a nonretarded age-mate whose cognitive system has matured at a faster rate. Further, while cognitive level has an obvious effect on performance, so does its speed of maturation. At any particular stage of development, the individual's cognitive level is comprised of the sum total of cognitive processes available or mastered. This cognitive collection constitutes the information-processing system that mediates both inputs from the environment and responses that the individual makes in efforts to adapt. The quality and nature of this information-processing system clearly has profound and pervasive effects on behavior at every age.

In sum, although many thinkers disagree with me, I believe that it is only by reference to differences in the rate of development and final level of formal cognitive functioning that the distinction between intellectually retarded and nonretarded people can be reliably and consistently drawn, and their behavioral differences understood.

Cognitive versus Motivational Determinants of Behavior

Now that I have constructed a reasonable and, in my opinion, valid frame of reference concerning the essential differences between individuals with and without mental retardation, it becomes my task to convince the reader that overemphasizing this basically sound position has resulted, at best, in incomplete and, at worst, totally erroneous explanations for the behavior of retarded persons. Let me be clear on this matter. As stated earlier, the cognitive functioning of retarded individuals, which is poorer in quality than that of individuals of average intellect, has a profound and pervasive influence on their general behavior. The crucial questions here are: Just how profound and just how pervasive is this influence, and how does it vary across tasks with which they are confronted? What must be grasped is that the behavior of retarded people, like that of all human beings, reflects more than the formal cognitive processes that we have been discussing up to this point.

Since there is considerable agreement that a deficiency in cognitive functioning is the essential defining feature of mental retardation, it is easy to see why workers have concentrated on cognitive determinants, and have underemphasized, if not almost totally excluded, other factors influencing the behavior of those with mental retardation. There is clearly a tendency in the scientific literature to attribute all of the atypical behavior of retarded groups to their cognitive deficiency. We appear to be so awed with the cognitive shortcomings inherent in mental retardation that we are led into tautologies in which we assert that retarded individuals behave the way they do because they are retarded. More sophisticated theoretical efforts have attempted to avoid this circularity, attributing behavioral differences between retarded and nonretarded individuals, not to the global phenomenon of mental retardation, but rather to some specific hypothesized defect or behavioral deficiency thought to characterize intellectually retarded functioning. Thus, over the years, ideas have been put forth that retarded people suffer from a relative impermeability of the boundaries between regions in the cognitive structure (see Chapter 5); primary and secondary rigidity caused by subcortical and cortical malformations, respectively (Goldstein, 1942–43); inadequate neural satiation related to brain modifiability or cortical conductivity (Spitz, 1963); impaired attention directing mechanisms (Merrill & O'Dekirk, 1994; Zeaman, 1959); a relative brevity in the persistence of stimulus trace (Siegel & Foshee, 1960); and improper development of verbal processes resulting in a dissociation between the verbal and motor systems (Luria, 1956; O'Connor & Hermelin, 1959).

I have long taken an adversarial stance toward the need to invoke such concepts when explaining differences in behavior between groups of MA-matched, cultural-familial retarded and nonretarded groups (e.g., Zigler, 1967). However, I have also gone on record as believing that these theoretical formulations are unquestionably valuable in that they lead us away from a rather sterile global approach toward a more fine-grained analysis of the cognitive processes of both retarded and nonretarded individuals. Thus, my contentions aside, included in this list are concepts that lie at the center of some of the most important programmatic theoretical efforts in the area of mental retardation.

These concepts also comprise one side of the developmental versus difference controversy over the nature of mental retardation, about which

I have written at length (Zigler, 1969; Zigler & Balla, 1982; Zigler & Hodapp, 1986). Difference theorists contend that all mental retardation stems from underlying organic dysfunctions that result in specific deficits in cognitive functioning and atypical cognitive development. Developmental theorists believe that this description applies only to individuals whose retardation is caused by organic impairments. They view individuals with cultural-familial retardation as representing the lower portion of the normal distribution of intelligence. As such, they should follow the same overall pattern of development as nonimpaired individuals, but they will progress at a slower rate and ultimately attain a lower asymptote of cognitive functioning. These predictions are referred to as the similar structure and similar sequence hypotheses, respectively. To date, the majority of the research favors the developmental model (see Weisz, Chapter 2, and Bennett-Gates & Zigler, 1998).

I do not choose here to pick the winner of the developmental-difference controversy. The listing here of the difference positions is presented only to highlight the fact that the bulk of theoretical and empirical efforts in the field long concentrated on the cognitive shortcomings of the retarded individual. As this list of hypothesized cognitive deficiencies grew over the years, it became common to explain all differences in behavior between nonretarded and retarded individuals with a selection of one defect or another that appeared even remotely relevant to the behavioral differences in question. Having been misinterpreted in the past, I want to be perfectly clear here. My statement is in no way an indictment of the theoretician who is carefully exploring the cognitive variable that interests him or her. It is an indictment of the after-the-fact "theorizing" that allows the thinker to avoid coming to grips with the complexities of the subject matter.

While no exception can be taken to circumscribed cognitive hypotheses concerning mental retardation, I must assert again that any cognitive theory cannot be a complete theory of the behavior of retarded people because their behavior, like that of any other group of humans, reflects factors other than cognitive ones. While the analogy is far from perfect, it should be noted that as a group, children of lower socioeconomic status (SES) have lower IQs than middle-SES children. However, when differences are found in the behavior of children in the two classes, the IQ difference is but one of many factors considered in interpreting them. Workers look closely at the children's social environments, educational histories, the child-rearing practices to which they have been subjected, and the attitudes, motives, goals, and experiences that they bring to the assessment situation. In contrast, when we deal with children with mental retardation, we often seem to assume that the cognitive deficiency from which they suffer is such a pervasive determinant of their total functioning as to make them impervious to the effects of influences known to affect the behavior of everyone else.

This assumption can clearly be seen in the research paradigm favored in the early decades of empirical work in mental retardation. Many studies directed at illuminating differences in cognitive functioning employed comparisons of institutionalized retarded children, whose preinstitutional lives were frequently spent in the very lowest segment of the lowest socioeconomic class, with middle-SES children who resided at home. Such groups differed not only with respect to the quality of their cognitive functioning as defined by the IQ, but also with respect to their total life histories and the nature of their current social-psychological interactions. Although individuals with mental retardation are generally no longer institutionalized, they are still subjected to relatively more social deprivation and rejection than are those of normal intellect. Modern scientists are ready – even anxious – to invoke these experiences in explaining the behavior of children from lower-income families. Yet, in the case of retarded individuals, we still rely so heavily on their cognitive deficiencies that we tend to ignore environmental events known to be central in the genesis of the personality of individuals of normal intellect.

In defense of workers who employed this paradigm, it can be argued that one need not be very sensitive to motivational or personality differences between groups compared on tasks thought to be essentially cognitive in nature. In my opinion, such an argument is an erroneous one. Although it is unquestionably true that the effects of particular motivational and emotional factors will vary as a function of the particular task employed, the performance on no single task can be considered the inexorable product of cognitive functioning, totally uninfluenced by other systems. Evidence in support of this point can be found in numerous studies employing tasks thought to be cognitive in nature, where differences in performance have been found to be associated with social class in IQ-matched individuals of normal intellect, and related to institutional status in IQ-matched individuals of retarded intellect. This leads me to reject the often implicitly held view that the cognitive deficiencies of the retarded individual are so ubiquitous and massive in their effects that we may safely ignore personality variables that also distinguish our retarded subjects from their nonretarded comparison group. This strikes me as little more than a reaffirmation of a sound experimental dictum: You cannot safely attribute a difference in performance on a dependent variable to a known difference in subject characteristics (e.g., IQ) if the populations also differ on other factors that could reasonably affect, or have been demonstrated to affect, performance on the dependent measure.

The overly cognitive deterministic approach to the behavior of people with mental retardation appears to stem from more than the implicit or explicit assumptions criticized here. It is also the result of the relative absence of a sound and extensive body of empirical work dealing with personality factors in the behavior of retarded individuals. The dearth of such work has invariably been noted by scholars faced with the task of reviewing the literature on personality functioning in mental retardation (e.g., Gardner, 1968; Heber, 1964). Had such a body of work developed over the years, it unquestionably would have played a moderating role with respect to the narrow cognitive approach that we have been discussing.

Personality Myths

Not only has surprisingly little work been done on the development and structure of personality in retarded individuals, but many of the views advanced have been surprisingly inadequate, and, in some instances, patently ridiculous. In a paper written years ago, Susan Harter and I pointed out how in the early part of this century the viewpoint became popular that individuals of retarded intellect were essentially immoral, degenerate, and depraved. To represent this point of view, we quoted a 1912 statement made by one of our nation's pioneer figures in mental retardation, Walter Fernald:

> The feebleminded are a parasitic, predatory class, never capable of self-support or of managing their own affairs. . . . Feebleminded women are almost invariably immoral and . . . usually become carriers of venereal disease or give birth to children who are as defective as themselves. . . . Every feebleminded person, especially the high-grade imbecile, is a potential criminal, needing only the proper environment and opportunity for the development and expression of his criminal tendencies. (In Zigler & Harter, 1969, p. 1066.)

Unfortunately, the next half-century did not witness much abatement in our cliché-ridden and stereotypical thinking on the personality of retarded people (Gardner, 1968; Mautner, 1959). Several writers (Wolfensberger & Menolascino, 1968; Zigler, 1966) noted how this deficit approach was sometimes carried to the extreme view that retarded persons represent some sort of subspecies or homogenous group of less-than-human organisms. Not until the battle that led to passage of the Education for All Handicapped

Children Act of 1975 (now called the Individuals with Disabilities Education Act) did the realization grow that retarded individuals are fully human.

One cannot help but wonder why simplistic and prejudicial views about the personality of retarded people were perpetuated for so long. I believe that some of this error can be traced directly to a common, but not necessary, outcome of the taxonomic practice of categorizing and labeling. As mentioned earlier, people can be fairly easily differentiated with respect to the rate of their cognitive development and the ultimate level of cognition achieved. Consistent with the taxonomic activities that permeate much of the scientific endeavor, this ability to differentiate quickly lends itself to the categorizing and labeling of individuals along some dimension of intellectual adequacy. The grossest example of this is the typical textbook presentation of the distribution of intelligence, in which a line is arbitrarily drawn through the distribution so that it intersects the abscissa at the point representing an IQ of 70, with everyone below this point categorized as mentally retarded.

If one is not careful, this straightforward and certainly defensible practice can subtly and deleteriously influence our general views concerning the essential nature of intellectually retarded individuals. If one fails to appreciate both the arbitrary nature of the 70 IQ cut-off point and the fact that we are dividing people on nothing more than the grossest overall measure of cognitive functioning, it is but a short step to the formulation that all those falling below this point are subnormal. Since the conceptual distance between "subnormal" and "abnormal" – the latter with its age-old connotation of disease and defect – is minimal, the final easy step is to regard those on the retarded side of the fence as a homogenous group of organisms defective in all spheres of functioning and forever separated by their very nature from all persons possessing higher IQs.

Again, clarity is in order. There is no question that retarded individuals differ from nonretarded individuals in cognitive functioning. However, we must be on guard not to generalize from this fact and create a general difference orientation in our approach to the behavior of people with mental retardation. Unfortunately, just such a difference orientation long suffused our thinking in this area. The bulk of our effort was directed at discovering how retarded individuals are different from more intelligent members of society, and very little attention was paid to how they are similar. While the difference approach might have had a certain viability in the early stages of the investigation of cognitive differences between retarded and nonretarded groups, its value shrinks drastically when we are confronted with the issue of personality differences. Indeed, the difference orientation in the personality sphere becomes totally indefensible when it generates stereotypes of personality functioning applied to all retarded individuals. The great heterogeneity in personality that we can grossly observe in a random sample of retarded individuals makes it rather unlikely that a particular set of personality traits is an invariable feature of low intelligence. Rather than attributing inherent personality characteristics to mental retardation, it would be more parsimonious to view the development of personality in retarded individuals as no different in nature than the development of personality in individuals of normal intellect.

Personality Development

Once we accept such a view, we can turn our attention away from personality traits thought to manifest themselves as a consequence of intellectual retardation and toward those particular experiences in the socialization process that give rise to the relatively long-lasting emotional and motivational factors that constitute the personality structure. Once we shift orientation in this way, we allow ourselves to discover that the personality of a retarded individual will be like that of someone who is not retarded in those instances where the two have had similar socialization histories. We might also expect differences to the extent that their socialization histories differ. Furthermore, we would not expect a personality pattern unique to mental retardation and shared by those whose intellectual features led us to label them as retarded. Rather, we would anticipate variation in the personality functioning of a retarded group to the extent that the group members have had different life experiences, just as we would anticipate such differences among individuals of normal intellect who have had differing experiential histories. If we take this mindset to the study of variations in personality functioning between groups of retarded and nonretarded individuals, as well as intragroup variation, we can begin to look for their sources – a search that will be far more productive than one confined to stereotypes and IQ scores.

If the process of personality development is the same regardless of IQ level, how do we explain the common finding of stylistic differences between groups of retarded children and middle-SES children of normal intellect? This finding does not contradict my thesis at all if we remember that many retarded children have had very deprived and atypical social histories. Again, however, we must recognize that the specific atypical features of their experiences, and the extent to which they are atypical, may vary from one retarded child to the next. Two sets of parents who are themselves retarded may provide quite different rearing environments for their children. At one extreme, we may find a retarded child who is ultimately removed from the home, not because of low intelligence, but because the home represents an especially poor environment. At the other extreme, a retarded set of parents may provide their children with a relatively normal home even though it might differ in certain important respects – values, goals, attitudes, and opportunities for learning – from a home in which the family is of average or superior intelligence.

In the first example, the child not only experiences a quite different socialization history while still living at home, but also differs from the child in the second situation to the extent that residential placement has its own effects on personality. Given the fact that much of our knowledge about personality features in mental retardation was derived from comparisons of institutionalized retarded children with children of average intellect who lived at home, one cannot help but wonder how many of the differences discovered reflected the effects of institutionalization, the factors that led to the child's institutionalization, or some complex interaction between these factors, rather than some purely cognitive aspect of mental retardation.

To add even more complexity, the socialization histories of cultural-familial retarded persons differ markedly from the histories of those retarded individuals who are organically impaired. Those with organic etiologies do not show the same gross differences from the nonretarded population in the frequency of good versus poor family environments. They do differ, however, from both the cultural-familial retarded and nonretarded populations in their pattern of cognitive development. Because of genes, biochemistry, or environmental insult, their cognitive apparatus is damaged and/or its functioning impaired. Their intellectual performance therefore has operating features that deviate from the norm. Years ago (Zigler, 1967), I proposed a two-group approach to mental retardation in which cultural-familial retardation was conceptualized as representing the lower part of the normal distribution of intelligence. Thus the same rules that govern normal development would apply. Retarded individuals with organic etiologies were treated as having their own distribution located to the left of the normal curve, with a small amount of overlap. Their cognitive development would follow different rules imposed by the particular type of damage their neural systems had suffered.

Amazing advances in medical research have now pinpointed many types of damage and their results in behavior and development. (See Dyken's discussion in Chapter 11 as well as Burack, Hodapp, & Zigler, 1988.) Yet these leaps in science have not uncovered any new explanations for cultural-familial retardation, supporting my belief that these individuals received a genetic draw that places them at the lower end of the normal IQ distribution – which, by definition, must have a low end as well as a high end. Furthermore, genes are not linked to personality as closely as they are to intelligence, although scientists are beginning to identify certain behavioral phenotypes in specific types of organic retardation.

In the face of this complexity, we need not consider the problem unassailable, nor need we assert that each retarded child is so unique that it is impossible to isolate the ontogenesis of those factors that are important in influencing level of functioning. I believe we should conceptualize retarded persons as essentially rational human beings, responding to environmental events in much the same way as individuals of normal intellect. Then (unless science eventually proves otherwise), we can allow our knowledge of normal personality development to give direction to our efforts.

This does not mean that we can ignore the importance of lowered intelligence per se, since personality traits and behavior patterns do not develop in a vacuum. However, in some instances, the personality characteristics of retarded individuals will reflect environmental factors that have little or nothing to do with intellectual endowment. For example, many of the effects of residential placement may be constant regardless of the person's intelligence level. In other instances, we must think in terms of an interaction – that is, given a lowered intellectual ability, a person will have certain experiences and develop certain behavior patterns different from those of a person with greater intellectual endowment. An obvious example is the greater amount of failure that retarded individuals typically experience. But, again, what must be emphasized is that the behavior pattern developed as a result of this history may not differ in kind or ontogenesis from that developed by individuals of normal intellect who, by some environmental circumstance, also experience an inordinate amount of failure. By the same token, if retarded persons can somehow be guaranteed a more typical history of success, we would expect their behavior to be more typical, independent of their intellectual level.

This last statement – alluding to the improvement of behavior through the manipulation of the environmental events that affect motivational structure – leads me to raise a note of caution. Rather knowledgeable workers in the area of mental retardation (Milgram, 1969; Zeaman, 1968) have attributed a motivational theory of mental retardation to me. This is an error. I have never asserted, nor am I now asserting, that the essential nature of the deficiency in retarded functioning is motivational. As I hope I have made clear in this presentation, as well as in many other writings, I consider the essential difference between retarded and nonretarded individuals to be cognitive. Thus, no amount of change in the motivational structure of retarded persons will make them intellectually normal, when normalcy is defined in terms of those formal cognitive processes discussed at the beginning of this chapter. However, we can speak of improving the performance of a retarded individual on a task, through the manipulation of motivational factors, to the extent that performance on that task is influenced by more than the cognitive demands it poses.

This point becomes an especially crucial one when dealing with the everyday social competence of the retarded individual. Even a complete overhaul of the motivational structure will not make it possible for him or her to become a nuclear physicist. However, rather circumscribed changes in motivation may make the difference between successful and unsuccessful employment at an occupation that has cognitive demands within the limits of that person's cognitive ability. I have been impressed by the repeated demonstrations that the performance of many retarded people on a variety of tasks is poorer than would be predicted from their general level of cognitive ability, typically defined by their MAs. It is my view that a great deal, if not all, of this deficit in performance is due to the attenuating effects of motivational factors. However, even if these effects were extinguished so that the individual functioned optimally in a manner commensurate with his or her general level of cognitive ability, that person would still be intellectually retarded in comparisons with same-aged individuals of normal intellect. Thus, a concern with motivational factors in the performance of retarded individuals holds no promise of a dramatic cure for mental retardation, defined in terms of its essential cognitive foundation. A motivational approach does hold the promise of teaching us how to help people with mental retardation to utilize their intellectual capacity optimally.

Although not terribly dramatic, such a goal is at least realistic. It is also of the utmost social importance in light of the now well-documented evidence that the everyday adjustment and/or competence of the majority of retarded people residing in our society is more a function of personality than it is of cognitive ability. Such evidence bolsters a recurring theme in my thinking – as important as the formal cognitive processes are, their roles have been overestimated, especially with respect to those everyday demands of society that we consider when assessing individual social competence.

The Rise and Fall of Studies of Personality

Over the years, my colleagues and I have attempted to delineate and, sometimes, experimentally manipulate a number of motivational variables not necessarily unique to the performance of retarded persons, but ones commonly observed in their behavior as a group. We have been interested in discovering the particular experiences that give rise to particular motives, attitudes, and styles of problem solving, and how variation in these experiences leads to variation in the personality structure of individuals of both retarded and normal intellect. We have, in certain instances, been especially interested in demonstrating that the performance of retarded persons, which has generally been attributed to cognitive shortcomings, is actually the product of particular motives. This interest does not mean that we invariably championed the importance of motivational over cognitive variables, since it is clear that these two classes of variables can, independently and in interaction, both influence performance on any given task. It was only through a fine-grained analysis of performance on a variety of tasks, by a number of groups of retarded and nonretarded subjects with varying socialization histories, that we were able to attribute particular aspects of performance to motivational factors. We remain aware that while it is conceptually feasible to draw a distinction between cognitive and motivational operants in behavior, this division is extremely difficult if not totally artificial in practice.

Our contributions to the understanding of personality functioning in mental retardation began at a time when care and treatment practices were radically different than they are today. Many of the participants in our (and others') research resided in institutions where they experienced much more social deprivation than later generations of retarded individuals, most of whom reside in the community. Yet many of the personality features we identified were not peculiar to institutional residents but were also observed to some extent in our noninstitutional groups. Traits such as low expectancy of success, fear of failure, need for social reinforcement, outerdirectedness, and overdependency (all topics in this book) were often found to affect our retarded subjects regardless of where they lived. This is not really surprising because people of low intelligence undoubtedly fail more, rely more on adults to help them, and experience social rejection a lot more than other people with greater intellectual endowment. This is as true today as it was when institutions were common. In fact, now that children with mental retardation are exposed more to nonretarded peers in mainstreamed or fully inclusive classrooms, their shortcomings may be more obvious and the effects on motivation more pronounced. (This is an empirical question that unfortunately has not been given the serious attention that it – and the retarded children affected – deserve.)

Nor does the demise of the residential institution erase the relevance of social deprivation to the behavior of retarded individuals. Even though our ability to identify specific causes of mental retardation has become highly sophisticated over the years, about half of the retarded population is still classified as having a cultural-familial etiology (Zigler & Hodapp, 1986). This type of retardation is most common in the lower socioeconomic class, which can be a more socially depriving environment than that available in wealthier surroundings. Thus, social deprivation can still be a driving factor in the performance and personality development of many individuals with mental retardation.

Most unfortunately, the serious study of personality features in mental retardation has dwindled in recent decades. An exception is the increased attention to psychiatric disorders and dual diagnosis in the clinical literature. Perhaps the importance of this type of work was overshadowed by the exciting advances that have occurred in biogenetic and biochemical fields. A review of the mental retardation literature since 1975 revealed that the number of studies published each year (about 1,000) remained relatively constant (King et al., 1997). The focus, however, shifted. In the last decade, proportionately more work was conducted in the areas of diagnosis, classification, epidemiology, and genetics than in psychology, etiology, or rehabilitation. I have no complaints with the interest in nonpsychological features of mental retardation. My complaint is that, like the narrow interest in low IQ in earlier years, the rest of the retarded person is being ignored. Yet that person still has a personality – a complex array of motivational and emotional features that permeate his or her everyday functioning. And unlike the categorical issues or genetic properties, these are features we can work with to help that functioning be more adaptive. The rest of this book describes the theoretical and empirical bases of the motivational approach to mental retardation and some practical applications directed at enabling retarded individuals to live happier and more productive lives.

References

American Association on Mental Retardation. (1992). *Mental retardation: Definition, classification, and systems of supports* (9th ed.). Washington, DC: Author.

American Psychiatric Association. (1994). *Diagnostic and statistical manual of mental disorders* (4th ed.). Washington, DC: Author.

Bennett-Gates, D., & Zigler, E. (1998). Resolving the developmental-difference debate: An evaluation of the triarchic and systems theory models. In J.A. Burack, R. Hodapp, & E. Zigler (eds.), *Handbook of mental retardation and development* (pp. 115–131). New York: Cambridge University Press.

Burack, J.A., Hodapp, R.M., & Zigler, E. (1988). Issues in the classification of mental retardation: Differentiating among organic etiologies. *Journal of Child Psychology, 29,* 765–779.

Gardner, W.I. (1968). Personality characteristics of the mentally retarded: Review and critique. In H.J. Prehm, L.A. Hamerlynck, & J.E. Crosson (eds.), *Behavioral research in mental retardation* (No. 1, pp. 53–68). Eugene, OR: University of Oregon, Rehabilitation Research and Training Center in Mental Retardation.

Goldstein, K. (1942–43). Concerning rigidity. *Character and Personality, 11,* 209–226.

Heber, R.F. (1964). Personality. In H.A. Stevens & R. Heber (eds.), *Mental retardation: A review of research* (pp. 143–174). Chicago: University of Chicago Press.

Jacobson, J.W., & Mulick, J. (eds.). (1996). *Manual of diagnosis and professional practice in mental retardation.* Washington, DC: American Psychological Association.

King, B.H., State, M.W., Shah, B., Davanzo, P., & Dykens, E. (1997). Mental retardation: A review of the past 10 years. Part I. *Child and Adolescent Psychiatry, 36,* 1656–1663.

Luria, A.R. (1956). *Problems of a higher nervous activity in the normal and nonnormal child.* Moscow: Akad. Pedag. Nauk RSFSR.

MacMillan, D.L., Gresham, F.M., & Siperstein, G.N. (1993). Conceptual and psychometric concerns about the 1992 AAMR definition of mental retardation. *American Journal on Mental Retardation, 98,* 325–335.

Mautner, H. (1959). *Mental retardation: Its care, treatment and physiological base.* Elmsford, NY: Pergamon.

Merrill, E.C., & O'Dekirk, J.M. (1994). Visual selective attention and mental retardation. *Cognitive Neuropsychology, 11,* 117–132.

Milgram, N.A. (1969). The rationale and irrational in Zigler's motivational approach to mental retardation. *American Journal of Mental Deficiency, 73,* 527–532.

O'Connor, N., & Hermelin, B. (1959). Discrimination and reversal learning in imbeciles. *Abnormal and Social Psychology, 59,* 409–413.

Siegel, P.S., & Foshee, J.G. (1960). Molar variability in the mentally defective. *Abnormal and Social Psychology, 61,* 141–143.

Spitz, H.H. (1963). Field theory in mental deficiency. In N.R. Ellis (ed.), *Handbook of mental deficiency* (pp. 11–40). New York: McGraw-Hill.

Tuddenham, R.D. (1962). The nature and measurement of intelligence. In L. Postman (ed.), *Psychology in the making* (pp. 469–525). New York: Knopf.

Wolfensberger, W., & Menolascino, F. (1968). Basic considerations in evaluating ability of drugs to stimulate cognitive development in retardates. *American Journal of Mental Deficiency, 73*, 414–423.

Zeaman, D. (1959). Discrimination learning in retardates. *Training School Bulletin, 56*, 62–67.

Zeaman, D. (1968). Review of N. R. Ellis, *International review of research in mental retardation: Vol. 1. Contemporary Psychology, 13*, 142–143.

Zigler, E. (1966). Research on personality structure in the retardate. In N.R. Ellis (ed.), *International review of research in mental retardation* (Vol. 1, pp. 77–108). New York: Academic Press.

(1967). Familial mental retardation: A continuing dilemma. *Science, 155*, 292–298.

(1969). Developmental versus difference theories of mental retardation and the problem of motivation. *American Journal of Mental Deficiency, 73*, 536–556.

(1987). The definition and classification of mental retardation. *Upsala Journal of Medical Science, Supplement*, 1–10.

Zigler, E., & Balla, D. (1982). Motivational and personality factors in the performance of the retarded. In E. Zigler & D. Balla (eds.), *Mental retardation: The developmental-difference controversy* (pp. 9–26). Hillsdale, NJ: Erlbaum.

Zigler, E., & Harter, S. (1969). Socialization of the mentally retarded. In D.A. Goslin & D.C. Glass (eds.), *Handbook of socialization theory and research* (pp. 1065–1102). New York: Rand McNally.

Zigler, E., & Hodapp, R.M. (1986). *Understanding mental retardation.* New York: Cambridge University Press.

2 Cognitive Performance and Learned Helplessness in Mentally Retarded Persons

John R. Weisz

An enduring legacy of Edward Zigler's decades-long research program has been an intriguing picture of the personality and motivational characteristics of mentally retarded persons. Although Zigler's developmental perspective on mental retardation is in large part a model of cognitive development, efforts to understand the overt performance of retarded persons on a variety of ostensibly cognitive tasks have led to the study of personality and motivational factors that influence such performance – and, more broadly, the adaptation – of mentally retarded people. This chapter describes a body of work that involves both features of the Zigler tradition. First, we consider research on the cognitive performance of retarded and nonretarded groups. Second, we consider research on one particular personality-motivational factor – learned helplessness – that may help to explain some of the findings on cognitive performance.

Research on Cognitive Development and Performance

My own venture into the study of personality and motivation grew out of efforts to study cognitive development in retarded and nonretarded individuals. As a graduate student at Yale, I grew interested in the developmental-difference controversy through reading Ed Zigler's work and discussing the issues with him. This interest eventually led to research and to a series of three literature reviews designed to summarize the state of the evidence on what has come to be known as the developmental vs. difference controversy.

The controversy involves several theories that cluster around two opposite poles. At one pole is the "developmental position," articulated by Edward Zigler and his colleagues (e.g., Zigler, 1969; Zigler & Balla, 1982). This position applies specifically to the more than half of all mentally

17

retarded persons who are classified as having cultural-familial retardation.[1] Intellectual deficits in this group do not result from specific, identifiable organic or genetic anomalies (e.g., Down syndrome or focused brain damage), IQ levels rarely fall below 45, and – to fit a strict definition – these individuals have at least one other immediate family member who is also mentally retarded.

Retarded individuals in this cultural-familial group, according to the developmental position, pass through steps or stages of cognitive development in the same order as nonretarded individuals. However, the two groups are said to differ in two respects. First, retarded people pass through the stages at a slower pace, and end their cognitive development at a lower level, than do nonretarded persons. We have labeled this aspect of the developmental position the similar-sequence hypothesis (Weisz & Zigler, 1979). The developmental position also holds that cultural-familial retarded persons and nonretarded persons who are similar in *level* of cognitive development (typically, operationally defined as mental age) will also be similar to one another in the formal cognitive processes they employ in reasoning and solving problems. We have labeled this aspect of the developmental position the similar-structure hypothesis (Weisz & Zigler, 1979; Weisz & Yeates, 1981; Weisz, Weiss, & Bromfield, 1986).

At the opposite pole in the controversy is a heterogeneous group of theories, each differing from the developmental position in some significant respect (see, for example, Ellis & Cavalier, 1982; Milgram, 1973). Because of Zigler's perception that these theories emphasize differences between retarded and nonretarded groups more than does his own, he has labeled them collectively the "difference position" (for example, Zigler, 1969). Some difference theories emphasize retarded-nonretarded differences in stages of cognitive development, whereas others predict differences in the cognitive processes employed by retarded and nonretarded people at similar levels of cognitive development. In other words, developmental and difference theories differ with respect to both the similar-sequence hypothesis and the similar-structure hypothesis. Our reviews of the evidence were organized around these two hypotheses.

---

1. Limiting the developmental perspective to the cultural-familial group seems appropriate in that the population of retarded people who have specific physiological deficits and genetic anomalies are apt to show a more heterogeneous array of cognitive processes that are difficult to encompass within a single cognitive theory. Retarded people without such specific deficits – the cultural-familial group – are thought to represent the natural lower end of the normal distribution of intelligence. As such, they are subject to the provisions of the general theory.

Tests of the Similar-Sequence Hypothesis

First, we consider the similar-sequence hypothesis. Some theoretical support for this hypothesis can be found in the Piagetian literature (see, e.g., Piaget, 1953, 1956). Piaget (1956) argued that "the minimum program for establishment of stages is the recognition of a distinct chronology, in the sense of a constant order of succession" (p. 13). Kohlberg (1969, 1971), building on Piaget's perspective, argued that certain cognitive-developmental stage sequences might well be similar across individuals because the stages are rooted in certain invariant characteristics of the environment and of the nervous system. Kohlberg also maintained that the stages of understanding described by Piaget might partake of certain "inherent orderings" dictated by logic, and independent of differences among developing individuals. As Kohlberg put it, "The invariance of sequence in the development of a concept or category is not dependent upon a prepatterned unfolding of neural patterns; it must depend upon a logical analysis of the concept itself" (1969, p. 355). To the extent that a given sequence of cognitive stages does depend upon a logical order (e.g., stage 3 involves reorganizing a network of thought patterns that first developed in stage 2), one might predict that the order of cognitive stages would be similar for retarded and nonretarded youngsters. Moreover, it could even be argued that if an inherent logic dictates the order of stages, the similar-sequence hypothesis might well apply to all mentally retarded people, not just the cultural-familial population.

It is possible, however, to derive quite a different hypothesis from the Piagetian literature. Milgram (1973) did so. After reviewing Piagetian research with mentally retarded groups (see Inhelder, 1968) and discussing Piaget's perspective with Piaget himself, Milgram concluded that the stages or levels of the retarded person's cognitive development may be different from those of the nonretarded person in some important ways. For example, Milgram argued that "when a retardate moves from one cognitive level to the next, traces of the previous level persist much longer, and the retardate is more likely to regress to earlier, long-practiced modes of thought" (p. 206). This apparent difference position differs from the similar sequence hypothesis in two ways: (a) It implies that the cognitive stages of retarded and nonretarded groups may be qualitatively different, and (b) it implies that in contrast to the monotonic sequences described by Piaget for non-retarded youngsters, retarded individuals may under some conditions move backward from more mature to less mature levels of thought.

The conflicting hypotheses advanced by Zigler (1969) and Milgram

(1973) are both linked to the Piagetian literature. This is reasonable because Piagetian theory and research are cast explicitly in terms of cognitive stages. Moreover, the Piagetian research literature includes numerous tasks designed to assess those stage levels. Thus, Piagetian research provides a particularly appropriate body of evidence bearing on the similar-sequence hypothesis. This evidence was the focus of our first review (Weisz & Zigler, 1979), in which we summarized the findings of several types of Piagetian evidence bearing on the hypothesis.

Cross-Sectional and Order-Difficulty Evidence: Studies Using Only Retarded Samples. One general way of testing the similar-sequence hypothesis is with cross-sectional research in which groups of mentally retarded children at more than one developmental level are tested with multiple Piagetian tasks. A finding that the direction of performance differences between developmental levels is the same for mentally retarded groups as for nonretarded groups constitutes support for the similar-sequence hypothesis. A second general approach is to compare the relative difficulty levels of the various tests or items. The assumption is that the item passed by the largest number of subjects reflects the process that develops earliest, the item passed by the fewest subjects reflects the process that develops latest, and so forth. If the rank-ordering of difficulty levels within a nonretarded group matches the rank-ordering among the retarded, this constitutes a second form of support for the similar sequence hypothesis. One may also apply formal scaling procedures (e.g., Green, 1956) to such ordinal data, such that developmental sequences can be inferred from the pattern of passes and failures for each individual subject. If retarded groups show pass-fail patterns fitting the same stage sequence that has been demonstrated for nonretarded subjects in other samples, then the similar-sequence hypothesis is supported.

Numerous investigators have employed some type of cross-sectional research, order-of-difficulty research, or combination of the two in ways that are germane to the similar-sequence hypothesis (see list of studies in Weisz & Zigler, 1979). First, we consider studies that have included only mentally retarded samples. In several of these studies, it is difficult to determine whether the samples included only cultural-familial retarded individuals. However, the studies have generally supported the hypothesis that the order of cognitive stages in groups of retarded persons closely resembles the order found in nonretarded groups. This conclusion has been supported in studies of conservation of mass, weight, and volume (Marchi,

1971); qualitative identity, quantitative identity, and equivalence conservation (Roodin, Sullivan, & Rybash, 1976); identity and equivalence conservation (McManis, 1969); numerical concepts (see Mannix, 1960; Singh & Stott, 1975, for an exception to this pattern, see Lister, 1972); concepts of space (Houssiadas & Brown, 1967; Stearns & Borkowski, 1969); the logic of relations (e.g., "Show me your right hand, your left; show me my right hand, my left," Lane & Kinder, 1939); and moral judgment (Abel, 1941).

Cross-Sectional and Order-Difficulty Evidence: Studies Using Both Retarded and Nonretarded Samples. Unlike the research described in the previous paragraph, some studies have directly compared the performance of retarded and nonretarded groups in the same experiment. In these studies, too, method descriptions often leave open the question of whether the samples may have included noncultural-familial retarded persons. The question may be academic, however, because the findings consistently indicate that the order of difficulty of various Piagetian tasks is the same for retarded and nonretarded groups. This is the case in studies of conservation concepts (Achenbach, 1969; Gruen & Vore, 1972) and concepts of time (Lovell & Slater, 1960; Montroy, McManis, & Bell, 1971). It is also the case for a diverse collection of Piagetian concepts, including (a) generic and gender identity, various conservations, magic and dream concepts, class inclusion, role taking, and the logic of relations (see DeVries, 1970, 1973a, 1973b, 1974), and (b) additive classification, multiplicative classification, seriation, and multiplication of asymmetrical transitive relations (i.e., coordinating size and color seriation in a two-dimensional array; see Lovell, Healey, & Rowland, 1962; Lovell, Mitchell, & Everett, 1962).

Longitudinal Evidence. Longitudinal research certainly provides the most powerful test of the similar-sequence hypothesis. Thus, there is special interest in a longitudinal study by Stephens and colleagues (see Stephens, Mahaney, & McLaughlin, 1972; Stephens & McLaughlin, 1974; Stephens et al., 1974) in the late 1960s and early 1970s. The investigators tested seventy-five retarded and seventy-five nonretarded persons on multiple Piagetian tasks at two points in time, two years apart. The assessments included eleven measures of moral judgment and twenty-nine measures of cognitive development across four additional conceptual domains (conservation, logic and classification, operativity and symbolic imagery, and combinatory logic). Over the two-year longitudinal period, both the retarded and nonretarded groups showed significant improvement on nearly all of the measures, suggesting that the direction of development on these tasks was similar among the retarded and nonretarded groups.[2]

Status of Evidence on the Similar-Sequence Hypothesis. With but a few exceptions, the bulk of the evidence reviewed here is consistent with the similar-sequence hypothesis. This conclusion is tempered somewhat by the irregular quality of the evidence. The cross-sectional data reviewed here would have been more informative if they had been based more often on individual pass-fail patterns subjected to a scaling analysis (e.g., Green, 1956; Guttman, 1950). And the longitudinal research would have been more helpful if the reports of change in group means and percentages over time had been replaced or supplemented by data on the number of individuals in each group showing specific developmental patterns over time. Although the quality of the data could be stronger, it is certainly true that the great preponderance of the evidence to date appears consistent with the similar-sequence hypothesis (for a detailed review, see Weisz & Zigler, 1979).

Tests of the Similar-Structure Hypothesis

In a second and third review (Weiss, Weisz, & Bromfield, 1986; Weisz & Yeates, 1981), we examined tests of the similar-structure hypothesis. These tests involved comparisons of cognitive performance by cultural-familial mentally retarded groups and nonretarded groups who are similar in level of development. As noted earlier, this hypothesis is the part of the developmental position (e.g., Zigler, 1969) that holds that retarded and nonretarded groups matched for developmental level (usually operationally defined as MA) will have similar ability within a variety of cognitive domains.

The similar-structure hypothesis is opposed by two quite dissimilar "difference" positions. One of these is the view that retarded people will show cognitive ability that is inferior to that of nonretarded people of similar developmental level. As an example, Milgram (1973) argued that at

---

2. On nine of the moral judgment measures, the direction of change over two years was the same for both the retarded and nonretarded subjects. However, Mahaney and Stephens (1974) reported instances when "the improvement which occurred in one area of moral judgment was not maintained when opinions were solicited on another, but similar, situation" (1974, p. 137). These "oscillations" occurred more often among retarded than nonretarded subjects. This finding is difficult to interpret, given Kohlberg's (1974) criticism of the Stephens et al. measures: "Empirical research confirms the fact that Piaget's moral stage measures do not meet the criteria of structural stages" (p. 142).

any given level of development, the retarded person's reasoning is especially likely to contain traces of more primitive developmental stages, and especially prone to show regression to those earlier stages. Consequently, Milgram argued, retarded groups are likely to score lower on cognitive measures than are MA-matched nonretarded groups. As Milgram put it, "Given tasks without a ceiling or floor effect for the general MA of the subjects being used, the retarded will dependably demonstrate an equal-MA deficit" (1973, p. 209). In contrast to Milgram, Kohlberg (1968) argued that mentally retarded people should be *more* advanced cognitively than their nonretarded MA peers. His reasoning was that cognitive development depends heavily on the child's "general experience" in the world. Because retarded people of a given MA have lived longer than nonretarded people of the same MA, those who are retarded should have a more extensive base of general experience and thus be more advanced cognitively.

To summarize, three theoretical positions differ sharply on what will be found when retarded and nonretarded groups are matched for MA and given tests of cognitive performance. One position (Zigler, 1969) maintains that no reliable group differences will be found; another (Milgram, 1973) holds that mentally retarded groups will prove to be inferior; yet another (Kohlberg, 1968) predicts that retarded groups will prove superior to non-retarded groups of similar MA.

Piagetian Tests of the Similar-Structure Hypothesis. In one review relevant to these three conflicting predictions, Keith Yeates and I (Weisz & Yeates, 1981) surveyed the findings of 32 experiments comparing the performance of MA-matched retarded and nonretarded groups on various Piagetian tasks. The 32 studies included 113 different comparisons across the following areas of conceptual development: additive composition, animism, artificialism, causality, classification, class inclusion, conservation (of area, color, continuous quantity, discontinuous quantity, length, mass, number, two-dimensional space, volume, and weight), dream concepts, extensive qualities, generic identity, gross qualities, identity concepts, intensive qualities, logical contradiction, magic concepts, moral judgment, perceptual decentering, perspective taking, probability, realism, relative thinking, role taking, seriation, time concepts, and transitivity.

The concepts and age groups studied provided reasonably broad coverage of the preoperational and concrete operational periods. The findings as a whole showed a rather mixed picture concerning the similar-structure hypothesis. Of the 113 group comparisons, 82 (73 percent) yielded results consistent with the hypothesis, 26 (23 percent) supported the difference position taken by Milgram (1973), and 5 (4 percent) supported Kohlberg's (1968) view that retarded groups would be superior to their nonretarded MA peers.

We took a closer look at the studies, trying to distinguish between those studies in which an effort was made to include in the retarded sample only those individuals who were not suffering from some specific organic impairment or genetic anomaly – that is, cases showing at least one of the defining features of cultural-familial mental retardation, the only group for which the similar-structure hypothesis has been proposed. Of the 113 total comparisons, only 39 involved groups that met this standard; of these 39, only 4 (10 percent) yielded results inconsistent with the similar-structure hypothesis.

As a second means of taking a "closer look" at the data, we used a counting method, relying on the fact that if a null hypothesis is true, then differences between any two groups across independent studies should approximate a normal distribution. Accordingly, the proportion of significant differences in either direction should be equal to the alpha level that has been selected (see Binder, 1963; Grant, 1962; Greenwald, 1975). Following this reasoning, the array of differences actually obtained across the studies can be compared with the hypothetical distribution by means of the chi-square test. In such a test, the expectation, assuming a normal distribution around a "no difference" mean, would be that 10 percent of the studies would yield significant group differences (i.e., 5 percent on each tail) and that 90 percent would yield no reliable group differences. Thus, the similar-structure hypothesis would be supported by a distribution of findings in which 90 percent of the comparisons showed no reliable retarded-nonretarded group difference, 5 percent showed significant differences in the direction predicted by Milgram (1973), and 5 percent showed significant differences in the direction predicted by Kohlberg (1968).

In the Weisz-Yeates review, we compared this expected distribution of studies to the obtained distribution via chi-square tests. (See Weisz & Yeates, 1981, p. 171, for caveats regarding the use of chi-square with such data.) When the tests were calculated separately for studies that excluded organically impaired retarded subjects (the "etiology controlled" studies) and studies that did not (the "etiology uncontrolled" studies), two different patterns emerged. In the etiology-uncontrolled studies, more comparisons than expected by chance supported Milgram's (1973) difference position. Among the etiology-controlled studies, however – that is, the studies whose samples approximated the selection criteria specified by Zigler and others for fair tests of the developmental position – the distribution was not significantly different from that which the similar-structure hypothesis predicts ($p > 0.50$). Thus, a close examination of the evidence revealed considerable support in the Piagetian literature for the similar-structure hypothesis.

Information-Processing Tests of the Similar-Structure Hypothesis. In a subsequent review of the evidence, Bahr Weiss, Richard Bromfield, and I (Weiss, Weisz, & Bromfield, 1986) focused on cognitive processes that fall not within the Piagetian tradition but rather within the broad information-processing experimental research tradition. The survey included twenty-four studies, involving fifty-nine comparisons of retarded and nonretarded groups on such cognitive processes as selective attention, input organization, memory, paired-associate learning, incidental learning, discrimination learning and learning-set formation, concept usage and matching, hypothesis-testing behavior, and even humor. To be included in this review, studies had to meet three methodological criteria, reflecting concerns raised in the preceding critique. The retarded samples had to be (a) matched on MA with a nonretarded group, (b) screened to exclude organically impaired individuals, and (c) noninstitutionalized. Studies that meet all three criteria are relatively rare in this field. This is reflected in the fact that 203 studies out of our initial pool of 227 (89 percent) were eliminated for failure to meet one or more of the criteria.

A gross examination of findings across the fifty-nine retarded-nonretarded group comparisons suggested the possibility of an empirical stand-off: 52 percent of the fifty-nine comparisons revealed no significant retarded-nonretarded difference, and another 45 percent revealed significant differences favoring the nonretarded group. Only 3 percent (two comparisons) revealed significant differences favoring Kohlberg's (1968) prediction that the retarded group would outperform the nonretarded group. Thus, about half the findings supported the similar-structure hypothesis and about half ran counter to it. However, as suggested earlier, (see also Weisz & Yeates, 1981), box score tallies of this sort are not the most appropriate means of testing the similar-structure hypothesis.

Because the similar-structure hypothesis is essentially a null hypothesis, it is most appropriately tested against an expected normal distribution of group differences, the distribution one would expect if the hypothesis were in fact valid (see Binder, 1963; Grant, 1962; Greenwald, 1975). We carried out such a test with these data, first using a chi-square test (as in Weisz & Yeates, 1981), then using a meta-analysis. The chi-square test showed a highly significant deviation from the distribution expected under the null hypothesis: Many more comparisons than would be expected under the null showed nonretarded groups outperforming the retarded comparison groups.

To carry out the meta-analysis, we computed the Z-score equivalent (Rosenthal, 1978) for the probability of the group effect (the retarded-nonretarded comparison) in each study (i.e., F and t values for each group effect were converted). We then computed a mean of these Z-score equivalents, averaging across the various group comparisons. The similar-structure hypothesis would have been supported by a mean Z of 0 (or a figure not significantly different from 0). But the meta-analysis revealed a highly significant difference, across studies, between the performance of the retarded and nonretarded groups, mean $Z = 1.32$; test of mean $Z = 0$: t (52) = 5.37, $p < 0.0001$. Retarded subjects performed significantly worse than nonretarded subjects, averaged across tasks and subject samples.

We followed up on this finding by trying to identify the cognitive domains in which retarded and nonretarded groups differed most significantly. Two such domains were the areas of (a) memory and (b) discrimination learning and learning-set formation. In the area of discrimination learning and learning-set formation, a chi-square test for homogeneity of group differences revealed that retarded-nonretarded group differences were not consistent across studies. Two of the most striking group differences were in the area of learning-set formation. In the area of memory, our test for homogeneity of differences again revealed that inferior performance by retarded subjects was not uniform across studies. Deficits were found in the performance of retarded groups on visual short-term memory (STM), nonserial auditory STM, cross-modal STM, and visual paired-associate learning. One area in which nonretarded groups showed consistent superiority was verbal explanation of the strategies they used in the various tasks. By contrast, retarded and nonretarded groups performed equally well in tests of incidental learning, and retarded groups tended to outperform their nonretarded MA peers on tests of distractibility and selective attention. Of special interest, retarded groups failed to show performance deficits on most tests of more integrated or higher-order cognitive behaviors such as concept usage and matching, and hypothesis testing. This finding seems to run counter to Spitz's (1976) hypothesis that retarded individuals are particularly deficient in cognitive areas that have developed relatively recently in human evolution.

Interpreting the Similar-Structure Evidence

What can we conclude from the two bodies of research just reviewed – that is, the information-processing findings and the Piagetian findings bearing on the similar-structure hypothesis? The most obvious possibility is that the similar-structure hypothesis may be generally valid for the conceptual domains studied by Piagetian investigators, but not for at least some of the cognitive domains in the information-processing tradition. On the other hand, several alternative interpretations should be considered.

Artifactual Explanations. Various artifacts might possibly explain the discrepancy between the Piagetian findings and the information-processing findings. One such artifact might be a subtle form of experimenter selectivity and bias. Investigators who carry out Piagetian studies may be more likely than those who conduct information-processing studies to favor the developmental hypothesis, which is, after all, closely linked to Piagetian theory (see Zigler, 1969; Zigler & Balla, 1982). Through various inadvertent forms of experimenter bias (see, e.g., Rosenthal, 1966), the two groups of investigators might have tended to find results supporting their respective a priori points of view. Such bias might help explain some of the inconsistencies across studies; however, it does not seem likely that the bias could fully account for the strong consistency in the Piagetian research literature.

Other artifactual explanations may merit consideration. For instance, it could be argued that Piagetian tasks are more susceptible than information-processing tasks to ceiling and floor effects (see Milgram, 1973), or that the information-processing studies used inferior procedures for screening out organically impaired retarded persons. Such explanations, while potentially plausible, do not seem any better equipped than the experimenter bias explanation to account for the strong consistency within the Piagetian evidence and the sharp contrast between that evidence and the information-processing findings. Thus, it seems that other interpretations have to be considered.

Interpretations Favoring the Difference Position. One set of interpretations favors the general difference position. It could be argued that the kinds of cognitive tasks most likely to reveal true cognitive deficits in mentally retarded people are those within the information-processing tradition. Information-processing research, after all, developed out of a search for individual and group differences. The Piagetian tradition, by contrast, grew out of a search for commonalities that underlie development. Thus, Piagetian research may have evolved toward the use of tasks that are sensitive to developmental change but not to differences between individuals or groups at similar levels of development. This might help to explain why a review of Piagetian evidence would support the similar-structure hypothesis, whereas a review of information-processing evidence would not. Even this explanation, though, would not cover why there were marked retarded-nonretarded group differences in some information-processing domains but not in others. To account for this aspect of the findings, we may have to consider the types of information-processing tasks that revealed significant group differences.

My research team also investigated the possibility that tasks requiring substantial amounts of verbal processing were especially likely to yield significant retarded-nonretarded group differences. We had independent ratings made of whether stimuli used in each information-processing experiment were predominantly verbal or nonverbal; a chi-square test revealed that a marginally higher proportion of the comparisons showed retarded-nonretarded group differences when verbal stimuli were used than when nonverbal stimuli were used ($p < 0.07$). This in turn suggested the possibility that tasks requiring substantial activity in the left cerebral hemisphere might reveal the most pronounced deficit in mentally retarded persons. A number of other researchers have argued that retarded persons are particularly deficient in verbal skills (see, e.g., Clarke & Clarke, 1965; Ingalls, 1978) and that the left hemisphere is more efficient than the right at verbal processing (Bradshaw & Nettleton, 1981). Could it be true that cultural-familial retarded people are particularly deficient in left hemisphere processing? Such a deficit might even help to explain the fact that retarded-nonretarded performance differences were found on information-processing tasks but not Piagetian tasks, because there is some evidence that processing of most Piagetian tasks occurs primarily in the right hemisphere.

Several other difference theories provide possible explanations for the pattern of findings summarized above. For example, verbal mediation theory (Borkowski & Wanschura, 1974) proposes that retarded persons are deficient in the production of verbal mediators. The theory could account for some but not all of the findings we reviewed. We also considered inhibition theory (Heal & Johnson, 1970), which holds that retarded persons are often unable to properly inhibit learned responses or suppress extraneous stimulus input when such actions would be adaptive. This theory, too, could account for only some of the information-processing findings. Indeed, it seems clear that no single difference position is comprehensive enough to explain all our findings.

Interpretations Favoring the Developmental Position. Other interpretations of the information-processing and Piagetian findings can be offered that favor the developmental position. One such interpretation focuses on the issue of ecological validity. A case can be made for the notion that most Piagetian tasks are more "lifelike" or ecologically valid than most information-processing tasks. Consider, for example, the contrast between the task of making moral judgments about lifelike dilemmas and the task of learning to discriminate between colored shapes. Even the manner in which Piagetian tasks are administered tends to be more conversational and natural than the more academic approach that is typically used to assess memory skills, discrimination learning, and so forth. It is possible that the mentally retarded participants in the research discussed earlier showed inferior performance on the information-processing tasks in part because they found those tasks relatively unengaging. Moreover, the academic nature of the tasks may have reminded them of school tasks with which they had a history of difficulty.

A related interpretation that is consistent with the developmental position is that retarded and nonretarded children differ significantly on some noncognitive variable such as motivation or expectancy of success that may influence performance on some types of tasks (e.g., information-processing) more than others (e.g., Piagetian) (see, e.g., Zigler, 1971, 1973). It is certainly important to recognize that the cognitive performance of cultural-familial retarded persons is likely to be influenced by factors other than cognitive ability alone. Indeed, efforts to identify such extracognitive factors and trace their impact have generated one of the richest legacies of the developmental-difference controversy. Edward Zigler and his colleagues have spearheaded these efforts, demonstrating the existence and impact of such factors as outerdirectedness, low expectancy of success, wariness of adults, and atypical reward preference (see, e.g., Tanaka et al., 1998; Yando & Zigler, 1971; Zigler, 1971, 1973; Zigler, Bennett-Gates, & Hodapp, chapter 9). An extensive program of research by Zigler and colleagues (see, e.g., Zigler & Balla, 1982; Zigler & Hodapp, 1986) indicates that retarded and nonretarded individuals of similar MA differ in a number of motivational and personality characteristics that can influence performance on cognitive tasks.

Such evidence is important; alone, however, it does not completely validate a motivational explanation for observed differences among MA-matched groups on cognitive tasks. Motivational differences might exist concurrently with group differences in cognitive ability. To rule out a cognitive ability explanation, investigators need to test whether, when motivational differences are controlled, differences between retarded and nonretarded subjects on cognitive task performance are no longer significant.

Data available in the information-processing studies permitted us to carry out a rough approximation to such a test. In several of these studies, subjects were told they would receive some form of reward for good performance. We (in Weiss et al., 1986) tested whether the presence or absence of such presumably motivation-enhancing manipulations affected the outcome of retarded-nonretarded group comparisons. We found only a trend: Studies that included such manipulations were somewhat less likely to show group differences, but not significantly ($p < 0.25$). It is certainly possible that efforts in these studies to manipulate motivation were inadequate. It could be argued, for example, that a simple *reward-for-good-performance* manipulation in a single study cannot be expected to erase major motivational deficits created by a retarded person's lifetime of adverse experience with cognitive tasks. It could also be argued that the reward manipulations in these studies failed to address the most critical motivational or personality factors that undermine performance.

The Piaget vs. Tower of Hanoi Study: An Example of How to Test Motivation and Personality Process Explanations. These concerns highlight the need for theorists and investigators who emphasize the role of personality and motivational factors to propose and test quite specific hypotheses – that is, hypotheses that specify which of these factors (for a list of potentially relevant factors, see Zigler, 1971, 1973) will undermine performance on which cognitive tasks, and how the effects of these factors can most fairly be operationally defined. In this context, a study by Kreitler, Bennett-Gates, and Zigler (1998) is a good exemplar. This study directly compared the performance of retarded and nonretarded individuals on a gamelike Piagetian conservation of area task and a more "academic" information-processing task known as *Tower of Hanoi* (rearranging the order of a stack of disks or cans, under a set of restrictive rules). In one condition, with each task, a pretest game ("marble in the hole") was used in an effort to create a success experience and thus reduce levels of failure expectancy in the participants. The success experience had no measurable impact on the performance of retarded participants on the Piagetian conservation task; retarded and nonretarded groups performed similarly on this task regardless of whether the experimenters began with the success experience. On the *Tower of Hanoi* information-processing task, however, the prior success experience had marked beneficial effects on the retarded group; retarded subjects who had no preliminary success experience showed significantly poorer performance than the nonretarded group on the information-processing tasks, but retarded subjects in the early success condition showed no such performance deficit. These findings are consistent with the notion that deficient information-processing task performance by mentally retarded youth, relative to their nonretarded MA peers, is due to a specific motivational factor — that is, the tendency of retarded individuals to begin academic-type tasks with an expectancy of failure (see also MacMillan, 1969; MacMillan & Keogh, 1971; Zigler, 1973).

Another Information-Processing Finding and Its Implications

One other finding of the information-processing meta-analysis warrants discussion at this point, because it relates to a somewhat different theme for research on personality and motivational factors. The meta-analysis showed a significant interaction of IQ and MA: As the average MA of subjects in the information-processing experiments increased, so did the likelihood of significant retarded-nonretarded performance differences. What factor or factors might change with increasing MA that might in turn be related to increasing performance deficits in mentally retarded youngsters? Several possibilities may be found in the work of Zigler and colleagues; for example, such processes as expectancy of failure, and outer-directedness (see, e.g., MacMillan, 1969; MacMillan & Keogh, 1971; Zigler, 1971, 1973) may grow more pronounced in retarded individuals as they mature, due to accumulating failure experiences and experiences in which relying on others for guidance has paid off. However, another factor may need to be considered, one that bears several similarities to factors Zigler and colleagues have identified as important but that grows out of a very different body of research and theoretical literature. This additional factor is learned helplessness.

Research on Learned Helplessness in Mentally Retarded Persons

The learned helplessness syndrome has been conceptualized in a number of different ways (see, e.g., Abramson, Seligman, & Teasdale, 1978; Garber & Seligman, 1980; Seligman, 1975), but most accounts applied to humans include the following two components: (a) a subjective perception by individuals that they cannot exert control over certain salient outcomes, and (b) corresponding deficits in response initiation or perseverance. My own interactions with mentally retarded youngsters in and out of school settings have led me to suspect that the helplessness construct may hold some explanatory power for this population. I suspect that mentally retarded youngsters often do anticipate low levels of control over outcomes in the school-achievement domain, and that they often show deficits in the application of their cognitive abilities in school – for example, in problem-solving situations.

Studies of Helplessness-Like Performance Deficits

Studies designed to explore this possibility have been few in number and preliminary in nature. Nonetheless, they do provide a point of departure for helplessness research on mentally retarded groups, and they may help to suggest useful directions for future empirical efforts. The initial studies dealt primarily with performance deficits. My first effort in this regard was a study of learned helplessness in cultural-familial retarded and non-retarded children who were matched at three levels of ability: MA levels 5½, 7½, and 9½ years (Weisz, 1979). The sample included not only retarded and intellectually average children, but groups of high-IQ children as well.

I used four operational definitions of helplessness. (a) To gauge perseverance following failure, children were presented with a puzzle and allowed to complete it successfully; then they were presented with a second puzzle and were stopped before completing it, in an apparent failure. They were then asked to decide whether to repeat the failure puzzle or to repeat the one at which they had just succeeded. Using a similar procedure, Dweck and Bush (1976) had found that children who ascribed their failures to uncontrollable factors (a defining characteristic of learned helplessness) were less likely to persevere at the failed task than children who believed their failures were due to controllable factors.

(b) A second operational definition was a set of response-initiation measures, some adapted from Floor and Rosen (1975). As one example, children were trained to turn off a buzzer in a reaction-time task; later, the experimenter left the child alone and activated the buzzer with a remote control switch. The length of time the child tolerated the unpleasant noise before initiating a controlling response (i.e., shutting off the buzzer) was scored, together with other measures (e.g., latency to correct the experimenter who had called the child by the wrong name), to form an overall response initiation score.

(c) Two questionnaires were also used. In one, teachers estimated each child's likelihood of initiating controlling responses in a variety of classroom situations – for example, when the child faced a new activity that looked difficult. In a second questionnaire, the children selected causal attributions for various favorable and unfavorable outcomes at school and at home. On a similar measure, Diener and Dweck (1978) had found that children who attributed unfavorable outcomes to their own insufficient effort (presumably regarding their failures as reversible through increased effort) showed low levels of helplessness.

Results with all three youth-report measures (but not the teacher questionnaire) involved IQ × MA interactions that bore a noticeable resemblance to the IQ × MA interaction seen in the information-processing meta-analyses discussed earlier. All three helplessness measures showed the retarded youth to be more helpless than the nonretarded youth, but only at one or both of the upper MA levels. One interpretation of this pattern is that retarded children may learn helplessness gradually, over years of development.

(d) Although the operational definitions of helplessness that we employed in our initial study may have been appropriate for the context of that research, they were not the most commonly employed means of assessing the construct. A more commonly used procedure for gauging helplessness involves the creation of a series of uncontrollable aversive experiences, often problem-solving activities that entail a series of failures. The way people respond to these failures, particularly their perseverance in continuing to apply their abilities, is used as an index of their resistance to helplessness.

I used measures of this type in a study (Weisz, 1981a) designed to investigate whether retarded children might be more susceptible to a helpless response pattern than would MA-matched nonretarded children. In the study, retarded and nonretarded children with mean MAs of about 9½ years completed a series of concept-formation problems, then were given feedback indicating that they had the wrong answers during four successive test problems. These problems followed a series of similar training problems involving veridical feedback that was frequently positive.

The two groups performed similarly on the training problems, suggesting that they were similar not only in MA but also in their ability to solve problems of this type. Yet the groups diverged markedly when the performance feedback became negative. Under the "failure feedback" condition, retarded children showed a highly significant decline in their use of effective strategies, from early to late test problems. Nonretarded children, by contrast, did not show a significant decline, and in fact showed a slight increase in their use of effective strategies over the course of the "failure" problems. The pattern of results suggests that there is at least one situation in which negative feedback can provoke a kind of "giving up" on the part of mentally retarded youngsters.

The study also included a new means of assessing teachers' ratings of their pupils' helplessness in the classroom. In the Helpless Behavior Checklist, teachers were presented with a series of brief behavior descriptions and asked to indicate whether each was "not true," "somewhat or sometimes true," or "very true or often true" of the target child. Some of the items involved helpless attributions (e.g., "Says 'I can't do it,' when having trouble with the work"); some involved helpless behavior (e.g., "When running into difficulty, gives up and quits trying"). On both attributions and behavior, teachers rated retarded subjects significantly more helpless than their nonretarded peers.

Relevant Findings from Other Investigators. Findings of other investigators have supported and extended ideas growing out of our early work. For example, Rholes, Blackwell, Jordan, and Walters (1980) found that susceptibility to learned helplessness, assessed via different measures than ours, increased among nonretarded children as the age of the children increased from kindergarten through late elementary years. Such a trend is consistent with our suggestion (closely related to Zigler, 1971) that retarded youngsters accumulate failure experiences and feedback suggesting low ability and low probability of personal control over events, across years of development – experiences that foster developmental increases in susceptibility to helplessness.

A study by Gargiulo and Sullivan (1986) compared the performance of MA-matched retarded and nonretarded groups (MA means: 9.18, 9.27; CA means: 13.95, 8.80) on four of the measures I had used (in Weisz, 1979; Weisz, 1981) as operational definitions of helplessness: (a) the puzzle repetition task (children choose to repeat a puzzle they had previously completed vs. previously failed), (b) the voluntary response initiation task (e.g., "accidental" buzzer, wrong name), (c) the children's attribution questionnaire, and (d) the teachers' Helpless Behavior Checklist. On all four measures, the retarded group scored as more helpless than the nonretarded group (all $ps < 0.003$).[3]

Extending the study of helplessness and mental retardation in a new direction, Reynolds and Miller (1985) administered questionnaire measures of both helplessness (their own Mastery Orientation Inventory) and depres-

---

3. Gargiulo and O'Sullivan also found that the various measures designed to tap helplessness showed quite low intercorrelations within the retarded group, but moderate intercorrelations (range: .05–.50) in the nonretarded group; they concluded that these "measures of learned helplessness are not interchangeable . . ." (1986, p. 205).

sion (the Reynolds Adolescent Depression Scale) to age-, gender-, and race-matched retarded and nonretarded groups (mean age about 17 years). Retarded adolescents showed higher scores on both the helplessness questionnaire ($p < 0.001$) and the depression questionnaire ($p < 0.001$). Depression scale means showed the mentally retarded teens significantly higher on symptom clusters reflecting somatic (e.g., feeling sick), self-evaluative (e.g., feelings of worthlessness, self-pity), and behavioral (e.g., crying, irritability) components, but not mood (e.g., dysphoria) or vegetative symptoms (e.g., sleep, fatigue).

In one of the earliest efforts in this area, Floor and Rosen (1975) employed an interesting array of helplessness measures with retarded and nonretarded groups. The measures included a self-report passive-dependency scale (e.g., "Do you wish you were still a child?"), a locus of control scale, a coping behavior questionnaire (e.g., "What would you do if your wallet were stolen?"), and a series of in vivo response initiation tests (e.g., Phone rings while person is alone in office. Does person answer it?). The measures employed were intriguing, and the group differences generally showed higher levels of helplessness in the retarded groups than the nonretarded group. However, the fact that the retarded and nonretarded groups were matched not on MA, but on chronological age – as in the Reynolds and Miller (1985) study (see preceding paragraph) – means that the findings have only limited relevance to the issues under discussion in this chapter.

State of the Evidence on Retarded-Nonretarded Group Differences in Helplessness and Related Conditions. To summarize, data from our research (Weisz, 1979) and that of Gargiulo and Sullivan (1986), using the same four helplessness measures, show higher levels of helplessness in retarded groups than in nonretarded groups of similar MA, provided that the MA level is relatively high (e.g., MA means of 9). Data from our research and that of Rholes et al. (1980) suggest the possibility that susceptibility to helplessness may increase in retarded individuals with increasing maturity. And the findings of Reynolds and Miller (1985) raise the possibility that helplessness in retarded individuals may also be associated with depressive symptoms.

Probing the Etiology of Helplessness in Retarded Youth

If retarded youngsters do develop a marked susceptibility to helplessness, why is this so? Our research has generated several possible answers. First, our observations in classrooms (Raber & Weisz, 1981) have suggested that retarded children receive feedback patterns that foster a helpless orientation. They receive relatively frequent negative feedback, and this could lead them to begin a variety of school-like tasks with a readiness to anticipate failure (see MacMillan, 1969; Zigler & Balla, 1982); this readiness may be activated when the problems get tough, or when early errors begin to pile up. Importantly, a high proportion of the negative feedback that mentally retarded children receive appears to be performance-related and relevant to their cognitive abilities. This particular pattern has been linked to helplessness in earlier research with nonretarded youngsters (see Dweck et al., 1978). The pattern can foster a tendency to attribute failures to low ability, a stable, uncontrollable cause. Children who receive such feedback patterns have been found to show performance debilitation in response to feedback suggesting failure (see Dweck et al., 1978).

More on the Etiology of Helplessness: Judgments and Attributions of Nonretarded Persons in Response to the "Mentally Retarded" Label. It is also possible that helplessness is fostered in mentally retarded people by the judgments and attributions that are made about them by nonretarded people. Specifically, nonretarded people may interpret failure by a retarded person in ways that lead them to tolerate or even encourage low levels of perseverance. To explore this possibility, we have carried out several studies of how the judgments and attributions of nonretarded people are influenced by the "mentally retarded" label.

To illustrate the reasoning underlying our research, let us consider attributions that nonretarded people might make for failure by a child labeled mentally retarded. A defining characteristic of mental retardation is low ability. Because low ability is such a salient attribute of retarded children, it may be emphasized in causal attributions for such children even when they are being compared with nonretarded children of similar ability. Such reasoning would illustrate attributional overextension, the extension of a salient causal ascription (e.g., low ability) beyond its logical limits (see Weisz, 1981b). If such overextension were to occur when adults make judgments about a retarded child, the resulting emphasis on the causal importance of low ability might (following Kelley, 1973) lead the adults to discount the role of other plausible causal factors such as insufficient effort. Adults who believe that a child's failure at a task resulted primarily from low ability and not from insufficient effort are not likely to encourage that child to persist at the task. Instead, they may allow the child to give up, thus essentially condoning helpless behavior.

In an initial effort to explore this line of reasoning, I carried out a series of three studies (Weisz, 1981) in which college students made judgments about a problem-solving failure by a mentally retarded child and an unlabeled child of equal MA. In study 1, the students made judgments about either the retarded or the unlabeled child (i.e., a between-groups design). In study 2, all judgments were made about both children (i.e., a repeated-measures design). In both studies, low ability was rated as a significantly more important cause of failure for the retarded than for the unlabeled child, insufficient effort was rated more important for the unlabeled child, and the unlabeled child was rated as more likely to succeed at the task in future attempts. In study 3, college students were given both the "retarded child" pattern of expectancies and attributions and the unlabeled child pattern, derived from studies 1 and 2. After reading both descriptions, applied to hypothetical children, the students were asked to indicate how likely it was that they would urge each child to persevere following failure. As expected, the students reported that the retarded child pattern would make them less likely to urge perseverance than would the unlabeled child pattern.

The attributional pattern identified in Weisz (1981a) was further supported in a study by Bromfield (1983) using a videotaped experience of child failure. The tape showed a "teacher" and a young girl interacting for about five minutes. The child succeeded at one block-design problem, but then struggled with the next block design problem throughout the remainder of the tape, never succeeding. Half the college students who viewed the tape were told that the child was mentally retarded; half were not. All students were given identical information about the child's MA, achievement test performance, and ability at block-design problems. Despite this fact, the students who thought they were viewing a mentally retarded child made markedly different judgments about what they had seen than did the other students. Subjects in the retarded child condition were significantly more likely than the other subjects to (a) attribute the child's failure to insufficient ability, (b) predict future failure at the block-design problem with the same teacher, and (c) predict future failure at the block-design problem even with a more experienced teacher. In fact, subjects in the retarded child condition actually rated the child as lower in block-design ability than did the other subjects, despite the fact that all subjects had been given exactly the same block-design ability scores. The two groups did not differ in their attributions to low effort or in their judgments as to how much they would have encouraged the child to persist at the block-design problem. With these two exceptions, the results replicated the findings of Weisz (1981a).

Are some groups of nonretarded people more susceptible than others to being influenced by the mentally retarded label? We explored this question in two studies. In one, Keith Yeates and I (Yeates & Weisz, 1982) used vignettes to compare the susceptibility of various adult groups to label effects. We found that adults who had limited experience with mentally retarded people (i.e., university undergraduates and regular classroom teachers) showed relatively strong label effects of the sort discussed here; more experienced adults (i.e., graduate students in special education and special education teachers) did not. Interestingly, we also found that adults who endorsed the similar-structure hypothesis on a separately administered questionnaire were less susceptible to label effects than were adults who rejected the hypothesis.

In a related study, Bromfield, Weisz, and Messer (1986) used the videotape described earlier to assess susceptibility to the effects of the mentally retarded label by nonretarded third, sixth, and ninth graders. Consistent with developmental literature on person perception and social cognition, we found that label effects were negligible among the youngest group, strong among sixth graders, and even stronger among ninth graders. This suggests that the attributional and other judgmental processes of interest here may take shape over the course of development in nonretarded people.

Taken together, our vignette and videotape attributional research suggests that some of the adults in the retarded youngster's world, and even some of the retarded child's older peers, may be influenced in benevolent but potentially harmful ways by the mentally retarded label. The label, applied to a child who has failed a problem-solving task, may lead nonretarded people into a potentially helplessness-promoting pattern of attributions and behavior with respect to the labeled child. I do not suggest that this is the sole cause of the helpless behavior sometimes shown by mentally retarded individuals, but if it is one of the causes, it may be one of the most remediable. If nonretarded people who directly influence the lives of mentally retarded people — for example, teachers, parents, siblings, and classmates — were aware of the ways retarded people do and do not differ cognitively from nonretarded people, the judgmental patterns we have identified might be less pronounced. This notion is supported by the finding (in Yeates & Weisz, 1982) that helplessness-fostering judgmental patterns are generally not found among adults who believe that retarded and nonretarded groups at similar cognitive-developmental levels are similar in cognitive ability.

Does Institutionalization Foster Development of Helplessness? Some investigators have suggested that institutional living – which was long part of the experience of many retarded individuals and thus part of the empirical work that spawned current theories – may promote the development of helplessness. Rosen, Floor, and Baxter (1971) and DeVellis (1977), for example, emphasized that retarded persons living in institutions frequently experience a lack of control over outcomes, and are often exposed to noncontingent reward and punishment – conditions that have been shown to stimulate helplessness in experiments with both (nonretarded) people and infrahuman species. Both Rosen et al. and DeVellis argue that institutionalized retarded individuals show characteristic symptoms of helplessness. Although these authors make an intuitively appealing case (consistent in some ways with the perspective of Balla and Zigler, 1982), the only study I know of in which helplessness measures were used with both institutionalized and noninstitutionalized retarded groups (Floor & Rosen, 1975) reported no significant group difference on any of the measures. Thus, while institutional living may conceivably contribute to the development of helplessness in mentally retarded individuals, we lack hard evidence, to date, to support this possibility.

Future Directions for Research on Helplessness and Mental Retardation

A significant limitation of the preceding findings, save those of Raber and Weisz (1980), is that they provide no direct information on the ways children and adults behave in everyday life. Laboratory analog studies are useful devices, particularly at early stages in the development of a field (Weisz, 1978), but the findings they yield will have much greater credibility if they are replicated and extended in naturally occurring contexts. Developing observational measures of helplessness would be an extremely useful contribution to this field of inquiry.

Another useful direction for future research is suggested by Abramson et al.'s (1978) notion that learned helplessness may assume a number of forms, some more devastating than others. Helplessness may be broadly generalized ("I expect to be helpless in many situations.") or specific to particular problems or contexts. It may be chronic or acute. It may also be personal ("I am helpless, but others in this situation would not be.") or universal ("Everyone would be helpless here."). People's standing on these dimensions may carry significant implications for other aspects of their functioning. For example, individuals who believe that everyone in the same situation would be helpless may feel depressed but without a loss of self-esteem; however, those who perceive their helplessness as personal may well suffer a loss of self-esteem. What particular forms of helplessness do retarded children suffer, and how do these affect their emotional responses to failure and other adversities? These questions could form the basis for a very useful research agenda.

Ultimately, a key focus of research may need to be prevention and remediation. A number of strategies for alleviating helplessness have already shown promise (Andrews & Debus, 1978; Chapin & Dyck, 1976; Dweck, 1975), and some have begun to propose ways of alleviating helplessness in retarded individuals specifically (see, e.g., Stamatelos & Mott, 1983). But such applications in the mental retardation field should probably await evidence on the situations in which retarded individuals are particularly susceptible to helplessness, and on the forms of helplessness to which they are most likely to fall prey. If research continues to indicate that preventive and therapeutic interventions are needed, it would be difficult indeed to imagine a more important task for researchers in the field than that of refining and testing the effects of such interventions.

There can be little doubt that retarded individuals draw from a more limited reservoir of cognitive potential than do nonretarded individuals. For this reason, it is important to promote, in whatever ways we can, optimum expression of the abilities retarded children do possess. One means of doing this is to identify noncognitive factors that may undermine expression of those abilities, and the evidence reviewed here suggests that one such factor may be learned helplessness. Thus, continued efforts to understand, and ultimately to minimize, susceptibility to helplessness may hold significant benefits for retarded children in their pursuit of competence and independence.

Concluding Comment: Cognitive and Extracognitive Processes

The findings reviewed here — addressing cognitive processes, helplessness, and labeling effects — may ultimately converge in a potentially useful way. Considered together, they may help sharpen our picture of (a) the cognitive capabilities of retarded people, (b) circumstances in which retarded people may perform below the level of those capabilities, and (c) judgments and behavior by nonretarded people in the retarded person's environment that may contribute to such subability performance. The picture assembled here is probably best viewed as a set of hypotheses to be explored in further research. Such research – weaving together the study of cognitive abilities and such extracognitive factors as learned helplessness – may enrich our understanding of why cultural-familial retarded people behave as they do. If so, the research will fit nicely into the tradition now associated with the venerable developmental position on cultural-familial mental retardation as articulated and studied by Edward Zigler and his colleagues.

References

Abel, T.M. (1941). Moral judgments among subnormals. *Journal of Abnormal and Social Psychology, 36,* 378–392.

Abramson, L.Y., Seligman, M.E.P., & Teasdale, J.D. (1978). Learned helplessness in humans: Critique and reformulation. *Journal of Abnormal Psychology, 87,* 49–74.

Achenbach, T.M. (1969). Conservation of illusion-distorted identity: Its relation to MA and CA in normals and retardates. *Child Development, 40,* 663–679.

Balla, D., & Zigler, E. (1982). Impact of institutional experience on the behavior and development of retarded persons. In E. Zigler & D. Balla (eds.), *Mental retardation: The developmental-difference controversy* (pp. 41–60). Hillsdale, NJ: Erlbaum.

Binder, A. (1963). Further consideration on testing the null hypothesis and the strategy and tactics of investigating theoretical models. *Psychological Review, 70,* 107–115.

Borkowski, J.G., & Wanschura, P.B. (1974). Mediational processes in the retarded. In N.R. Ellis (ed.), *International review of research in mental retardation* (Vol. 7, pp. 1–54). New York: Academic Press.

Bradshaw, J.L., & Nettleton, N.C. (1981). The nature of hemispheric specialization in man. *Behavioral and Brain Sciences, 4,* 51–91.

Bromfield, R.N. (1983). *Effects of the "mentally retarded" label on perceptions of a child's failure.* Unpublished masters thesis, University of North Carolina at Chapel Hill.

Bromfield, R., Weisz, J.R., & Messer, T. (1986). Children's judgments and attributions in response to the "mentally retarded" label: A developmental approach. *Journal of Abnormal Psychology, 95,* 81–87.

Clarke, A.M., & Clarke, A.D.B. (1965). *Mental deficiency: The changing outlook.* New York: Free Press.

DeVellis, R.F. (1977). Learned helplessness in institutions. *Mental Retardation, 21,* 10–13.

DeVries, R. (1970). The development of role taking as reflected by behavior of bright, average, and retarded children in a social guessing game. *Child Development, 41,* 759–770.

(1973a). *Performance on Piaget-type tasks of high-IQ, average-IQ and low-IQ children*. Chicago: University of Illinois at Chicago Circle (ERIC Document Reproduction Service No. ED086, 374/PS007 129).

(1973b). *The two intelligences of bright, average, and retarded children*. Chicago: University of Illinois at Chicago Circle (ERIC Document Reproduction Service No. ED079/102/SE 016 419).

(1974). Relationships among Piagetian, IQ, and achievement assessments. *Child Development, 45,* 746–756.

Diener, C.S., & Dweck, C.S. (1978). An analysis of learned helplessness: Continuous changes in performance, strategy, and achievement cognitions following failure. *Journal of Personality and Social Psychology, 36,* 451–62.

Dweck, C.S., & Bush, E.S. (1976). Sex differences in learned helplessness: 1. Differential debilitation with peer and adult evaluators. *Developmental Psychology, 12,* 147–156.

Dweck, C.S., Davidson, W., Nelson, S., & Enna, B. (1978). Sex differences in learned helplessness: II. The contingencies of evaluative feedback in the classroom: III. An experimental analysis. *Developmental Psychology, 14,* 268–276.

Ellis, N.R., & Cavalier, A.R. (1982). Research perspectives in mental retardation. In E. Zigler & D. Balla (eds.), *Mental retardation: The developmental-difference controversy* (pp. 121–152). Hillsdale, NJ: Erlbaum.

Floor, L., & Rosen, M. (1975). Investigating the phenomenon of helplessness in mentally retarded adults. *American Journal of Mental Deficiency, 79,* 565–572.

Garber, J., & Seligman, M.E.P. (eds.). (1980). *Human helplessness: Theory and application*. New York: Academic Press.

Gargiulo, R.M., & O'Sullivan, P.S. (1986). Mildly mentally retarded and nonretarded children's learned helplessness. *American Journal of Mental Deficiency, 91,* 203–206.

Gargiulo, R.M., O'Sullivan, P.S., & Barr, N.J. (1987). Learned helplessness in reflective and impulsive mentally retarded and nonretarded children. *Bulletin of the Psychonomic Society, 25,* 269–272.

Grant, D.H. (1962). Testing the null hypothesis and the strategy and tactics of investigating theoretical models. *Psychological Review, 69,* 54–61.

Green, B.F. (1956). A method for scalogram analysis using summary statistics. *Psychometrika, 21,* 79–88.

Greenwald, A.G. (1975). Consequence of prejudice against the null hypothesis. *Psychological Bulletin, 82,* 1–20.

Gruen, G.E., & Vore, D.A. (1972). Development of conservation in normal and retarded children. *Developmental Psychology, 6,* 146–157.

Guttman, L. (1950). The basis of scalogram analysis. In S.A. Stouffer et al. (eds.), *Measurement and prediction* (Vol. 4). Princeton, NJ: Princeton University Press.

Heal, L.W., & Johnson, J.T., Jr. (1970). Inhibition deficits in retardate learning and attention. In N.R. Ellis (ed.), *International review of research in mental retardation* (Vol. 4, pp. 107–150). New York: Academic Press.

Houssiadas, L., & Brown, L.B. (1967). The coordination of perspectives by mentally retarded children. *Journal of Genetic Psychology, 110,* 211–215.

Hunt, J.McV. (1974). Discussion: Developmental gains in reasoning. *American Journal of Mental Deficiency, 79,* 127–133.

Ingalls, R.P. (1978). *Mental retardation: The changing outlook.* New York: Wiley.

Inhelder, B. (1968). *The diagnosis of reasoning in the mentally retarded.* New York: Day (originally published in 1943).

Kelley, H.H. (1973). The process of causal attribution. *American Psychologist, 28,* 107–128.

Kohlberg, L. (1968). Early education: A cognitive-developmental view. *Child Development, 39,* 1013–1062.

(1969). Stage and sequence: The cognitive-developmental approach to socialization. In D. Goslin (ed.), *Handbook of socialization theory and research.* Chicago: Rand McNally.

(1971). From is to ought: How to commit the naturalistic fallacy and get away with it in the study of moral development. In Kohlberg, L. (1974). Discussion: Development gains in moral judgment. *American Journal of Mental Deficiency, 79,* 142–146.

Kreitler, S., Bennett-Gates, D., & Zigler, E. (1998). *The developmental-difference controversy in mental retardation: Piaget versus the Tower of Hanoi.* New Haven, CT: Yale University.

Lane, E.B., & Kinder, E.F. (1939). Relativism in the thinking of subnormal subjects as measured by certain of Piaget's tests. *Journal of Genetic Psychology, 54,* 107–118.

Lister, C. (1972). The development of ESN children's understanding of conservation in a range of attribute situations. *British Journal of Educational Psychology, 42,* 14–22.

Lovell, K., Healey, D., & Rowland, A.D. (1962). Growth of some geometric concepts. *Child Development, 33,* 751–767.

Lovell, K., Mitchell, B., & Everett, I.R. (1962). An experimental study of the growth of some logical structures. *British Journal of Psychology, 53,* 175–188.

Lovell, K., & Slater, A. (1960). The growth of the concept of time: A comparative study. *Child Psychology and Psychiatry, 1,* 179–190.

MacMillan, D.L. (1969). Motivational differences: Cultural-familial retardates vs. normal subjects on expectancy for failure. *American Journal of Mental Deficiency, 74,* 254–258.

MacMillan, D.L., & Keogh, B.K. (1971). Normal and retarded children's expectancy for failure. *Developmental Psychology, 4,* 343–348.

McManis, D.L. (1969). Conservation of identity and equivalence of quantity by retardates. *Journal of Genetic Psychology, 115,* 63–69.

Mahaney, E.J., & Stevens, B. (1974). Two-year gains in moral judgment by retarded and nonretarded persons. *American Journal of Mental Deficiency, 79,* 139–141.

Mannix, J.B. (1960). The number concepts of a group of E.S.N. children. *British Journal of Educational Psychology, 30,* 180–181.

Marchi, J.U. (1971). *Comparison of selected Piagetian tasks with the Wechsler Intelligence Scale for Children as measures of mental retardation.* Doctoral dissertation, University of California, Berkeley. *Dissertation Abstracts International, 31,* 6442A (University Microfilms No. 71–51, 833).

Milgram, N.A. (1973). Cognition and language in mental retardation: Distinctions and implications. In D.K. Routh (ed.), *The experimental psychology of mental retardation.* Chicago: Aldine.

Montroy, P., McManis, D., & Bell, T. (1971). Development of time concepts in normal and retarded children. *Psychological Reports, 28,* 895–902.

Piaget, J. (1953). *The origins of intelligence in the child.* London: Routledge & Kegan Paul.

(1956). The general problem of the psychobiological development of the child. *Discussions on Child Development, 4,* 3–27.

Raber, S.M., & Weisz, J.R. (1981). Teacher feedback to mentally retarded and nonretarded children. *American Journal of Mental Deficiency, 86,* 148–156.

Reynolds, W.M., & Miller, K.L. (1985). Depression and learned helplessness in mentally retarded and nonmentally retarded adolescents: An initial investigation. *Applied Research in Mental Retardation, 6,* 295–306.

Rholes, W.S., Blackwell, J., Jordan, C., & Walters, C. (1980). A developmental study of learned helplessness. *Developmental Psychology, 16,* 616–624.

Roodin, P.A., Sullivan, L., & Rybash, J.M. (1976). Effects of a memory aid on three types of conservation in institutionalized retarded children. *Journal of Genetic Psychology, 129,* 253–259.

Rosen, M., Floor, L., & Baxter, D. (1971). The institutional personality. *British Journal of Mental Subnormality, 17,* 2–8.

Rosenthal, R. (1966). *Experimenter effects in behavioral research.* New York: Appleton Century Crofts.

(1978). Combining results of independent studies. *Psychological Bulletin, 85,* 185–193.

Rosenthal, R., & Rubin, D.B. (1982). Comparing effect sizes of independent studies. *Psychological Bulletin, 92,* 500–504.

Seligman, M.E.P. (1975). *Helplessness: On depression, development, and death.* San Francisco: Freeman.

Singh, N.N., & Stott, G. (1975). The conservation of number in mental retardates. *Australian Journal of Mental Retardation, 3,* 215–221.

Spitz, H.H. (1976). Toward a relative psychology of mental retardation, with a special emphasis on evolution. In N.R. Ellis (ed.), *International review of research in mental retardation* (Vol. 8, pp. 35–56). New York: Academic Press.

Stamatelos, T., & Mott, D.W. (1983). Learned helplessness in persons with mental retardation: Art as a client-centered treatment modality. *The Arts in Psychotherapy, 10,* 241–249.

Stearns, K., & Borkowski, J.G. (1969). The development of conservation and horizontal-vertical space perception in mental retardation. *American Journal of Mental Deficiency, 73,* 785–790.

Stephens, B., Mahaney, E.J., & McLaughlin, J.A. (1972). Mental ages for achievement of Piagetian reasoning tasks. *Education and Training of the Mentally Retarded, 7,* 124–128.

Stephens, B., McLaughlin, J.A., Hunt, J., Mahaney, E.J., Kohlberg, L., Moore, B., & Aronfreed, J. (1974). Symposium: Developmental gains in the moral reasoning, moral judgment, and moral conduct of retarded and nonretarded persons. *American Journal of Mental Deficiency, 79,* 113–161.

Stephens, B., & McLaughlin, J.A. (1974). Two-year gains in reasoning by retarded and nonretarded persons. *American Journal of Mental Deficiency, 79,* 116–126.

Tanaka, M., Bennett-Gates, D., Malakoff, M.E., & Zigler, E. (1998). *Development of outerdirectedness in individuals with and without mental retardation.* New Haven, CT: Yale University.

Weiss, B., Weisz, J.R., & Bromfield, R. (1986). Performance of retarded and nonretarded persons on information-processing tasks: Further tests of the similar structure hypothesis. *Psychological Bulletin, 100,* 157–175.

Weisz, J.R. (1979). Perceived control and learned helplessness among mentally retarded and nonretarded children: A developmental analysis. *Developmental Psychology, 15,* 311–319.

(1981a). Effects of the "mentally retarded" label on adult judgments about child failure. *Journal of Abnormal Psychology, 90,* 371–374.

(1981b). Learned helplessness in black and white children identified by their schools as retarded and nonretarded: Performance deterioration in response to failure. *Developmental Psychology, 17,* 499–508.

Weisz, J.R., & Yeates, K.O. (1981). Cognitive development in retarded and nonretarded persons: Piagetian tests of the similar structure hypothesis. *Psychological Bulletin, 90,* 153–178.

Weisz, J.R., & Zigler, E. (1979). Cognitive development in retarded and nonretarded persons: Piagetian tests of the similar sequence hypothesis. *Psychological Bulletin, 86,* 831–851.

Yeates, K.O., & Weisz, J.R. (1985). On being called mentally retarded: Do developmental and professional perspectives limit labeling effects? *American Journal of Mental Deficiency, 90,* 349–352.

Yando, R., & Zigler, E. (1971). Outerdirectedness in the problem solving of institutionalized and noninstitutionalized normal and retarded children. *Developmental Psychology, 4,* 277–288.

Zigler, E. (1969). Development versus difference theories of mental retardation and the problem of motivation. *American Journal of Mental Deficiency, 73,* 536–556.

(1971). The retarded child as a whole person. In H.E. Adams, & W.K. Boardman (Eds.), *Advances in experimental clinical psychology.* Oxford: Pergamon.

(1987). The definition and classification of mental retardation. *Upsala Journal of Medical Science, Supplement, 13,* 1–10.

(1973). Why retarded children do not perform up to the level of their ability. In R.M. Allen, A.D. Cortazzo, & R. Toister (Eds.), *Theories of cognitive development: Implications for the mentally retarded.* Coral Gables, FL: University of Miami Press.

Zigler, E., & Balla, D. (eds.) (1982). *Mental retardation: The developmental difference controversy.* Hillsdale, NJ: Erlbaum.

Zigler, E., & Hodapp, R.M. (1986). *Understanding mental retardation.* New York: Cambridge University Press.

3 Developmental and Experiential Variables in the Self-Images of People with Mild Mental Retardation

Marion Glick[1]

The self-image has long been a central construct in personality theory (e.g., Allport, 1955; James, 1890; Rogers, 1951). A person's self-image, while shaped by experience, also organizes experience and motivates behavior. In research with children, adolescents, and adults, more positive self-images have been found to correlate with achievement, resolve to learn, greater internal locus of control, and greater resilience and stress resistance (Garmezy, 1983; Harter, 1983; Luthar, Zigler, & Goldstein, 1992; Sternberg & Kolligan, 1990; Switzky, 1997). These correlations may reflect the effect of positive experiences and adaptive personality characteristics (e.g., achievement, stress resistance) on the self-image rather than that of the self-image on adaptation. Most likely, the self-image is both a determinant and a consequence of experience and behavior. If achievement gives rise to academic self-esteem or perceived competence in that area (Harter, 1983), such self-esteem can lead to greater resolve to learn and the development of more effective learning strategies, as discussed by Switzky (1997).

The manner in which people with mental retardation view themselves should influence their functioning, just as it influences functioning in the general population. Moreover, people with mental retardation frequently encounter certain experiences (e.g., a disproportionately high incidence of failure, social stigmatization) that might adversely affect their self-images (Weisz, 1981; Zigler, 1971). Yet relatively little research has examined self-images in people with mental retardation. In part, this paucity of research reflects issues of measurement. A person's self-image is known only to the person; thus, effective measurement requires self-report. Concerns have been raised about the accuracy of such self-report in people with mental retardation, given their limited cognitive and language abilities (Zetlin,

1. The research studies described in this chapter were supported by Research Grant 03008 from the National Institute of Child Health and Human Development. I thank Ellen Weld, Daniel Loevins, and Elizabeth Pruett for their help in data collection and content coding for the study by Glick, Bybee, and Zigler (1997).

47

Heriot, & Turner, 1985). As the research to be reported in this chapter will indicate, when appropriate instruments are used, assessment of self-image seems possible for people with mild mental retardation and mental ages (MAs) of nine years or older.

The paucity of research on self-image in people with mental retardation may also reflect a preoccupation with cognitive functioning that for many years dominated research on mental retardation. As discussed by Zigler (1971), this focus on the cognitive functioning and intellectual ineffiencies of people with mental retardation was such that little attention was paid to the many other factors that also influence behavior. The major thrust of Zigler's research in mental retardation has been to look at the whole person, and thus to examine ways in which personality and motivational charac- teristics arising from certain life experiences interact with the person's developmental abilities to determine behavior on both cognitive and non- cognitive tasks (e.g., Achenbach & Zigler, 1968; Hodapp, Burack, & Zigler, 1990; Zigler, 1966, 1971; Zigler & Balla, 1982; Zigler, Balla, & Butterfield, 1968; Zigler & Burack, 1989; Zigler & Hodapp, 1986, 1991).

Zigler's developmental position on mental retardation differentiates cultural-familial mental retardation from forms of mental retardation with organic etiologies. Individuals with familial mental retardation display no known organic etiology, primarily function within the mild range of mental retardation, and comprise approximately 50 percent of people with mental retardation (Zigler & Hodapp, 1986). The developmental position assumes that these individuals represent the lower range of the normal distribution of intelligence. People with familial mental retardation are presumed to differ from the general population only in that development proceeds more slowly and attains a lower upper limit (Hodapp et al., 1990; Zigler, 1969; Zigler & Hodapp, 1986). Consequently, the principles of development that characterize individuals without mental retardation are assumed to apply also to people with cultural-familial retardation. Recent evidence suggests that the developmental framework can also be applied to people with various organic forms of mental retardation (Cicchetti & Pogge-Hesse, 1982; Hodapp & Zigler, 1995, 1997). When matched for mental age, indi- viduals with familial mental retardation and those without mental retarda- tion should perform similarly on cognitive tasks (Weisz & Zigler, 1979; Zigler, 1969). Where differences in cognitive performance appear despite identical MA, the assumption is that these differences reflect the operation of certain personality and motivational variables that arise from life experi- ences that people with mental retardation often encounter, such as social deprivation and frequent experiences of failure. These personality and mo- tivational variables are the topic of this book.

Like the other personality and motivational variables investigated by Zigler and his colleagues, self-images are presumed to be influenced by life experiences and to affect performance. In addition, because they are concepts, self-images are presumed to be influenced by the person's level of cognitive development. Thus, the research on self-image conducted by Zigler and his colleagues over a period of forty years examines the influences both of cognitive development and of life experiences. The underlying formulations and findings from this research will be reviewed in this chapter.

The cognitive-developmental interpretation of self-image and supporting research will be presented first. This interpretation derives from basic principles that define normative development, and should be applicable to people with familial mental retardation and to those without mental retardation. Similarly, self-images are central in the functioning of both groups. For these reasons, this cognitive-developmental approach has been advanced through studies of normative child development, of children and adolescents with mild mental retardation, and of adults and children with emotional disorders (see Glick & Zigler, 1985). In presenting the cognitive-developmental interpretation, the focus will be on research with individuals without mental retardation.

The development of self-images in people with mental retardation will be discussed in the second section of the chapter. The developmental position on mental retardation generates the expectation that when matched for MA, individuals with mental retardation and those without should manifest self-images indicative of the same cognitive-developmental level. In light of the focus of the developmental approach to mental retardation on personality characteristics that arise from particular life experiences, a major concern in the research on the self-images of people with mental retardation has been with experiential variables that may moderate the unfolding of the developmental sequence.

Recent findings concerning various self-images of adolescents with mild mental retardation, correlations among measures, and relationships to depression will be presented in the third section of the chapter.

A Cognitive-Developmental Interpretation of Self-Image

Achenbach and Zigler (1963) first advanced the cognitive-developmental interpretation of self-image disparity. They posited that increased disparity between the real self-image (the person's current view of self) and the ideal self-image (the ideal person that he or she would like to be) was a natural concomitant of normal growth and development. This formulation was based on two developmental principles. First, in accordance with the developmental principles of Werner (1948) and Piaget (1951), higher levels of development entail greater cognitive differentiation. In any cognition, therefore, the more developmentally advanced person tends to employ more categories and finer distinctions within each category than a person functioning at a lower developmental level. This greater differentiation should result in a greater likelihood for disparity between a person's conceptualization of the real self and the ideal self. The second principle is that with development, individuals incorporate increasingly complex social demands and expectations (Zigler & Glick, 1986; Zigler & Phillips, 1960). The greater self-demands at higher developmental levels and the guilt associated with failure to meet these demands should also lead to greater disparity between the real and ideal self-images at higher developmental levels. This hypothesized relationship between self-image disparity and guilt has been supported by findings that in both children and young adults, guilt is correlated with greater self-image disparity and a higher ideal self-image (Bybee & Zigler, 1991).

This cognitive-developmental interpretation of self-image disparity stands in marked contrast to the more traditional view, first advanced by Rogers and Dymond (1954), that greater real-ideal disparity indicates a lack of positive self-regard and hence maladjustment. This Rogerian interpretation of greater real-ideal disparity as an indicator of maladjustment has retained some followers (e.g., Higgins, Klein, & Strauman, 1985).

Findings from many studies with a variety of populations have supported the cognitive-developmental interpretation of self-image disparity. In studies with nonretarded children and adolescents, greater self-image disparity has been found to be related to higher developmental functioning as indicated by each of the following variables: (a) older chronological age, (b) higher IQ as a reflection of level of cognitive ability, (c) the presence of thought rather than action symptoms, with expression in thought presumed to reflect developmentally higher functioning (Piaget, 1951; Werner, 1948), and (d) evidence of nonegocentric thought in a role-taking task and greater maturity in moral reasoning (Bybee, 1986; Glick & Zigler, 1985; Katz & Zigler, 1967; Katz, Zigler, & Zalk, 1975; Leahy & Huard, 1976; Luthar et al., 1992; Phillips & Zigler, 1980). In all these studies, a more positive ideal self-image was also correlated with developmentally higher functioning. In some studies, a less positive real self-image appeared at higher developmental levels (Katz & Zigler, 1967; Phillips & Zigler, 1980). Research with adult psychiatric and nonpsychiatric patients likewise revealed greater self-image disparity and more differentiation of other aspects of the self-image

Table 3.1. *Developmental differences in self-image*

Developmental variables	Self-image measure	
	Real-ideal disparity	Ideal
Older chronological age	greater	higher
Higher IQ	greater	higher
Thought rather than action symptoms	greater	higher
Nonegocentric reasoning	greater	higher
Greater maturity in moral reasoning	greater	higher
Better coping (adult patients)	greater	——

for patients with higher developmental functioning as indicated by coping effectiveness (Achenbach & Zigler, 1963; Mylet, Styfco, & Zigler, 1979). Contrary to the Rogerian interpretation, psychiatric and nonpsychiatric patients did not differ in self-image disparity.

The major developmental differences found in the self-image research are summarized in Table 3.1. The consistent finding that greater real-ideal disparity characterizes developmentally higher functioning accords with the developmental interpretation first advanced by Achenbach and Zigler (1963). Equally consistent has been the finding that more positive ideal self-images are associated with developmentally higher functioning in childhood and adolescence. This relationship between developmental level and ideal self-images, although not posited by Achenbach and Zigler, may reflect two developmental processes (Glick & Zigler, 1985). The first is the greater incorporation of societal demands and values at higher developmental levels that Achenbach and Zigler discussed in reference to self-image disparity. The second is the capacity for abstract hypothetical thinking that emerges at higher developmental levels (Piaget, 1951; Werner, 1948). If differentiated from and conceptualized as distinct from the real self, the ideal self-image is after all an abstraction.

The Influences of Cognitive Development and Experiential Variables on Self-Image

Zigler's developmental position on mental retardation and the cognitive-developmental interpretation of self-image generate two directions for research on the self-images of people with mental retardation. The first concerns cognitive-developmental changes in self-images that should be associated with differences in mental age (MA). Higher MA should be associated with developmentally higher characteristics of the self-image:

greater real-ideal self-image disparity and higher ideal self-images. As described previously, the developmental position posits that individuals with familial retardation differ from the general population only in that development proceeds more slowly and attains a lower upper limit. Thus, when matched for MA, the cognitive performance of these individuals and those without mental retardation should be similar.

The second area of research concerns experiential variables that can give rise to personality and motivational characteristics that can affect the unfolding of the developmental sequence. As underscored in this book, such variables are a central focus of the developmental position on mental retardation.

Developmental Level, Institutionalization, and Mental Retardation

Based on the assumption that self-image disparity is influenced by general cognitive-developmental factors and by particular psychodynamic factors that are outgrowths of a person's unique life experiences, Zigler, Balla, and Watson (1972) investigated self-image disparity in institutionalized and noninstitutionalized children and adolescents with mild mental retardation and with average IQ. Three subgroups of institutionalized and three subgroups of noninstitutionalized boys were studied: (a) adolescents with mild mental retardation, (b) younger children of average intelligence matched by MA with the retarded group, and (c) adolescents of average intelligence matched by CA with the retarded group. The adolescents with mental retardation were exclusively of familial etiology, and had no gross motor or sensory disorders. The mean chronological ages (with mental ages in parentheses) of the adolescents with mental retardation were 16.2 (10.5) for the institutionalized subsample and 14.5 (10.0) for the noninstitutionalized subsample. These means for the participants of average intelligence were: 10.9 (10.4) for the younger institutionalized group, 16.1 (15.4) for the older institutionalized group, 9.8 (10.7) for the younger noninstitutionalized group, and 16.1 (16.0) for the older noninstitutionalized group. The self-image items were those used previously by Katz and Zigler (1967), and they were presented in two formats: a six-alternative questionnaire and an adjective checklist. A correlation of .40 between disparity scores on the questionnaire and on the checklist provided some evidence of the construct validity of the measures.

The findings in this study supported an interpretation of self-image as influenced by both cognitive-developmental and experiential-psychodynamic factors. Consistent with the cognitive-developmental interpretation and the research findings summarized in the previous section, the children at the higher MA levels (older children, both institutionalized and noninstitutionalized) displayed (a) greater real-ideal self-image disparity (as measured by both the questionnaire and adjective checklist), (b) higher ideal self-images (as measured by the questionnaire), and (c) lower real self-images (as measured by the adjective checklist) than children of lower MA (adolescents with mild mental retardation and younger children of average intelligence, within both the institutionalized and noninstitutionalized subsamples).

The remaining results of the study pointed to psychodynamic features of the self-concept that appeared to be outgrowths of the individuals' unique life histories. The institutionalized boys, regardless of mental age or mental retardation status, had lower real and lower ideal self-image scores than noninstitutionalized children. Even though they displayed lower ideal self-images, the institutionalized boys showed greater self-image disparity than the noninstitutionalized boys because of their very low real self-images. The children and adolescents living in institutions thus appeared both to have very low senses of self-esteem and to set low standards for themselves. Compared with children of the same MA without mental retardation, the children with mild mental retardation had lower ideal self-images, and thus displayed less self-image disparity.

Whether the differences between the institutionalized and noninstitutionalized groups reflected the effects of institutionalization per se, or were outgrowths of negative experiences that frequently precede institutionalization, could not be determined in the study by Zigler et al. (1972). However, length of institutionalization was not related to any self-image measure. Thus, length of institutional residence did not appear to affect the children's self-images. In addition, as will be discussed later in this section, findings by Bybee, Ennis, and Zigler (1990) suggest that the effects of institutionalization may be dependent on numerous variables, including the quality of institutional care.

The lower ideal self-images found by Zigler et al. (1972) for children with mental retardation may reflect the experiences with failure that these children frequently encounter. Such experiences can lead to the lowering of aspirations and to an orientation toward avoidance of failure rather than striving to succeed (Weisz, 1981; Zigler, 1971).

Developmental Level and Experiences Associated with Mental Retardation

Leahy, Balla, and Zigler (1982) also reported lower ideal self-images in children with mental retardation. They examined children with familial mental retardation (mean CA = 11.9, mean MA = 6.9) and two groups of children of nonretarded intelligence: a younger group matched to those with mental retardation by MA (mean CA = 6.9, mean MA = 7.7) and an older group matched to those with mental retardation by CA (CA = 11.6, MA = 13.9). Institutionalization was not a variable in this study; the subsample with mental retardation attended special education classes in public schools. Real and ideal self-images were assessed using two formats: (1) the Katz-Zigler (1967) adjective checklist used by Zigler et al. (1972), and (2) a picture instrument representing the Katz–Zigler items (Phillips & Zigler, 1980).

In accordance with the cognitive-developmental formulation, more positive ideal self-images appeared at higher MA levels. The influence of experiential-psychodynamic factors was reflected in the less positive ideal and real self-images of the children with mental retardation. As was found by Zigler et al. (1972), the children with mental retardation had significantly less positive ideal self-images on both formats than children of average ability in either group (those matched by MA and those matched by CA). In addition, on the checklist measure, the real self-images of the children with mental retardation were found to be lower that those of either intellectually average group. Being labeled mentally retarded and placed in a self-contained special education class may result in both a less positive view of the self and in lowered aspirations (ideal self-image).

Quality of Institutional Care and Domains of the Self-Concept

Bybee et al. (1990) examined self-concepts and outerdirectedness in two groups of adolescents with mental retardation: (a) adolescents residing in an institution widely recognized for providing high quality care, and (b) adolescents residing at home who attended day school with the institutionalized group. The mean CA (with MA in parentheses) for the institutionalized and noninstitutionalized subsamples were 15.8 (9.4) and 15.4 (9.1), respectively.

The Perceived Competence Scale for Children (Harter, 1982) was used to assess the adolescents' real self-images in four domains: cognitive, social, physical, and global (or general) self-worth. No evidence was found that residing in a high-quality institution adversely affected the adolescents' self-images; the institutionalized and noninstitutionalized subsamples did not differ in any self-image scores.

Concerning the four self-concept domains, both groups of adolescents (institutionalized and noninstitutionalized) rated themselves significantly more positively on the global self-worth and cognitive subscales than on the social and physical abilities subscales. The social and physical abilities domains therefore appear to be salient areas of self-perceived deficiency for adolescents with mental retardation. The lower scores in the social domain are consistent with findings that people with mental retardation frequently display deficits in social interaction skills (Greenspan, 1979; Zigler & Hodapp, 1986). The lower scores in the physical abilities domain may reflect handicaps and problems with motor coordination that are found frequently in people with mental retardation who attend special schools or reside in institutions (Zigler & Hodapp, 1986).

The higher self-rating the adolescents gave on general (global) self-worth compared with some specific content domains seemed particularly encouraging. Adolescents with mental retardation may be able to maintain a view of themselves as worthwhile despite their recognition of limitations in specific areas. Although the adolescents' higher self-ratings in the cognitive domain seem surprising, social comparison processes offer a possible explanation (Harter, 1985a; Widaman et al., 1992). Renick and Harter (1989) found that mainstreamed children with learning disabilities and IQs in the normal range rated themselves lower on the cognitive subscale of the Perceived Competence Scale for Children than did nonhandicapped children in regular classes. By contrast, ratings by mainstreamed children with mild mental retardation on the cognitive subscale did not differ significantly from those provided by nonhandicapped children in their classes (Silon & Harter, 1985).

The format of the Perceived Competence Scale encourages the use of a social comparison group. Further analysis revealed that the children with learning disabilities and those with mental retardation used different comparison groups in rating themselves. Whereas in rating their cognitive competence, the children with learning disabilities compared themselves to nonhandicapped children in regular classes, children with mental retardation, even if mainstreamed, compared themselves to other children with mental retardation. If children with mental retardation, even when mainstreamed, use the scholastic performance of other mentally retarded children in judging their own cognitive competence, adolescents with mental retardation who attend a special school and may reside in an institution might well compare themselves with other students with mental retardation in the special school when rating their own cognitive competence.

Summary

The studies reviewed in this section revealed the influences of both cognitive-developmental and experiential variables on the self-images of chil-

Table 3.2. *Self-image in mental retardation:*
Developmental and experiential variables

	Self-image measure	
Variables	Real	Ideal
Cognitive-developmental		
Older MA		higher
Experiential		
Institutionalization[a]	lower	lower
Mental retardation	lower[b]	lower

[a]Effects found by Zigler et al. (1972) but not by Bybee et al. (1990). Many variables including quality of institutional care appear to influence this effect.
[b]Effect found by Leahy et al. (1982) but not by Zigler et al. (1972).

dren and adolescents with mild mental retardation. The major findings are summarized in Table 3.2. Consistent with the cognitive-developmental interpretation of self-image and with the developmental position on mental retardation, higher ideal self-images were found at higher mental age levels (Leahy et al., 1982; Zigler et al., 1972). Zigler et al. (1972) also found greater real-ideal self-image disparity at higher MA levels. These findings closely parallel results obtained in research with nonretarded individuals. As described previously, that research consistently found greater self-image disparity and higher ideal self-images at higher developmental levels.

A major emphasis in the developmental position has been on experiential variables that give rise to personality and motivational characteristics that may modify performance on cognitive tasks. As Table 3.2 indicates, children in institutions, both with and without mental retardation, could display less positive real self-images and lowered aspirations (ideal self-images) than their noninstitutionalized counterparts. However, where quality of care was high, institutional living did not affect self-images. Even at equivalent MA levels, children and adolescents with mental retardation displayed lower aspirations, and in one study, less positive real self-images than children without mental retardation. Social stigmatization and failure are frequently encountered by people with mental retardation, and these experiences can lower feelings of self-worth and expectations about future achievement.

In the developmental research on self-image, the influence of experiential variables was first examined in individuals with mental retardation. Subsequent studies extended this focus to individuals without mental retardation. The findings of Katz et al. (1975) suggested that social stigmatization resulting from being labeled emotionally disturbed and placed in special education classes negatively affected children's real self-images. Ethnicity and low socioeconomic status were found particularly to affect children's ideal self-images (Phillips & Zigler, 1980).

A strength of the cognitive-developmental interpretation of self-image is that from its inception the research has encompassed diverse populations. Despite the disparate populations, the underlying developmental issues have remained constant with the theoretical formulation proceeding along a single line. Thus, the research on normative development has enhanced understanding of special populations, and research with special populations has elucidated processes in the normative development of self-image (Glick, 1998).

A Closer Examination of Various Self-Images of Adolescents with Mild Mental Retardation

In an extension of our earlier work, Glick, Bybee, and Zigler (1997) examined three types of self-image and their relation to depression among adolescents with mild mental retardation in a large urban school system. The first concern of the study was with the construct validity of self-image measures for individuals with mild mental retardation. The second concern was to broaden understanding of these individuals' self-images through the use of spontaneous self-description and the inclusion of the negative future self-image, which Ogilvie (1987) termed the "undesired self." The third concern was to examine the relationships among self-images and depression.

The ability of people with mental retardation to adequately comprehend self-image questionnaires – and thus whether such measures are appropriate for these individuals – has been questioned. Zetlin et al. (1985) analyzed responses to questionnaires with a yes-no format by adult participants with IQs ranging from 28 to 65 ($M = 51$). They reported the majority of responses to be ambiguous and problematic to score. However, level of mental retardation was not addressed in the analyses, and only the yes-no format was examined. Sigelman, Budd, Winer, Schoenrock, and Martin (1982) analyzed responses of three samples of children and adults with mental retardation to alternatively structured questions. The mean IQs of the samples ranged from 40 to 48. They found major problems with acquiescence response bias when a yes-no format was used, but valid responses given by the majority of the samples to a multiple-choice questionnaire.

Few participants were found to be able to respond to open-ended question-naires. Furthermore, at higher IQ levels, accuracy increased and response bias decreased.

Zigler's developmental position concerns individuals in the mild range of mental retardation with no known organic etiology. Studies derived from this formulation have included older children and adolescents with mild mental retardation whose MAs corresponded to chronological ages for which the self-image measures were appropriate. The consistency of the developmental findings of the studies just reviewed provides one indication that the self-image measures used were appropriate.

Glick et al. (1997) examined the responses of adolescents with mild mental retardation both to a modified version of the Katz–Zigler (1967) real and ideal self-image scales and to the Self-Perception Profile for Children (Harter, 1985b). Inasmuch as both the Katz–Zigler real self-image and the Harter scales assess current view of self, a significant correlation between the measures would reflect construct validity. The contents of the adolescent's spontaneous descriptions of their real, ideal, and negative future images of self should also shed light on the degree to which the concepts were understood.

Spontaneous self-descriptions were requested not only to illuminate the adolescents' understandings of self-concepts but to broaden knowledge about their views of self. Most research on self-image has used reactive measures on which participants rate themselves on dimensions provided by the researcher; these dimensions often have little salience for the individual (McGuire, 1984). Spontaneous self-descriptions, by contrast, entail characteristics salient to the person's own view of self, and such descriptions include many contents not included in standardized inventories (Bybee, Glick, & Zigler, 1990; McGuire, 1984). Knowledge about self-perception was further extended through inclusion of the negative future self-image. Ogilvie (1987) discussed the importance of this self-image, the "undesired self" – what the individual fears he or she might become. He proposed this as an important contrast to the ideal self-image. Being less abstract and more experience-based than the ideal self-image, the undesired self may be an important dimension whereby individuals gauge satisfaction with life (Ogilvie, 1987).

Major theories of depression have long posited a relationship between low self-esteem and depression (Abramson, Seligman, & Teasdale, 1978; Beck, 1967; Freud, 1917/1986; Pyszczynski & Greenberg, 1987). This assumption, common to the theories, is supported by findings that for adolescents without mental retardation, a lower real self-image correlates with greater depression (Allgood-Merten, Lewinsohn, & Hops, 1990; Doerfler et al., 1988; Harter & Jackson, 1993; Luthar et al., 1992; Renouf & Harter, 1990). A similar correlation between self-image and depression for adolescents with mild mental retardation would provide further evidence for the validity of self-image measures for these adolescents, and would also extend understanding about depression in people with mild mental retardation.

Participants in the Glick et al. (1997) study were twenty adolescents (nine male, eleven female) in special education classes for mental retardation in a large urban school system. Their mean IQ was 66.0 (range = 49–74) and their mean age was 13 years 3 months (range = 12 years 2 months to 17 years 1 month). Eleven students were African-American, eight were Hispanic, and one was Caucasian.

Self-image measures were (a) spontaneous descriptions of real, ideal, and negative future self-images, (b) the Katz–Zigler (1967) real and ideal self-image scales, and (c) the Self-Perception Profile for Children (Harter, 1985b). For each of the three spontaneous self-descriptions, the students were asked to provide five ideas. Responding was facilitated through the use of a sentence completion format (e.g., "I am a person who . . . " [real self-image]; "I don't want to be a person who . . . " [negative future self-image]. The Katz–Zigler scales have been used in all investigations of the cognitive-developmental approach to self-image, and have demonstrated good reliability for individuals at the MA levels of the participants in this study. Based on pilot research, real and ideal self-images were each assessed using ten of the twenty items of the measure, and four response alternatives were offered for each item – ranging from "I am a lot like this" to "I am not at all like this." Documentation of the reliability and validity of the Self-Perception Profile for Children is provided by Harter (1982, 1985b). Depression was measured using the Children's Depression Inventory, or CDI (Kovacs, 1983). The CDI, the most thoroughly researched self-report measure of childhood depression, has been employed frequently as a criterion measure in studies of depressed versus nondepressed children, and as a point of comparison in the validation of other depression measures. It has also been used with children with mental retardation (Matson, Barrett, & Helsel, 1988).

All measures were administered orally. Each participant was seen in three individual interview sessions. In the first session, spontaneous real and then spontaneous ideal self-descriptions were elicited first. Following this, the Katz–Zigler real and ideal self-image scales were administered. At the end of the first session, participants completed several true-false and

Likert-type screening items (Senatore, Matson, & Kazdin, 1985) in order to assess their accuracy in responding to such formats. All participants responded accurately on these items. In the second session, spontaneous descriptions of negative future self-images were elicited followed by the Self-Perception Profile for Children (Harter, 1985b). The CDI was administered in the third session.

The order of administration of measures was determined by a number of considerations. As has been traditional in self-image research, the real self-image was described before the ideal in both spontaneous description and the Katz–Zigler questionnaire. To reduce the influence of real and ideal self-descriptions on descriptions of the negative future self-image, the latter descriptions were elicited some days later at the beginning of the second session. Of the self-image measures, the Harter (1985b) scale is the most structured and the spontaneous descriptions the least structured. To reduce the influence of the more structured measures, spontaneous descriptions were elicited first, followed by the Katz–Zigler and the Harter self-image measures. The CDI was administered last so that responses to this scale would not influence self-image measures. The true-false and Likert-type screening items were administered at the end of the first session to minimize their influence on other measures. The instructions for all other measures in the study emphasized that there are no right or wrong answers. By contrast, the screening items were designed to have correct and incorrect responses.

Correlations Among Self-Image Measures and Depression

The students showed much consistency in their responses to the Katz–Zigler real self-image scale and the Harter Self-Perception measure. As indicated in Table 3.3, overall scores on these two assessments of real self-image were highly intercorrelated, and more positive real self-images on both measures correlated with lower depression. Katz–Zigler ideal self-image scores were not correlated with depression. With respect to the domains of the Self-Perception Profile (Harter, 1985), two domains (physical appearance and social acceptance) were unrelated to scores on the other domains, the CDI, and the Katz–Zigler real self-image. The majority of the remaining domains were intercorrelated and related to depression and Katz–Zigler real self-image scores (see Table 3.4).

The consistency of the students' responses across self-image measures and across the majority of domains of the Harter Self-Perception Scale support the construct validity of these assessments with adolescents with

Table 3.3. *Correlations among self-image measures and depression*

Measure	?	3
1. Real self-image (Katz–Zigler)	.72***	.47*
2. Self-perception (Harter)	——	.56**
3. Children's Depression Inventory		

*p < .05
**p < .01
***p < .001

Table 3.4. *Correlations of self-perception domains with Katz–Zigler and CDI scores*

Measure	2	3	4	5	6
Domains (Harter)					
1. Athletic competence	.22	.49*	.29	.49*	.12
2. Behavioral conduct	——	.50*	.85****	.64**	.64**
3. Scholastic competence		——	.35	.38	.63**
4. Global self-worth			——	.64**	.42[a]
5. Real self-image (Katz–Zigler)				——	.47**
6. Children's Depression Inventory					——

*p < .05
**p < .01
****p < .0001
[a]p = .06

mild mental retardation. The relationships of less positive real self-images to greater depression mirror the findings obtained for adolescents without mental retardation described previously. That the correlations with depression appeared also in adolescents with mild mental retardation provides further indication that the real self-image measures can appropriately be used with these individuals.

Examination of the correlates of the content domains of the Harter scale points particularly to the importance of the behavioral conduct domain for a sense of self-worth and absence of depression in adolescents with mild mental retardation. Behavioral conduct subscores correlated highly not only with global self-worth subscores ($r = .85$, $p < .0001$) but with the Katz–Zigler measure of real self-image ($r = .635$, $p < .003$) and with the absence of depression ($r = .636$, $p < .003$). Furthermore, as will be indi-

Table 3.5. *Frequently mentioned contents of spontaneous self-descriptions*

Content category	Percentage of students mentioning
Real self-image	
Helpful, caring	70
Well behaved	45
Other personality traits (e.g., happy, do my best)	60
Academic	55
Athletic	30
Sociable, friendly	25
Interests, hobbies	25
Ideal self-image	
Specific occupation	95
Desired personality traits	45
Occupational success/satisfaction	25
Educational goals	—
Athletic	20
Negative future self-image	
Mean, angry, fighting	60
Other negative personality traits	45
Criminality	45
Drug/alcohol abuse	30
Undesired specific occupation	25
Injury, illness, death	25

cated, the content category involving being well-behaved, respectful, and not starting trouble was mentioned by almost half of the adolescents in their spontaneous descriptions of the real self-image. The adolescents' emphasis on behaving well may in part reflect a focus on this dimension by teachers. Nevertheless, the salience of this dimension for the adolescents is heartening. Behavioral conduct is important in life adjustment (e.g., Goleman, 1995), and it is an aspect of functioning that is achievable for individuals with mild mental retardation just as for those of average intelligence.

Contents of Spontaneous Descriptions of Real, Ideal, and Negative Future Self-Images

Table 3.5 presents the content categories the adolescents mentioned most frequently in spontaneous descriptions of real, ideal, and negative future self-images, and the percentages of students who mentioned these categories in at least one of the five self-descriptive items they gave for the image.

Inspection of Table 3.5 points to the appropriateness of the contents to the different self-images. Both the contents and the phrasings of the adolescents' descriptions of the real self-image focus on present characteristics, whereas the emphasis in ideal self-descriptions was on future goals. As was found for children and adolescents without mental retardation (Bybee et al., 1990), the ideal self-image content mentioned most frequently by the adolescents with mild mental retardation was a specific occupation. The contents of the adolescents' descriptions of negative future self-images were clearly undesired.

Contents mentioned less frequently were likewise appropriate to the different self-images. For the real self-image, 15 percent of the students mentioned an aspect of physical appearance in at least one self-descriptive item, and 10 percent mentioned relations with current family members. For 20 percent of the subjects, at least one of the five self-descriptive items was classified as "other" primarily because of low frequency. Included in the "other" category were descriptions of liking: animals, travel, dating, particular foods or possessions; information about age, sex, religious affiliation; and a few responses that could not be coded by content category (e.g., "I am a human being," "I am still alive"). With respect to the ideal self-image, 15 percent of the adolescents mentioned relations with or helping their family in at least one ideal self-description, 10 percent mentioned marriage or having children, and 10 percent mentioned an aspect of physical appearance (e.g., pretty, being taller). For 15 percent of the adolescents, at least one of the five self-descriptive items was classified as "other," again primarily because of low frequency. Contents classified as "other" included being happy, travel, being like a specific person (e.g., Michael Jordan), living a long life. With respect to the negative future self-image, the content categories presented in Table 3.5 cover all responses except those categorized as "other." For 10 percent of the adolescents, at least one of the five negative future self-descriptions fell in the "other" content category because of low frequency. Responses in this category included seeing others hurt, making mistakes, and stopping church attendance.

In summary, the adolescents with mild mental retardation responded consistently and appropriately across a variety of measures of self-image. The domain of behavioral conduct appeared particularly salient to the adolescents' self-image. As has been found in individuals without mental retardation, lower real self-images were correlated with greater depression.

Self-Images of People with Mild Mental Retardation: Summary and Implications for Research and Intervention

The research presented in this chapter provides considerable evidence that adolescents with mild mental retardation can respond consistently and appropriately on many measures of self-image. Significant correlations appeared across various self-image measures, and responses in spontaneous self-descriptions were appropriate and meaningful. Furthermore, many of the findings with children and adolescents with mild mental retardation were similar to ones obtained for individuals without mental retardation. These similar findings include (a) greater real-ideal self-image disparity and higher ideal self-images at higher MA levels, (b) evidence that experiential variables can lower both the current view of self (real self-image) and aspirations (ideal self-image), and (c) the correlation of a lower real self-image with depression. The research thus supports the use of self-image measures both for further research on mild mental retardation and as one means for evaluating interventions.

Inasmuch as these measures appear appropriate and useful for adolescents, they may be useful also for adults with mild mental retardation. The degree to which self-image measures might be meaningful for understanding children with mild mental retardation or adolescents and adults with moderate mental retardation could be determined by further investigation. However, even if self-image measures were found to be useful only for adolescents and adults with mild mental retardation, the measures would in fact be applicable to the majority of people with mental retardation.

The fundamental assumption of the cognitive-developmental interpretation of self-image is that self-image disparity will be greater at higher developmental levels. Research with nonretarded children and adolescents has consistently supported this presupposition, and has also yielded consistent evidence that the ideal self-image is more positive at higher developmental levels. The greater real-ideal self-image disparity and the higher ideal self-images found at higher MA levels in children and adolescents with mild mental retardation points to the applicability of the cognitive-developmental interpretation to people with familial mental retardation. Furthermore, these findings support the fundamental assumption in the developmental position on mental retardation that the principles of development that characterize people without mental retardation apply also to individuals with cultural-familial mental retardation.

A concern in research has been that the life experiences of people with mental retardation – which can include high incidences of failure and social stigmatization – can lead to disproportionately high rates of depression (e.g., Benson, 1985; Jacobson, 1990; Prout & Schaefer, 1985). Although low self-esteem may as much result from as create depression, an implication of the correlation of various measures of the real self-image and depression is that efforts to reinforce a more positive real self-image could reduce depression for individuals with mental retardation. The salience of the behavioral conduct domain to overall self-esteem for the adolescents examined by Glick et al. (1997) suggests that this aspect of functioning might particularly be stressed in efforts to heighten self-esteem in people with mental retardation.

References

Abramson, L.Y., Seligman, M.E.P., & Teasdale, J.D. (1978). Learned helplessness in humans: Critique and reformulation. *Journal of Abnormal Psychology, 87,* 49–74.

Achenbach, T., & Zigler, E. (1963). Social competence and self-image disparity in psychiatric and nonpsychiatric patients. *Journal of Abnormal and Social Psychology, 67,* 197–205.

(1968). Cue-learning and problem-learning strategies in normal and retarded children. *Child Development, 3,* 827–848.

Allgood-Merten, B., Lewinsohn, P.M., & Hops, H. (1990). Sex differences and adolescent depression. *Journal of Abnormal Psychology, 99,* 55–63.

Allport, G.W. (1955). *Becoming: Basic considerations for a psychology of personality.* New Haven: Yale University Press.

Beck, A.T. (1967). *Depression: Clinical, experimental, and theoretical aspects.* New York: Hoeber.

Benson, B. (1985). Behavior disorders and mental retardation. Associations with age, sex, and levels of functioning in an outpatient clinic sample. *Applied Research in Mental Retardation, 6,* 79–85.

Bybee, J. (1986). *The self-image and guilt: Relationships to gender, developmental level, and classroom behavior.* Unpublished doctoral dissertation, Yale University, New Haven.

Bybee, J., Ennis, P., & Zigler, E. (1990). Effects of institutionalization on the self-concept and outerdirectedness of adolescents with mental retardation. *Exceptionality, 1,* 215–226.

Bybee, J., Glick, M., & Zigler, E. (1990). Differences across gender, grade level, and academic track in the content of the ideal self-image. *Sex Roles, 22,* 349–358.

Bybee, J., & Zigler, E. (1991). The self-image and guilt: A further test of the cognitive-developmental formulation. *Journal of Personality, 59,* 733–745.

Cicchetti, D., & Pogge-Hesse, P. (1982). Possible contributions of the study of organically retarded persons to developmental theory. In E. Zigler and D. Balla (eds.), *Mental retardation: The developmental-difference controversy.* Hillsdale, NJ: Erlbaum.

Doerfler, L.A., Felner, R.D., Rowlison, R.T., Raley, P.A., & Evans, E. (1988). Depression in children and adolescents: A comparative analysis of the utility and construct validity of two assessment measures. *Journal of Consulting and Clinical Psychology, 56,* 769–772.

Freud, S. (1986). Mourning and melancholia. In J. Coyne (ed.), *Essential papers on depression* (pp. 48–63). New York: New York University Press (original work published 1917).

Garmezy, N. (1983). Stressors of childhood. In N. Garmezy & M. Rutter (eds.). *Stress, coping, and development in children* (pp. 43–84). New York: McGraw-Hill.

Glick, M. (1998). A developmental approach to psychopathology in people with mild mental retardation. In J. Burack, R. Hodapp, & E. Zigler (eds.), *Handbook of mental retardation and development* (pp. 563–580). New York: Cambridge University Press.

Glick, M., Bybee, J., & Zigler, E. (1997). [Self-images of adolescents with mild mental retardation]. Unpublished raw data.

Glick, M., & Zigler, E. (1985). Self-image: A cognitive-developmental approach. In R. Leahy (ed.). *The development of self* (pp. 1–42). New York: Academic Press.

Goleman, D. (1995). *Emotional intelligence.* New York: Bantam.

Greenspan, S. (1979). Social intelligence in the retarded. In N. Ellis (ed.), *Handbook of mental deficiency, psychological theory and research.* Hillsdale, NJ: Erlbaum.

Harter, S. (1982). The Perceived Competence Scale for Children. *Child Development, 53,* 87–97.

    (1983). The development of the self-system. In M. Hetherington (ed.), *Handbook of child psychology: Social and personality development* (Vol. 4, pp. 275–385). New York: Wiley.

    (1985a). Processes underlying the construction, maintenance, and enhancement of the self-concept in children. In J. Suls and A. Greenwald (eds.), *Psychological perspectives on the self* (Vol. 3). Hillsdale, NJ: Erlbaum.

    (1985b). *Manual for the Self-Perception Profile for Children.* Unpublished manuscript, University of Denver.

Harter, S., & Jackson, B. (1993). Young adolescents' perception of the link between low self-worth and depressed affect. *Journal of Early Adolescence, 13,* 383–407.

Higgins, E. T., Klein, R., & Strauman, T. (1985). Self-concept discrepancy theory: A psychological model for distinguishing among different aspects of depression and anxiety. *Social Cognition, 3,* 51–76.

Hodapp, R. M., Burack, J. A., & Zigler, E. (1990). *Issues in the developmental approach to mental retardation.* New York: Cambridge University Press.

Hodapp, R. M., & Zigler, E. (1995). Past, present and future issues in the developmental approach to mental retardation. In D. Cicchetti & D. Cohen (eds.), *Manual of developmental psychopathology* (Vol. 2, pp. 299–331). New York: Wiley.

Hodapp, R. M., & Zigler, E. (1997). New issues in the developmental approach to mental retardation. In W. E. MacLean Jr. (ed.), *Handbook of mental deficiency, psychological theory and research* (3rd ed., pp. 115–136). Hillsdale, NJ: Erlbaum.

Jacobson, J.W. (1990). Do some mental disorders occur less frequently among persons with mental retardation? *American Journal on Mental Retardation, 94,* 596–602.

James, W. (1890). *Principles of psychology.* New York: Holt.

Katz, P., & Zigler, E. (1967). Self-image disparity: A developmental approach. *Journal of Personality and Social Psychology, 5,* 186–195.

Katz, P., Zigler, E., & Zalk, S. (1975). Children's self-image disparity: The effects of age, maladjustment, and action-thought orientation. *Developmental Psychology, 11,* 546–550.

Kovacs, M. (1983). *The Children's Depression Inventory: A self-rated depression scale for school-aged youngsters.* Unpublished manuscript, University of Pittsburgh School of Medicine.

Leahy, R., Balla, D., & Zigler, E. (1982). Role-taking, self-image, and imitation in retarded and nonretarded individuals. *American Journal of Mental Deficiency, 86,* 372–379.

Leahy, R. L. & Huard, C. (1976). Role taking and self-image disparity in children. *Developmental Psychology, 12,* 501–508.

Luthar, S. S., Zigler, E., & Goldstein, D. (1992). Psychosocial adjustment among intellectually gifted adolescents: The role of cognitive-developmental and experiential factors. *Journal of Child Psychology and Psychiatry, 33,* 361–373.

Matson, J., Barrett, R., & Helsel, W. (1988). Depression in mentally retarded children. *Research in Developmental Disabilities, 9,* 39–46.

McGuire, W.J. (1984). Search for the self: Going beyond self-esteem and the reactive self. In R.A. Zucker, J. Aronoff, & A.I. Rabin (eds.). *Personality and the prediction of behavior* (pp. 73–120). New York: Academic Press.

Mylet, M., Styfco, S. J., & Zigler, E. (1979). The interrelationship between self-image disparity and social competence, defensive style, and adjustment status. *Journal of Nervous and Mental Disease, 167,* 553–560.

Ogilvie, D.M. (1987). The undesired self: A neglected variable in personality research. *Journal of Personality and Social Psychology, 52,* 379–385.

Phillips, D.A., & Zigler, E. (1980). Children's self-image disparity: Effects of age, socioeconomic status, ethnicity, and gender. *Journal of Personality and Social Psychology, 39,* 689–700.

Piaget, J. (1951). Principle factors in determining evolution from childhood to adult life. In D. Rapaport (ed.), *Organization and pathology of thought* (pp. 154–175). New York: Columbia University Press.

Prout, H.T., & Schaefer, B.M. (1985). Self-reports of depression by community-based mildly mentally retarded adults. *American Journal of Mental Deficiency, 90,* 220–222.

Pyszczynski, T., & Greenberg, J. (1987). Self-regulatory perseveration and the depressive self-focusing style: A self-awareness theory of reactive depression. *Psychological Bulletin, 102,* 122–138.

Renick, M.J., & Harter, S. (1989). Impact of social comparisons on the developing self-perceptions of learning disabled students. *Journal of Educational Psychology, 81,* 631–638.

Renouf, A., & Harter, S. (1990). Low self-worth and anger as components of the depressive experience in young adolescents. *Development and Psychopathology, 2,* 293–310.

Rogers, C.R. (1951). *Client-centered therapy.* Boston: Houghton Mifflin.

Rogers, C.R., & Dymond, R.F. (eds.). (1954). *Psychotherapy and personality change.* Chicago: University of Chicago Press.

Senatore, V., Matson, J., & Kazdin, A. (1985). An inventory to assess psychopathology of mentally retarded adults. *American Journal of Mental Deficiency, 89,* 459–466.

Sigelman, C.K., Budd, E.C., Winer, J.L., Schoenrock, C.J., & Martin, P.W. (1982). Evaluating alternative techniques of questioning mentally retarded persons. *American Journal of Mental Deficiency, 86,* 511–518.

Silon, E.L., & Harter, S. (1985). Assessment of perceived competence, motivational orientation, and anxiety in segregated and mainstreamed educable mentally retarded children. *Journal of Educational Psychology, 77,* 217–230.

Sternberg, R., & Kolligan, J. (eds.). (1990). *Competence considered.* New Haven, CT: Yale University Press.

Switzky, H.N. (1997). Individual differences in personality and motivational systems in persons with mental retardation. In W.E. MacLean (ed.), *Ellis' handbook of mental deficiency, psychological theory and research,* (3rd ed., pp. 343–377). Hillsdale: NJ: Erlbaum.

Weisz, J. (1981). Learned helplessness in Black and White children identified by their schools as retarded and nonretarded: Performance deterioration in response to failure. *Developmental Psychology, 17,* 499–508.

Weisz, J., & Zigler, E. (1979). Cognitive development in retarded and nonretarded persons: Piagetian tests of the similar sequence hypothesis. *Psychological Bulletin, 86,* 831–851.

Werner, H. (1948). *Comparative psychology of mental development.* New York: Follett.

Widaman, K.F., MacMillan, D.L., Hemsley, R.E., Little, T.D., & Balow, I.H. (1992). Differences in adolescents' self-concept as a function of academic level, ethnicity, and gender. *American Journal on Mental Retardation, 96,* 387–403.

Zetlin, A.G., Heriot, M.J., & Turner, J.L. (1985). Self-concept measurement in mentally retarded adults: A micro-analysis of response styles. *Applied Research in Mental Retardation, 6,* 113–125.

Zigler, E. (1966). Motivational determinants in the performance of feebleminded children. *American Journal of Orthopsychiatry, 36,* 848–856.

(1969). Developmental versus difference theories of mental retardation and the problem of motivation. *American Journal of Mental Deficiency, 73,* 536–556.

(1971). The retarded child as a whole person. In H.E. Adams & W.K. Boardman (eds.), *Advances in experimental clinical psychology.* New York: Pergamon.

Zigler, E., & Balla, D. (eds.) (1982). *Mental retardation: The developmental-difference controversy.* Hillsdale, NJ: Erlbaum.

Zigler, E., Balla, D., & Butterfield, E.C. (1968). A longitudinal investigation of the relationship between preinstitutional social deprivation and social motivation in institutionalized retardates. *Journal of Personality and Social Psychology, 10,* 437–445.

Zigler, E., Balla, D., & Watson, N. (1972). Experiential determinants of self-image disparity in institutionalized and noninstitutionalized retarded and normal children. *Journal of Personality and Social Psychology, 23,* 81–87.

Zigler, E., & Burack, J. (1989). Personality development and the dually diagnosed person. *Research in Developmental Disabilities, 10,* 225–240.

Zigler, E., & Glick, M. (1986). *A developmental approach to adult psychopathology.* New York: Wiley.

Zigler, E., & Hodapp, R. (1986). *Understanding mental retardation.* New York: Cambridge University Press.

(1991). Behavioral functioning in individuals with mental retardation. *Annual Review of Psychology, 42,* 29–50.

Zigler, E., & Phillips, L. (1960). Social effectiveness and symptomatic behaviors. *Journal of Abnormal and Social Psychology, 63,* 264–271.

4   Intrinsic Motivation and Motivational Self-System Processes in Persons with Mental Retardation: A Theory of Motivational Orientation

Harvey N. Switzky

Introduction

This chapter has two purposes: to present to researchers and practitioners (a) a theory of motivational orientation as developed by a group of researchers that I have called the Peabody–Vanderbilt Group (Haywood, 1992; Haywood & Switzky, 1986; Switzky, 1997; Switzky & Haywood, 1991) and the evidence that supports their model, and (b) the beginnings of a newer, more coherent metatheory of personality and self-system processes for persons with mental retardation and an agenda for future research.

The psychological and educational literature of the last 30 years on the personality and motivational characteristics of individuals with mental retardation has mushroomed. Ironically, very little of what we know has been disseminated to those who are concerned with improving the lives of mentally retarded persons. Personality and motivational self-system processes are the fulcrum around which all other psychological, educational, and self-regulatory processes rotate to energize behavior and performance in mentally retarded persons. Personality and motivational self-system processes determine what information gets into the memory system, how that information is organized in memory, and what information is retrieved to enable persons with mental retardation to solve problems and behave in adaptive and appropriate ways.

Motivational and Self-System Processes in Persons with Mental Retardation: The Theory of Motivational Orientation

Prior to the 1960s, early concepts of personality and motivational process in persons with mental retardation were only loosely related to theoretical models derived from contemporary psychological thought, and virtually none of the models was based on any systematic study of the behavior of mentally retarded persons themselves. Researchers were concerned primarily with the role of cognitive processes and the differences in performance between persons with mental retardation compared with persons without mental retardation on different learning tasks, in an attempt to identify the deficits that were believed to characterize persons with mental retardation. Concerns with developmental and personality/motivational processes per se were deliberately ignored, and viewed more as confounding variables needing to be controlled so as to allow the researchers to more clearly focus on the infinitely more important cognitive and learning processes (Haywood & Switzky, 1986; Hodapp, Burack, & Zigler, 1990). The overwhelming cognitive emphasis in the area of mental retardation made motivational workers the iconoclasts of the field and made them huddle together in self-defense (E. Zigler, personal communication, August 7, 1995).

Over the last thirty years, there has been a veritable explosion of knowledge about the behavior of persons with mental retardation from a holistic, developmental, motivational, and cognitive perspective, recognizing the complex interplay of motivational processes with cognitive process within a developmental perspective (Haywood & Switzky, 1986; Merighi, Edison, & Zigler, 1990; Weisz, 1990; Zigler & Hodapp, 1991). See also Zigler (Chapter 1) and Weisz (Chapter 2). This point of view not only reflects a new concept of mental retardation, but also reflects contemporary psychological thought concerning the development of human beings as active problem-solvers (Lepper & Hodell, 1989; McCombs & Marzano, 1990; Paris & Newman, 1990; Sternberg & Berg, 1992; Zimmerman & Schunk, 1989). I view these trends as reflecting the accelerating integration between a psychology of mental retardation and a developmental psychology of human growth for all human beings (Borkowski et al., 1990; Feuerstein, Klein, & Tannenbaum, 1991; Haywood & Tzuriel, 1992; Hodapp et al., 1990; Pintrich & Schrauben, 1992).

Major historical attempts to conceptualize the behavior of persons with mental retardation in terms of personality and motivational constructs to explain the initiation, direction, intensity, and persistence of goal-directed behavior generally followed the dominant hypothetical constructs in vogue in psychological thought at the time, but "as through a glass darkly," since they were derived primarily from the behavior of nonretarded persons, and often forced, extended, and revised in order to incorporate and explain "motivated" behavior in persons with mental retardation.

The Peabody–Vanderbilt Group has for more than 30 years studied the operation of intrinsic motivation as the primary concept in a cognitive theory of motivational orientation (Haywood, 1992; Haywood & Switzky, 1986, 1992; Schultz & Switzky, 1990; Switzky, 1997; Switzky & Haywood, 1974, 1984, 1991, 1992; Switzky & Schultz, 1988). The central ideas are behavior for its own sake and its own reward, and that using one's cognitive resources to the fullest is intrinsically gratifying and motivating. The Peabody–Vanderbilt Group has investigated individual differences – both in mildly handicapped and in nonhandicapped persons, in task-intrinsic and task-extrinsic motivation – and how these differences affect behavior under specified conditions.

The theory of motivational orientation and its key concept of "intrinsic motivation" is related to White's (1959) theory of effectance motivation, but was more directly influenced by Hunt's (1963, 1971) conception of "motivation inherent in information processing and action"; the two-factor theory of work motivation formulated by Herzberg (Herzberg, 1966) and later by Bandura's social cognitive learning theories, especially his formulation of the self-system in reciprocal determinism (Bandura, 1978, 1986a, 1997); and Feuerstein's theory of mediational learning experiences (MLE) (Feuerstein, Rand, Hoffman, & Miller, 1980; Feuerstein, Klein, & Tannenbaum, 1991).

The term "intrinsic motivation" is used in somewhat different but overlapping ways as the theory of motivational orientation developed. Using Hunt's system, intrinsic motivation refers to what Hunt (1963, 1971) has called "motivation inherent in information processing and action." In this sense, it is behavior in the absence of external stimulation or the possibility of external consequences, arising from the expectation of the joy of the information-processing activity itself compared with extrinsic motivation, which refers to behavioral outcomes linked to the presence of external stimulation and the possibility of external consequences or reinforcement. According to this view, individuals explore for the satisfaction of taking in and processing new information (Haywood & Switzky, 1992; Hunt, 1971). Hunt (1963) proposed eight questions that a theory of motivation must answer:

1. *The instigation question.* What initiates behavior and what terminates behavior?
2. *The energization question.* What controls the vigor of an activity?
3. *The direction-hedonic question.* What controls the direction of behavior? What selects the cognitive activities individuals perform from among an array of available options?

4. *The cathexis question.* How do individuals choose objects, places, and persons they may form attachments with?
5. *The choice of response question.* What controls the particular response individuals finally make from among an array of responses?
6. *The choice of goals question.* What controls the particular end-goal individuals finally make from among an array of goals?
7. *The learning question.* How do we identify the factors that underlie and influence behavioral, conceptual change, and performance for individuals?
8. *The persistence question.* Why do individuals persist in using responses that fail to achieve their goals, and why do they persist in seeking goals they do not achieve?

In terms of Hunt's motivational questions (Haywood, 1992), intrinsic motivation instigates activity, especially mental activity, because activity is more pleasant and more exciting than inactivity. It leads to more vigorous behavior than does extrinsic motivation, thus energizing behavior. It directs behavior toward the more psychologically exciting or interesting of alternative paths. Intrinsic motivation aids in the formation of unique attachments/cathexes, specifically leading individuals to return to intrinsically motivating tasks. Choice, both of response and of goal, may constitute the most powerful function of intrinsic motivation. Given an array of choices, intrinsically motivated individuals will select responses that are more difficult to perform, and will move toward distant goals compared with extrinsically motivated persons. Intrinsic motivation will increase learning efficiency and the persistence of performance for individuals in using responses that fail to achieve their goals, and in pursuing goals that are not achieved, simply because it is the activity itself that is rewarding, and not the mere attainment of goals that is motivating. This aspect of motivation, controlled by the mere attainment of goals, is more typical of individuals who are extrinsically motivated.

A second use of the term intrinsic motivation (Haywood & Switzky, 1986) is embodied in the term "task-intrinsic" versus "task-extrinsic motivation," which is viewed as a learned personality trait by which individuals may be characterized in terms of the location of incentives that are effective in motivating their behavior rather than in the context in which tasks are performed. Individuals may be motivated by task-intrinsic factors (e.g., responsibility, challenge, creativity, opportunities to learn, and task achievement) or by task-extrinsic factors (ease, comfort, safety, security, health, and practical aspects of the environment). Individuals who are motivated by task-intrinsic factors are referred to as intrinsically motivated (IM), whereas individuals who are motivated by task-extrinsic factors are referred to as extrinsically motivated (EM). While all persons respond to each kind of incentive, it is the relative balance between the two sources of motivation – that is, the relative number of situations in which one is likely to be motivated by task-intrinsic versus task-extrinsic factors – that constitutes a stable and measurable personality trait. This aspect of the theory of motivational orientation was derived from the two-factor theory of work motivation formulated by Herzberg (1966).

Herzberg (1966), looking for sources of job satisfaction and dissatisfaction in industrial workers, asked them to think of times when they had been satisfied with their jobs and times when they had been so dissatisfied that they had thoughts of changing jobs, and then to identify the variables to which they attributed their dissatisfaction or satisfaction. In characterizing periods of dissatisfaction, the workers listed such variables as low pay; poor, unhealthy, hazardous, or uncomfortable work conditions; the context in which the job was performed; and lack of security – all conditions extrinsic to the job (to the task) itself – that is, task-extrinsic motivation. In characterizing periods of positive job satisfaction, instead of referring to the opposite poles of the dissatisfying task-extrinsic conditions, the workers listed such task-intrinsic variables as the sheer psychological satisfaction of doing a task, opportunities to learn new things, opportunities to exercise creativity, and taking responsibility or experiencing esthetic aspects of the job (the task) – all conditions intrinsic to the job (to the task) itself – that is, task-intrinsic motivation. Herzberg conceived of these variables not as lying on a single bipolar dimension, but as constituting two nonoverlaping dimensions that could vary simultaneously. Subsequent research revealed the power of the "motivator" variables (i.e., task-intrinsic factors in the theory of motivational orientation) over the "hygiene" variables (i.e., task-extrinsic factors in the theory of motivational orientation) in improving job satisfaction and job performance in a variety of industrial settings.

The Peabody–Vanderbilt Group (Haywood, 1992; Haywood & Switzky, 1986, 1992; Switzky & Haywood, 1984; Tzuriel, 1991) believes that the processes of thinking, learning, and problem-solving develop transactionally with task-intrinsic motivation and related attitudes about learning and thinking, self-concept variables, and habits of working, thinking, and learning. The group suggests that there is a transactional relationship between fluid intelligence, cognitive development, and the development of motivational orientation. (See Borkowski et al., 1990; Borkowski et al., 1992, for a related theory concerning the relationship among cognitive development, motivation, and problem-solving behavior.) The Peabody–Vanderbilt Group suggests that all children, regardless of their level of fluid intelligence, are born with a general motive to explore and gain mastery over their worlds – that is, with both curiosity and competence motives (Switzky, Haywood, & Isett 1974; Switzky, Ludwig, & Haywood, 1979). What happens to these motives is a direct function of the consequences, both direct and social, of their successive attempts to explore and to gain mastery of their world. Beginning with the Pavlovian orienting reflex, children's exploratory/mastery behaviors are supported with relative success or failure experiences, and these consequences constitute reinforcing conditions that lead to acceleration or deceleration of the behaviors. Parents' responses to the exploratory/mastery behaviors of their children's performance provide feedback on the success or failure of the outcomes.

Exploratory behaviors of relatively incompetent children (e.g., mentally retarded, learning disabled, behaviorally disordered, motoric or sensory-impaired) meet often with failure. These behaviors thus become increasingly less frequent, resulting in less inclination of these relatively incompetent children (a) to expose themselves to novel stimuli, (b) to derive information from their (less and less-frequent and less and less-intense) encounters with their environments, and (c) to accumulate basic knowledge about their worlds to evaluate, to understand, and to elaborate subsequent new information to induce generalizations about the rules and structures of their worlds. The deficient cognitive development of these children is directed toward the development of the personality trait of task-extrinsic motivation – that is, the tendency to attend to nontask and (therefore) nonfailure-producing aspects of the environment in order to avoid dissatisfaction and failure rather than to seek satisfaction and success. In contrast, relatively competent children engage similarly in initial attempts to explore and gain mastery. However, these attempts are met by successful feedback by parents and other socializing agents, thereby strengthening exploratory and curiosity behaviors, resulting in more inclination of these relatively competent children (a) to expose themselves to novel stimuli, (b) to derive more and more information from their encounters with their environments, (c) to accumulate more basic knowledge about their worlds in order to understand, and to elaborate subsequent new information to induce generalizations about the rules and structures of their worlds, and (d) to develop the personality trait of task-intrinsic motivation – that is, the tendency to seek success and satisfaction by attending to task-intrinsic aspects of the environment such as creativity, increased responsibility, new learning, psychological excitement, and task-intrinsic esthetics.

This personality trait of task-intrinsic motivation is later expressed as a greater frequency of choices of activities in response to task-intrinsic incentives than in response to task-extrinsic incentives. On the other hand, the personality trait of task-extrinsic motivation is later expressed as a greater frequency of choices of activities in response to task-extrinsic incentives than in response to task-intrinsic incentives. The cognitive and motivational aspects of individuals thus develop in a transactional way. For less competent individuals (e.g., mentally retarded, learning disabled, behaviorally disordered, motoric or sensory impaired), lack of external and social feedback of successful exploratory behavior by parents and other socializing agents results in fewer attempts at exploration and knowledge-acquisition and the creation of an extrinsic motivational orientation that creates the conditions of even less exploration and knowledge acquisition and a further slowing of cognitive development and an increasing extrinsic-motivational orientation that is known as the "poor get poorer" phenomenon) (Haywood, 1992; Haywood & Switzky, 1992). This phenomenon is related to the earlier concept of the "MA deficit" (Haywood & Switzky, 1986).

MA deficit refers to the observation that even if retarded persons are matched on mental age with nonretarded younger persons, the retarded persons do less well on a variety of measures of learning and behavioral effectiveness (Stevenson & Zigler, 1958; Zigler, 1971). For more competent individuals, the presence of external and social feedback of successful exploratory behavior by parents and other socializing agents results in accelerating attempts at exploration and knowledge acquisition, and the creation of an intrinsic-motivational orientation that creates the conditions of even more exploration and knowledge acquisition and an increasing intrinsic motivational orientation (the "rich get richer" phenomenon) (Haywood, 1992; Haywood & Switzky, 1992).

The primary instrument used by the Peabody–Vanderbilt Group to measure motivational orientation in mentally retarded as well as nonretarded persons is the Picture Choice Motivation Scale (PCMS) (Kunca & Haywood, 1969). In this scale, each item is a pair of pictures of people engaged in different activities, vocations, or endeavors determined to be qualitatively either EM or IM. For each of the twenty pictures illustrating an intrinsically motivated activity (e.g., opportunity to learn or challenge, intense psychological satisfaction, responsibility) or an extrinsically motivated activity (e.g., opportunity for safety, ease, comfort, security), the individual is asked which one is preferred. The final score used to classify the individual is the number of IM choices out of the twenty pairs. The PCMS is useful with persons from a mental age of 3 years up to adolescence, and has yielded test-retest reliability coefficients generally in the 0.80–0.90 range (Kunca & Haywood, 1969; Miller, Haywood, & Gimon, 1975; Switzky & Haywood, 1992). Several studies have shown that the PCMS yields an approximately normal distribution of scores down to about the mental age of 3 years, and that this distribution tends to become skewed (i.e., higher frequencies of intrinsic responses) with increasing chronological and mental age and psychometric intelligence up to middle adolescence (Call, 1968; Haywood, 1968a, 1968b; Haywood & Switzky, 1986; Switzky & Haywood, 1992). Generally, having an IM orientation is an increasing function of chronological age, mental age, psychometric intelligence, and social class. Usually, mentally retarded persons as a group are more EM compared with nonretarded persons of similar age. However, some mentally retarded persons are found to be IM. (See Switzky & Heal, 1990, for an extensive discussion of the construct validity of the PCMS.)

The theory of motivational orientation should predict the following results:

1. Having an IM orientation is helpful to both mentally retarded and nonretarded learners compared with having an EM orientation in terms of learning more effectively. However, having an IM orientation may have a greater impact on the performance of mentally retarded learners. Generally, these predictions have been confirmed. IM learners work harder and longer on a task compared with EM learners (Haywood, 1968a, 1968b; Haywood & Switzky, 1986; Haywood & Wachs, 1966; Schultz & Switzky, 1993; Zewdie, 1995).

2. There is an interaction between motivational orientation and incentives such that one must match incentive systems to the unique motivational orientations of individuals – that is, the performance of IM individuals will be optimally reinforced by task-intrinsic incentives, whereas the performance of EM individuals will be optimally reinforced by task-extrinsic incentives. Generally, these predictions have been strongly confirmed (Gambro & Switzky, 1991; Haywood & Switzky, 1975, 1985, 1986, 1992; Haywood & Weaver, 1967; Schultz & Switzky, 1990, 1993; Switzky & Haywood, 1974, 1984, 1991, 1992; Switzky & Heal, 1990; Switzky & Schultz, 1988).

3. IM persons may be characterized by self-monitored reinforcement systems that make them less dependent on external reinforcement conditions, while EM persons may be characterized by dependence on external reinforcement systems. IM children are more sensitive to task-intrinsic incentives, have high performance standards of internal self-reward, and are more likely to reinforce their own behavior, whereas EM children are

intensively outerdirected, have very low performance standards of internal self-reward, and are extremely sensitive to the external reinforcement environment. These predictions have been strongly confirmed (Gambro & Switzky, 1991; Haywood & Switzky, 1975, 1985, 1986, 1992; Switzky & Haywood, 1974, 1991, 1992).

IM Learners Learn More Effectively

IM learners may be characterized as "overachievers" and EM learners as "underachievers" on tests of school achievement, the efforts intensifying as the intelligence levels of the students decrease. In a set of studies (Haywood 1968a, 1968b; Switzky & Heal, 1990) relating motivational orientation to academic achievement levels on the reading, arithmetic, and spelling subtests of the Metropolitan Achievement Test for a sample of 10-year-old students in the Toronto, Canada, schools across three levels of intelligence (educable mentally retarded, IQs 65–80; intellectually average, IQs 95–109; intellectually superior, IQs 120 and above), the following results were noted:

1. Overachievers were found to be relatively more IM and underachievers relatively more EM in all three academic areas. Overachievers tended to be motivated to a greater extent by factors inherent in the performance of academic tasks, while underachievers tended to be motivated more by factors extrinsic to the task itself.

2. The differences in motivational orientation between overachievers and underachievers were largest for the group of educable mentally retarded students (EMR) and smallest for the group of intellectually superior students. The effects of motivational orientation intensified as the intellectual ability levels of the students decreased, so that a disproportionate number of lower ability students were assessed to be extrinsically motivated.

3. When the groups of students were matched on age, sex, and IQ, it was found that in all three achievement areas, IM students were achieving at a higher level than EM students. However, the effects varied with the level of intelligence. On average, the IM students in the average-IQ and EMR groups had achievement test scores about one full school year higher than those of the EM students in the same IQ group. The achievement of the IM EMR students was not different from that of the EM average-IQ students. Thus, there was compelling evidence (a) that intrinsic motivation is associated with higher school achievement, and (b) that the effects of the individ-

ual differences in motivational orientation appeared to be greater as IQ declined. While these students were not given the test of intrinsic motivation until they were 10 years old, retrospective examination of their school achievement scores showed that the achievement differences were already present in the first grade. Thus, having more of a relatively IM orientation can compensate by increasing performance levels in students of lower intelligence. Having more of a relatively EM motivation will decrease performance in students even below that predicted by their MA levels.

Schultz and Switzky (1993) examined how intrinsic motivation affected reading comprehension and mathematics achievement on the Basic Achievement Skills Individual Screener in a Midwestern group of urban minority elementary and junior high school students in the second through seventh grade (mean age = 11.4 years). Students with behavior disorders (BD) were compared with nonhandicapped peers. The purpose of the study was to demonstrate how differences in motivational orientation (IM vs. EM) contributed to the academic performance deficits often observed in children with behavior problems by using a design analogous to the one used by Haywood (1968a, 1968b) in which groups of students were matched on age, sex, and IQ, thereby potentiating the effects of motivational orientation on academic achievement. Previous studies (Schultz & Switzky, 1990; Switzky & Heal, 1990; Switzky & Schultz, 1988) suggested that the lower-than-expected school achievement in students with BD may result from an EM orientation to academic activities. Having an EM orientation may also further intensify existing problems in achievement resulting from students' subaverage intelligence or emotional problems. Having an IM orientation to academic activities may compensate for students' subaverage intelligence or emotional problems and raise levels of school achievement.

The expectation was that IM BD students would exhibit higher levels of scholastic achievement than EM BD students. Reading comprehension and mathematics achievement were the dependent measures. The results showed (a) both higher mathematics and reading achievement for the nonhandicapped students compared with the students with behavior disorders; (b) that IM students had higher reading comprehension than did EM students; and (c) that BD students exhibited significantly greater academic performance differences resulting from motivational orientation compared with their nonhandicapped peers. IM BD students had both higher mathematics and reading achievement than did EM BD students, whereas there was no difference between the IM and EM nonhandicapped students' mathematics and reading achievement. Individual differences in motivational orientation appeared to affect the academic performance of BD students more than that of their nonhandicapped peers.

These achievement differences reveal that children in both groups who are more motivated by factors intrinsic to learning tend to achieve at a higher level than children who are motivated by extrinsic factors. While these academic performance differences resulting from motivation orientation appear to be significant in both groups of children, they are much more important in students formally identified as behavior-disordered. IM BD students had substantially higher math and reading achievement test scores than did EM BD students. The results of this study support previous research (Haywood 1968a, 1968b; Haywood & Switzky, 1986; Switzky & Heal, 1990), which suggests that the lower-than-expected school achievement observed in many exceptional students (MR or BD) is associated with having an EM orientation to academic activities that may further intensify existing problems in achievement resulting from the students' subaverage intelligence or emotional problems. Having more of an IM orientation to academic activities may compensate for many exceptional students' subaverage intelligence or emotional problems, and may raise levels of school achievement.

There Is an Interaction Between Motivational Orientation and Incentives

IM persons may be characterized by self-monitored reinforcement systems that make them less dependent on external reinforcement conditions. IM persons are more sensitive to task-intrinsic incentives, have high performance standards of internal-self reward, and are more likely to self-reinforce their own behavior. EM persons may be characterized by dependence on external reinforcement systems that make them intensively outerdirected. EM persons have very low performance standards of internal self-reward, and are extremely sensitive to the external reinforcement environment.

There is an interaction between motivational orientation and incentives such that one must match incentive systems to the unique motivational orientations of individuals – that is, the performance of IM individuals will be optimally reinforced by task-intrinsic incentives, whereas the performance of EM individuals will be optimally reinforced by task-extrinsic incentives. This original formulation of the theory was first tested by Haywood and Weaver (1967) and then expanded by a whole series of studies (Gambro & Switzky, 1991; Haywood & Switzky, 1975, 1985, 1986, 1992; Schultz & Switzky, 1990, 1993; Switzky & Haywood, 1974, 1984, 1991, 1992; Switzky & Heal, 1990; Switzky & Schultz, 1988) that were interpreted in terms of Bandura's (1976, 1978, 1986a, 1993, 1997) social-cognitive learning theories, especially his theory of self-reinforcement, and his formulation of the self-system in reciprocal determinism. This approach stressed the importance of self-system processes reciprocally interacting with the external demand characteristics of the environment and the individual's own behavior.

In the social-cognitive view, people are neither driven by inner forces nor automatically shaped and controlled by external stimuli. Rather, human functioning is explained in terms of a model of triadic reciprocality in which behavior, cognitive and other personal factors, and environmental events all operate as interacting determinants of each other (Bandura, 1986a, p. 18). In social-cognitive theory, human agency operates within an interdependent causal structure involving reciprocal causation. In this transactional view of self and society, internal personal factors in the form of (a) cognitive, affective, and biological events, (b) behavior, and (c) environmental events all operate as interacting determinants that influence one another bidirectionally (Bandura, 1997, p. 6).

Haywood and Weaver (1967) showed that there was an interaction between the motivational orientation of institutionalized retarded children and adults and the incentives that are effective in a simple task. Relatively IM and strongly EM retarded persons participated in a repetitive motor task under one of four incentive conditions: (a) a ten-cent reward (strong EM incentive), (b) a one-cent reward (weak EM reward), (c) the promise of an opportunity to do another task (strong IM reward), and (d) no reward (control). EM subjects performed best under the ten-cent condition and worst under the task-incentive condition, while IM subjects showed the opposite behavior, performing best when offered only the opportunity to do another task and performing worst under the ten-cent incentive condition. In the control condition, IM subjects performed more vigorously than did EM subjects (see Haywood & Switzky, 1975).

Haywood and Switzky (1975) presented evidence that the behavior of IM and EM school-age children may be interpreted in terms of Bandura's (1993, 1997) concept of self-reinforcement. Bandura argued that individuals construct personal standards and self-incentives that they use to guide, motivate, and regulate their own behavior. Individuals do things that give them self-satisfaction, self-reward, and a sense of self-worth. Individuals refrain from behaving in ways that violate their personal standards because it will bring self-censure.

Haywood and Switzky (1975) found that it was possible to condition the verbal expression of motivation in IM and EM school-age children by contingent social reinforcement of statements that were counter to or supportive of the individual's own motivational orientation. Subjects in all contingent-reinforcement groups learned to discriminate IM from EM statements, with EM subjects demonstrating slightly more efficient learning, suggesting that the task-extrinsic verbal social reinforcement was more effective for them than for the IM children. In a noncontingent (control) condition, where responses were randomly reinforced, IM subjects increased their rate of IM verbalizations in spite of the lack of consistent external verbal social reinforcement, whereas EM subjects failed to show any significant change over trial blocks.

What was the source of the reinforcement for the IM subjects in the noncontingent (control) condition that increased their performance? It was self-reinforcement. As Bandura's (1976, 1993, 1997) concept of self-reinforcement suggested, IM persons may be characterized by self-monitored reinforcement systems that make them less dependent on external reinforcement conditions, while EM persons may be characterized by dependence on external reinforcement systems. Thus, EM children should be differentially more responsive than are IM children to social reinforcement, and consequently should show more efficient learning under such task-extrinsic incentives. When task-extrinsic incentives are presented noncontingently, EM children should not show any change in performance, while IM children (who are more sensitive to task-intrinsic incentives and more likely to self-reinforce their own behavior) should show changes in performance in spite of the absence of contingent conditions. So it is necessary to consider both the nature of the reinforcers and the individual differences in motivational orientation, as well as the relative strengths of an individual's self-monitored and externally imposed reinforcement systems, in order to predict performance under different reinforcement operations.

This analysis was dramatically confirmed in the next two studies, one with grade-school children (Switzky & Haywood, 1974) and the other with mildly mentally retarded adults (Haywood & Switzky, 1985). A later study (Zewdie, 1995), with inner-city African-American moderately mentally retarded adults in a sheltered workshop setting only partially replicated the results of the Haywood and Switzky (1985) study, but showed the strong effects of having an IM orientation on work production and work supervisor's ratings.

Switzky and Haywood (1974) showed that in order to predict performance under different reinforcement operations in school children in grades 2 through 5, it was necessary to consider (a) the internal or external control of the reinforcers, (b) individual differences in motivational orientation, and (c) the relative strengths of an individual's self-monitored and externally imposed reinforcements. Bandura and Perloff (1967) had compared the motor performance of children under self-monitored and externally imposed reinforcement, and found no differences between the two conditions. Both reinforcement conditions sustained responsivity, whereas the control conditions did not. Adding the dimension of individual differences in motivational orientation, Switzky and Haywood (1974) divided their participants into IM and EM samples and gave them the Bandura and Perloff task. Children were given a motor wheel-cranking task in which it was possible to vary the number of cranks of the wheel required to turn on a light on a column of lights, as well as the number of lights that had to be turned on to get a token. Tokens could be exchanged for prizes. In the self-monitored reinforcement condition, subjects selected their own schedules – that is, they decided how many cranks were needed to turn on a light and how many lights had to be turned on to earn a token. For each of these subjects, there was a yoked subject in the externally imposed reinforcement condition who had to follow the schedule selected by the self-monitored subject.

A dramatic interaction between the reinforcement conditions and the motivational orientations of the participants was found: (a) IM children worked harder, set leaner schedules of reinforcement, and maintained their performance longer than did EM children under self-monitored reinforcement conditions; (b) by contrast, EM children performed more vigorously and maintained their performance longer under conditions of externally imposed reinforcement. Thus, Bandura and Perloff's (1967) failure to find differential effects of these reinforcement systems may have been due to the canceling effects of individual differences in motivational orientation, with very strong differential effects interacting with such individual differences. These effects suggest that persons who are predominately IM are characterized by a self-regulatory system such that they are able to determine, choose, and pace their own behavior without direction from or reliance on external environmental sources. If external environmental controlling conditions are imposed, they will interfere with the operation of the IM individuals' self-regulatory system.

This latter inference is supported by a set of studies (Deci & Ryan, 1985; Lepper & Hodell, 1989; Morgan, 1984) showing generally that for individuals who are already IM, task-extrinsic incentive rewards interfere with task-intrinsic motivation. Conversely, individuals who are predominately EM are primarily under the control of a strongly developed external environmental reinforcement system, and need external direction from the environment in order to perform, which makes them less inclined to engage in internally generated self-regulated activities for their own sake. If forced to determine, choose, and pace their own behavior without direction from or reliance on external environmental sources, such individuals just shut down and perform very poorly.

The Haywood and Switzky (1985) study with mildly mentally retarded adults was based on the ideas that (a) self-regulation is extremely important to the ability of retarded persons to adjust to relatively independent living, and (b) the response of retarded persons to expectations of self-regulation or to expectations of externally imposed regulation depends on individual differences in task-intrinsic motivation. Since previous studies had shown that retarded persons are on average less IM than are nonretarded persons, self-regulation might be difficult to produce in retarded persons to the extent that motivational orientation and self-regulatory behavior are related. Haywood and Switzky also wanted to find out to what extent the incentive-system relationships previously established with normally developing school children were transportable to generally lower levels of intrinsic motivation – specifically the lower levels typically found in retarded persons.

The Haywood and Switzky (1985) experiment was designed as an analog of the Bandura and Perloff motor task, extending the Switzky and Haywood (1974) study to the work behavior of mildly retarded adults. The 1985 study was designed to adduce evidence on the relative efficacy of self-monitored and externally imposed reinforcement to IM and EM retarded persons – specifically with respect to their performance in work-related tasks.

The participants were mildly retarded IM and EM adults (mean age = 40.0 years) residing in a community-based intermediate care facility. Participants were assigned randomly to three conditions: self-regulated reinforcement, externally imposed reinforcement, and no-token control. Participants in the external-reinforcement group were matched individually to participants in the self-regulation group by sex, age, motivational orientation, and in a yoked manner, to schedule of reinforcement. Those in the control group were matched for sex, age, and motivational orientation with participants in the self-regulation group. All participants were given a work task consisting of placing a single flat or lock washer into each compartment of seven 18-compartment boxes placed side by side in a row. Work goals were set by placing a washer in the end-most compartment they intended to reach. Participants in the self-regulation condition set their own work goals, and after reaching them, determined the number of tokens they should get for their work. They also determined how long they would work. Tokens were exchanged for prizes at the end of the experimental session. Selections made by the self-regulation participants were imposed on participants in the external-reinforcement condition. In the control condition, the experimenter set the work goals, participants worked as long as they wished (with no indication of "pay" for their work), and were given a prize at the end. The principal dependent variable was the number of compartments filled (a measure of performance maintenance or task persistence).

IM mentally retarded participants worked harder (mean of 118 compartments filled) than did EM mentally retarded participants (mean of 80 compartments filled), confirming previous research with nonretarded school-aged children (Switzky & Haywood, 1974). There was also an interaction of condition and motivational orientation, the focus of principal interest in this study. In both the self-regulation and control conditions, IM mentally retarded participants filled more compartments than did EM mentally retarded participants, while IM and EM mentally retarded participants did not differ significantly under the external-reinforcement condition. IM participants also filled more of the compartments under the self-regulation condition than they did under the external-reinforcement condition. A higher level of intrinsic motivation was associated with more self-regulatory behavior than was a lower level of intrinsic motivation, replicating the Switzky and Haywood (1974) findings with nonretarded children, and the Haywood and Weaver (1967) findings with mentally retarded adults. These differences in performance between IM and EM persons are due to differences in their internal self-system characteristics. IM persons appear to respond chiefly to internal, cognitive, self-regulatory processes, whereas EM persons appear to respond chiefly to external, environmental influences. Further, IM persons appear to have a more strongly developed internal reinforcement system, whereas EM persons have a more strongly developed external reinforcement system.

The purpose of the Zewdie (1995) study was to replicate and extend the findings of Haywood and Switzky (1985) to get further evidence on the relative efficacy of self-monitored and externally imposed reinforcement for IM and EM moderately retarded persons. Zewdie (1995) also attempted to strengthen the ecological validity of the theory by observing the performance of workers with mental retardation in the real-world setting of the sheltered workshop.

The participants were primarily IM and EM moderately retarded African-American adults (mean age = 34.0 years). They were assigned randomly to three conditions: self-regulated reinforcement, externally imposed reinforcement, and no-token control. Those in the external-reinforcement group were matched individually to those in the self-regulation group by sex, age, motivational orientation, and in a yoked manner, to schedule of reinforcement. Those in the control group were matched for sex, age, and motivational orientation with participants in the self-regulation group. All participants were given a work task consisting of an eight-step relatively complex packing/assembly task involving packaging Chia Pets. They worked as long as they wished and by themselves.

Supervisors (who were blinded as to the motivational orientation) remained on the work floor where they could unobtrusively keep track of the participants' work goals and the number of tokens that they were awarding themselves. When participants completed their self-selected work goal under the self-regulated condition, they would inform the supervisor, at which time they traded their acquired tokens for a prize commensurate in value to the number of tokens accumulated.

Subjects in the external reinforcement condition were yoked to those in the self-regulation condition in terms of the work goal and the number of tokens received. The supervisor determined the work goal and the number of tokens that were dispensed. Subjects in the no-token condition were also yoked to those in the self-regulation condition in terms of the work goal. Supervisors set the work goal, and participants were allowed to work as long as they wished (with no indication of "pay" for their work). When finished working, they were given an unexpected prize in appreciation of their work.

Each participant's work was also rated by a supervisor on The Workshop Supervisor Behavioral Rating Scale (WSBR). This sixteen-item scale, specifically developed for this study, measured typical work skills and work behavior demands of sheltered workshop environments. Cronbach's coefficient alpha was .87, and test-retest reliability was .72 on the WSBR. Principal component analysis with varimax rotation was performed on the WSBR. Four factors were extracted. Factor 1 was named *independent work behavior,* and accounted for 46% of the variance. Items that loaded on Factor 1 were ability to work independently, motivation to work, persistence/ steadiness of work pace, speed, quality of work, initiating request for materials, working on monotonous work, and overall behavioral qualification. Factor 2 was named *collaborative work behavior,* and accounted for 12% of the variance. Items that loaded on Factor 2 were ability to follow directives, reaction to supervisor criticism, frustration tolerance, and odd or inappropriate behavior. Factor 3 was named *work habits,* and accounted for 11% of the variance. Items that loaded on Factor 3 were attendance, punctuality, and distractibility during work. Factor 4 was named *appearance behavior at work,* and accounted for 7% of the variance. Only one item loaded on Factor 4 – appearance and grooming.

Two dependent variables – the mean number of production units completed and the mean total minutes of work performed – were used as a measure of performance maintenance and task persistence. Supervisor ratings on the WSRB were analyzed using the factor scores on the four factors extracted by factor analysis. IM mentally retarded workers produced more units ($M = 31.00$ units) than EM mentally retarded workers ($M = 25.00$ units), replicating the Haywood and Switzky (1985) study. However, there were no interaction effects of motivational orientation and behavioral regulation condition.

IM workers worked longer ($M = 14.62$ minutes) than EM workers ($M = 13.20$ minutes). Workers in the self-reinforcement condition ($M = 15.96$ minutes) and in the external-reinforcement condition ($M = 14.05$ minutes) worked longer than workers in the no-token control condition ($M = 11.85$ minutes).

Analysis of the differences in component factor scores derived from the WSBR was carried out for the IM and EM workers. There was a significant difference between IM and EM workers on Factor 1. IM workers scored higher ($M = .33$ SD units) than did EM workers ($M = -.32$ SD units). No significant differences on other factor scores for the IM and EM workers were found. In general, the results replicate the Haywood and Switzky (1985) study, and provide additional construct and ecological validity to the theory of motivational orientation in real-world workshop settings even though the expected interaction of motivational orientation and behavioral regulation condition was not obtained. Perhaps these African-American moderately mentally retarded adults needed more training to understand the behavioral regulation conditions since they had considerably lower IQs than participants in the previous studies.

However, the core idea that differences in performance between IM and EM persons are due to differences in their internal self-system characteristics was strongly confirmed in the next set of studies, which were designed to further test the validity of the motivational orientation construct by investigating the effects of internal self-system influences and the role of the external demand characteristics of the environment in mildly retarded adults' (Switzky & Haywood, 1991) and in nonretarded young children's (Gambro & Switzky, 1991; Switzky & Haywood, 1992) self-regulatory behavior.

In the Switzky and Haywood (1991) study, the effects of external (environmental) and internal (cognitive) influences of self-regulatory behavior were investigated in IM and EM mildly mentally retarded adults (mean age = 37.3 years) residing in a community-based intermediate care facility. External environmental influences such as (a) stringent, variable, and lenient demand conditions, (b) instructional sets, (c) performance standards, and (d) schedules of self-reinforcement were varied. IM and EM participants were randomly assigned to three conditions of self-reinforcement task demands: (a) stringent (instructed to set very high performance standards, instructed to work as hard and fast as they could; experimenter modeled a lean schedule of reinforcement); (b) variable (not explicitly instructed as to how hard or fast to work, given choice of high or low performance standards, and experimenter modeled a schedule of reinforcement proportional in richness to the performance criterion chosen, i.e., more tokens for higher goals); or (c) lenient (not explicitly instructed as to how hard or fast to work, but rather allowed to set lower performance standards; experimenter modeled a rich schedule of reinforcement).

A motor/attention task was constructed, varying in seven levels of difficulty. The easiest had three and the hardest nine lines of geometric figures arranged randomly on a page. The task consisted of crossing out figures that matched a model (one initially crossed out) on each sheet. All participants were told to perform the task to get tokens that could be exchanged for prizes; the more tokens, the better the prize. After reaching their work goals (performance standards), they could pay themselves as many tokens from a nearby container as they thought their work had been worth. The dependent variables were (a) total work (sum of standards chosen over trials); (b) average performance standard chosen; (c) percentage of modeled standard (goal chosen as a percentage of the goal modeled by the experimenter); (d) schedule of reinforcement (items of work accomplished divided by the number of tokens paid to self); and (e) percentage of modeled schedule of reinforcement (schedule of reinforcement as a percentage of the schedule of reinforcement modeled by the experimenter).

It was expected that IM mildly retarded persons residing in quasi-institutional settings would perform more vigorously than EM persons under all imposed conditions since internal self-influences interact with external environmental influences in determining behavior. This was because IM persons have a more highly developed self-reinforcement system and as strongly developed an external reinforcement system as do EM persons, developed for coping in a setting – the community intermediate care facility – ruled primarily by external reinforcers. IM persons were expected to work harder, set higher performance standards, and set leaner schedules of self-reinforcement compared with EM persons.

Both external-environmental conditions (task-demand conditions) and internal-self characteristics (motivational orientation) had significant effects on the performance on the motor/attention task. Participants in the stringent-demand condition worked harder, set higher performance standards (higher goals), and arranged leaner schedules of self-reinforcement than did participants in the lenient-demand condition. IM participants worked harder, set higher performance standards (higher goals), and arranged leaner schedules of self-reinforcement than did EM participants over all demand conditions. Furthermore, IM subjects chose higher performance standards (higher goals) than had been demonstrated to them in the lenient-demand condition, and also arranged leaner schedules of self-reinforcement over all demand conditions than had been demonstrated to them, while EM subjects either copied the schedule set by the experimenter or set richer ones. Differences between IM and EM participants were most pronounced in the lenient-demand condition, suggesting that individual differences in motivational orientation will lead to the most divergent performances in situations where there is least external support and guidance.

Internal self-system characteristics of mentally retarded persons appear to interact reciprocally with external-demand characteristics of the environment to reveal substantial individual differences in self-reward behavior. These effects show that environmental (external) demand instructions do not operate in a vacuum. The recipients play an active role in selecting what information they extract from ongoing events and when and how they use that information and their own abilities. Persons do not simply react mechanically to situational influences; they actively process, interpret, and transfer them, supporting Bandura's concept of the self-system in reciprocal determinism (Bandura, 1976, 1978, 1986a, 1993, 1997). The results of this Switzky and Haywood study confirm modern concepts of the self-system and affirm the role of self-evaluative reactions in the self-regulation of behavior as applied to persons with mild mental retardation, as well as the results of the previous theories and research of the Peabody–Vanderbilt Group on the construct validity of motivational orientation.

Switzky and Haywood (1992) extended their earlier (1991) paradigm to middle-class nonretarded IM and EM preschool children (mean age = 4.7 years) in an attempt to investigate further the research validity of the motivational orientation construct by investigating the ontogenesis of intrinsic and extrinsic self-system characteristics and the interaction of ongoing behavior, with stringent and lenient environmental-demand conditions in young children's self-reinforcing behavior. Their goal was to determine at what age IM and EM self-system characteristics are present and functional in a population of young children. A stringent-demand condition – in the form of stringent instructional sets and criterion settings and lean schedules of self-reinforcement – and a lenient-demand condition – in the form of very lenient instructional sets and criterion settings and a very rich schedule of reinforcement – were provided to maintain performance on a motor/attention task. A motor/attention task was constructed, varying in four levels of difficulty ranging from three to nine lines of geometric figures arranged randomly on a page. The work task consisted of crossing out a geometric shape matching one initially crossed out on each sheet. The same dependent variables as in the Switzky and Haywood (1991) study were analyzed individually.

Again, both external and internal self-influences affected self-reinforcement performance on the motor/attention task. Children in the stringent-demand condition set a higher performance standard and arranged a leaner schedule of self-reinforcement than did children in the lenient-demand condition. EM children outperformed IM children on measures reflecting the strength of performance (total work behavior and total time working), presumably because of the higher incentive value of the reinforcers for the EM children. In previous research (Haywood & Switzky, 1985; Switzky & Haywood, 1974, 1991), subjects were not shown the reinforcers that were to be exchanged for the tokens until the end of the experiment. In this study, reinforcers that were to be obtained by the exchange of the tokens were shown to the children at the very beginning of the experiment, thereby potentiating the incentive value of the reinforcers for the EM children. On measures reflecting internal standards of self-regulation, IM children set a higher performance standard in the lenient-demand condition than did EM children. Also, IM children chose a higher performance standard than modeled in the lenient-demand condition than did EM children. This experiment shows that in preschool-age children, internal self-regulatory characteristics are present, well organized, and active, and interact with external-demand characteristics of the environment to reveal substantial individual differences in the patterns of self-reward behavior.

The purpose of the Gambro and Switzky (1991) study was to further test the research validity of the motivational orientation construct and the ontogenesis of IM and EM self-system characteristics and their interaction with external demand characteristics of the environment in another sample of middle-class nonretarded IM and EM preschool children (mean age = 4.8 years), by extending the Switzky and Haywood (1992) study in three ways: first, by including two tasks to test the durability of effects; second, by adding ecological validity through the use of more pragmatic tasks (letter recognition and object sorting) under lenient-demand conditions; third, by not showing the children the reinforcers that were to be exchanged for the tokens until the end of the experiment, thereby not emphasizing the external reinforcers. Because internal self-influences interact with external environmental influences in determining behavior, it was expected that IM young children would perform more vigorously under the lenient-demand condition for both tasks. This would follow because IM children probably would have a more developed self-reinforcement system than would EM children.

The dependent variable was total time on the two tasks in minutes. The analysis revealed a main effect of motivational orientation. IM children worked longer ($M = 11.4$ minutes) than EM children ($M = 8.4$ minutes), confirming expectations. The performance of young children with different motivational orientations showed significant individual differences in self-regulatory behavior when completing the two tasks under lenient-demand conditions with little emphasis placed on external reinforcers. As expected, IM young children spent more time on the tasks than EM young children. IM young children did not rely on external cues, but rather worked until their internal self-standards were satisfied. EM young children may have worked only until they felt they had earned enough tokens to obtain a prize. In the Switzky and Haywood (1992) study, external reinforcers were stressed, and the EM young children spent more time on tasks. In this study, external reinforcers were deemphasized, more realistic tasks were utilized, and the lenient-demand condition encouraged young children to use their internal self-system, with the result that the EM children did not work as long because of their dependence on external environmental conditions to guide their performance.

The Gambro and Switzky (1991) and Switzky and Haywood (1992) studies show that in children younger than 5 years of age, internal self-system characteristics of individuals are present and interact with external-demand characteristics of the environment to reveal substantial individual differences in patterns of self-reward behavior. This affirms the role of self-evaluative reactions in the self-regulation of behavior in very young children, and extends and confirms the theoretical model of motivational orientation developed by the Peabody–Vanderbilt Group on the construct validity of the motivational orientation concept to preprimary children.

Taken together, these five studies (Gambro & Switzky, 1991; Haywood & Switzky, 1986; Switzky & Haywood, 1974, 1991, 1992) suggest that individual differences in motivational orientation are associated with important dimensions of self-regulation, incentive-selection, goal setting, work performance, and perhaps most importantly, the satisfaction derived from the tasks themselves, both in mentally retarded and in nonretarded persons ranging from preschool and school-age children to adults. Bandura's model of the self-system (1976, 1978, 1986a, 1993, 1997), especially his concept of reciprocal determinism – that is, the continuous reciprocal interaction among the elements of behavior, internal cognitive processes than can affect perceptions and actions, and the external environment – deeply influenced the evolution of the motivational orientation construct of the Peabody–Vanderbilt Group and its research agenda. The research presented here supports Bandura's ideas and confirms related conceptions of the self-system, thus confirming the role of self-evaluative reactions in the self-regulation of behavior in persons with mild mental retardation and in normally developing preschool and school-age children (Borkowski et al., 1990, 1992; Deci & Ryan, 1985; Dweck & Leggett, 1988; Lepper & Hodell, 1989; McCombs & Marzano, 1990; Nicholls, 1989).

Bandura (1986b, 1997) has more recently written about the idea of personal agency – that is, the idea that individuals take responsibility for their actions and ascribe success and failure to the goals they choose, the resources they mobilize, and the effort they expend. Perceived self-efficacy – that is, beliefs concerning one's capabilities to organize and implement actions necessary to attain designated levels of performance – is one of the most important constructs in Bandura's (1986a, 1997) social-cognitive approach, and a critical component of personal agency. A strong belief in one's ability to use specific actions effectively (high perceived self-efficacy) enhances successful performance and feelings of pride, satisfaction, and self-respect (Schunk, 1990).

Bandura's (1986b, 1997) model of personal agency has some similarities to the Reciprocal Empowerment Model (REM) developed by McCombs and Marzano (1990), and McCombs and Whisler (1997). McCombs (1996) and her colleagues have built a model that assumes that within all persons there is a potential for positive functioning – for example, a wellspring of intrinsic self-esteem and a natural motivation to learn. The trick is to engage these powerful internal natural processes for creativity and growth by providing a socially supportive interpersonal environment that will put persons in touch with their intrinsic self-esteem, common sense, creativity, and intrinsic motivation to learn, as well as with their metacognitive competencies – which develop through training – so to allow persons to feel empowered, competent, and in control of their lives. This can only be accomplished through reciprocal social support of persons through quality positive support from the important others in their worlds (for example, parents, teachers, service providers). This social support can only occur to the extent that these important others themselves feel competent and in control, resulting in positive reciprocal empowerment and feedback for all the individuals in the loop.

The extension of the study of personal agency, perceived self-efficacy, and the REM to mentally retarded populations and preschool children may clarify our understanding of the operation of IM and EM within a framework that has been very successful in understanding self-regulation of behavior in older and more normative populations.

The theory of motivational orientation has also been strongly influenced by Feuerstein's theory of mediated learning experiences (MLE) (Feuerstein, Klein, & Tannenbaum, 1991; Feuerstein et al., 1980; Haywood, 1977; Haywood, Brooks, & Burns, 1986; Haywood & Tzuriel, 1992). Children acquire knowledge and understanding in two ways (Schultz & Switzky, 1990): (a) by learning through natural exposure to environmental stimuli where, because of their inborn intrinsic motivation to learn, they independently acquire very complex skills and abilities, and (b) by learning from significant others in their lives – that is, acquiring knowledge and understanding from parents and teachers of complex skills that are not easily learned independently. Depending on how they communicate and interact with children when they are passing on knowledge and understanding of skills, teachers and parents play an important role in maintaining and further shaping the natural ability in children to learn intrinsically by creating MLE, which arouse in children vigilance, curiosity, and sensitivity to the mediated stimuli, and create for and with the children temporal, spatial, and cause-effect relationships among stimuli (Schultz & Switzky, 1990; Tzuriel & Haywood, 1992). On the other hand, adult-child instructional interactions that lack this mediational quality tend to undermine the inborn intrinsic motivation that most children bring to the learning experiences they have with adults.

Thus, problem-solving behavior reflects the interaction of affective-motivational processes such as motivational orientation (Haywood & Switzky, 1992) and cognitive processes, including learned information-processing components of intelligence, the internal or mental processes that underlie intelligent behavior – metacognitive and higher-order control processes, performance components, and knowledge acquisition components (Borkowski et al., 1990, 1992; Carr, Borkowski, & Maxwell, 1991; Pressley, Borkowski, & Schneider, 1990) that allow individuals to use their fluid intelligence in an optimal fashion. Notice the similarities to the REM of McCombs (1996), McCombs and Marzano (1990), and McCombs and Whisler (1997).

In order to qualify as MLE, interaction between children and the mediating adult must meet the following criteria (Feuerstein et al., 1991; Haywood et al., 1986):

1. *Intentionality.* The mediating adult must tend to use the interactions to produce cognitive change in the child.
2. *Transcendence.* The intended change must be a generalizable one (a cognitive structural change that transcends the immediate situation and will permit children to apply new processes of thought in new situations).
3. *Communication of meaning and purpose.* The mediating adult communicates to children the long-range, structural, or developmental meaning and purpose of a shared activity or interaction (explains why they are doing a particular activity in cognitive terms).
4. *Mediation of a feeling of competence.* The mediating adult gives "feedback" on the children's performance by praising what is done correctly (by using correct and/or incorrect aspects of the children's performance, and thus attributing the children's achievement to their own efforts and learning strategies).
5. *Promotion of self-regulation of children's behavior.* Children's behavior is brought under control when they are able to focus on the problem or task at hand. Initially, operant controls may be needed to regulate children's behavior; however, these controls must be removed systematically (and gradually) so that behaviors are maintained with less direct extrinsic reinforcement.
6. *Sharing.* The children and the mediating adult share the quest for solutions to immediate problems and, more importantly, for the developmental change in the children's cognitive structures. The quest is shared because each has a defined role and function, and the interaction is characterized by mutual trust and confidence.

The more cognitive abilities, intrinsic motivation, and environmental opportunities children have, the more easily they learn. The greater the proportion they learn naturally and independently, the less the need for repeated and intense mediated learning experiences. Therefore, the need to utilize instructional guidelines that create MLEs is exacerbated in children with problems that impede their cognitive or motivational development, such as chaotic impoverished environments, mental retardation, learning disabilities, behavior disorders, and sensory and motoric disabilities. The affective-motivational factors (Haywood et al., 1992; Tzuriel, 1991) are basically thought of as an essential substrate for the proposed relationships among the components of MLE and cognitive modifiability that operate in a transactional fashion – that is, efficient mediation by parents can facilitate affective-motivational processes, which in turn encourage the adult mediators to adjust both the quality and the quantity of their mediation to match their children's responses (for example, reduce or increase efforts for children's engagement).

Moreover, MLEs must be used with all children to facilitate their intrinsic motivation and their reliance on internal self-system processes to increase their knowledge acquisition and knowledge usage. This expands their efficiency to solve problems and to decrease their extrinsic motivation and their overreliance and overdependence on environmental feedback, which will decrease their knowledge acquisition and knowledge use and make them less competent and less able to solve problems. MLEs have been successfully used in both normally developing, exceptional, and high-risk children and in adult populations to facilitate learning and intrinsic motivation (Feuerstein et al., 1991; Haywood & Tzuriel, 1991; Lidz, 1991a, 1991b; Savell, Twohig, & Rachford, 1986; Thoman, 1992).

Whitman (1990) has proposed a theoretical model of mental retardation as a disorder in self-regulation that overlaps somewhat with the current model of motivational orientation and its relationship to cognitive processes as evolved by the Peabody–Vanderbilt Group. Whitman (1990) argues that persons with mental retardation have great difficulty regulating their own behavior, and that in order to eliminate this problem, self-regulatory skills must be a primary goal of educators. The problem that I have with Whitman's general position is his over-generalization about the self-regulatory abilities of mentally retarded persons. The main thesis of the Peabody–Vanderbilt Group is that there are significant individual differences in persons with mental retardation to self-regulate their own behavior. Thus, different strategies are required for different subpopulations of mentally retarded persons (for example, intrinsically oriented vs. extrinsically oriented individuals).

The research of the Peabody–Vanderbilt Group has been most productive in helping us understand the influence of effectance motivation and motivational orientation (IM and EM) on the performance of retarded and nonretarded persons ranging from nonhandicapped preschoolers to school-age and middle-school children to mildly mentally retarded adults. There is much overlap between the ideas and constructs of Edward Zigler and his Yale Group and the Peabody–Vanderbilt Group about the operation of personality and motivational processes in persons with mental retardation. Together, the ideas of these groups form a complementary tapestry of overlapping ideas that help us understand those historically "overlooked motivational and environmental variables" that underlie individual differences in behavior in both mentally retarded and nonhandicapped persons.

An Agenda for Future Research

The Peabody–Vanderbilt Group has demonstrated that the active problem-solving performance of persons with mental retardation is a function of the complex interplay of personality and motivational processes within a developmental perspective, reflecting contemporary psychological thought. This work has supported the accelerating integration between a psychology of mental retardation and an overall developmental psychology of human growth applicable to both retarded and nonretarded persons. I believe that mental retardation researchers, few as they have been, have historically been more sensitive to individual differences in personality and motivational processes in the performance of learners with mental retardation, and have developed more elaborate models of motivational systems and self-system processes compared with other developmental psychologists studying nonhandicapped learners. Over the last decade and a half, however, contemporary developmental psychologists have become sensitized to the effects of motivational and self-system processes on outcome performances of nonhandicapped learners, and have developed extensive and insightful models of motivational self-system processes. These new models of motivation and self-system processes should be studied carefully by mental retardation researchers to help them refine models of motivation and future research endeavors.

As Weiner (1990) has documented, the study of motivation has been confounded with the study of learning without any real interest in developing cohesive, generalizable models of personality structure. Motivational theorists studying handicapped and nonhandicapped populations created measures of motivational constructs, and ignored the way their theoretical models related to the theoretical models of other motivational researchers or to the operational definitions of motivation of other motivational theorists. Developmental motivational theorists studying nonhandicapped populations have now developed more comprehensive cognitively based theories of motivation founded on the interrelated cognitions of causal ascriptions, efficacy and control beliefs, learned helplessness, and the goals for which persons are striving, within the context of a theory of self-system processes and a theory of intrinsic/extrinsic motivation (Bandura, 1997; DeCharms, 1984; Deci & Ryan, 1991; Dweck & Leggert, 1988; Lepper & Hodell, 1989; McCombs, 1996). In my opinion, Bandura's (1993, 1997) formulation of his theoretical model of self-efficacy is one of the better attempts to deal with the concerns expressed by Weiner (1990). Motivational researchers in the field of mental retardation have to make the same attempts as their colleagues in contemporary psychology to develop more cohesive, generalizable, highly focused, theoretically elaborate, and precise models of motivational systems applicable to persons with mental retardation.

The work of Dweck and Leggett (1988) and the related work of Nicholls (1989) concerning the perceptions of the reasons for task engagement must be evaluated by motivational researchers in the field of mental retardation as to their theoretical applicability to the motivational systems of mentally retarded persons. Among the reasons for task engagement are (a) goal-setting/goal values as a distinction among "learning goals"/"mastery goals"/"task goals" that motivate individuals to engage in tasks in order to develop mastery, understanding, increased competence, and learning new things, and (b) "performance goals"/"ego goals" that motivate individuals to validate their competence by obtaining positive judgments of their abilities (or avoiding negative ones) by engaging in tasks in order to do better than others, to demonstrate more intelligence than others, or to win approval from others.

Do the belief systems of mentally retarded learners concerning the nature of intelligence ("smartness") – that is, smartness as an "incremental" theory in which intelligence is viewed as something one can increase or as an "entity" theory in which intelligence is viewed as a fixed static trait – operate the same way to change goal structures in mentally retarded individuals as they do in nonhandicapped individuals (Nicholls, 1989)?

Bandura's (1993, 1997) expansion of his social-cognitive theory emphasizing the construct of personal agency and perceived self-efficacy stresses that individuals take responsibility for their actions, and impute success and failure to the goals they choose, the resources they mobilize, and the efforts they expend. Bandura also stresses the idea that beliefs concerning self-perceptions of one's abilities to organize and implement actions necessary to attain designated levels of performance to establish one's expectations and motivation have tremendous implications for motivational researchers in mental retardation. The Peabody–Vanderbilt Group has been heavily influenced by preliminary versions of Bandura's social-cognitive theory, and I expect that we will attempt to refine our models of motivation in persons with mental retardation by integrating aspects of Bandura's expanded theory, which has been so successful in accounting for behavioral outcomes in both nonhandicapped children and adults in so many different domains of performance.

Bandura (1993, 1997) has also tried to integrate his social-cognitive theory of self-regulation of motivation into the major contemporary psychological motivational theories dominating the current zeitgeist: attribution theory and causal attributions, expectancy-value theory and outcome expectancies, and goal theory and cognitized goals, in an attempt to lead the way to develop cohesive, generalizable models of personality structure and self-regulation. These attempts by Bandura surely need to be considered by all motivational researchers in the field of mental retardation in order to develop better motivational theories for persons with mental retardation.

Motivational theorists such as Decharms (1984), Deci and his colleagues (Deci & Ryan, 1985, 1991; Ryan & Connell, 1989), and Lepper and his colleagues (Lepper & Hodell, 1989) focused on such motivational constructs as autonomy and self-determination. They believe that individuals engage in activities initiated by their own volition and endorsed by their sense of self, rather than do things specifically to achieve some external reward or to avoid some external punishment. Individuals are intrinsically motivated when they perceive themselves as the cause of their own behavior – as possessing personal causation, having an internal locus of causality, having a feeling of choice – and when they can experience themselves as causal agents and view themselves as the originators of their own behaviors rather than as pawns of external forces. Additionally, intrinsically motivated individuals have strong needs for a sense of competence, self-determination, and challenge. Individuals are extrinsically motivated when they believe they are engaging in behavior because of controlling external environmental-demand conditions (e.g., external reinforcers, external constraints, pleasing another person, and having an external locus of causality).

These researchers have found that the demand conditions of the environment influence the individual's intrinsic motivation. "Informational" environments convey relevant information to the individual about competence at a task, thus supporting self-autonomy and intrinsic motivation. "Controlling" environments designed to bring about a particular behavioral outcome, usually by the use of extrinsic rewards, support dependency and extrinsic motivation in the individual by shifting the individual's perception away from autonomy and personal causation toward a perception of external causation that undermines intrinsic motivation. Motivational researchers in the field of mental retardation need to apply these principles to mentally retarded persons to determine the degree of informational and controlling components of the environment and ways in which service providers can facilitate the development of intrinsic motivation. Can they increase the informational qualities of the environment and decrease the controlling qualities of the environment to increase intrinsic motivation in persons with mental retardation? McCombs' theory of Reciprocal Empowerment may be important here (McCombs, 1996).

The Peabody–Vanderbilt Group of mental retardation researchers (Haywood & Switzky, 1986, 1992; Switzky, 1997), very early in the development of their theoretical models, believed strongly that the performance of mentally retarded persons reflected the interaction of intrinsic motivation and cognitive processes. Over the last fifteen years, this theme has increasingly dominated both motivational researchers and cognitive researchers, deriving from the mental retardation tradition (Borkowski et al., 1992; Feuerstein et al., 1991; Haywood & Tzuriel, 1992) and from developmental psychology (Dweck, 1986; Maehr & Pintrich, 1991; Nicholls, 1989; Paris & Newman, 1990; Pressley et al., 1990; Vye et al., 1988; Zimmerman, 1990). The efficient operation of cognitive processes and ability systems is vitally linked to motivational processes.

Only when personal-motivational processes are included in strategy training interventions will strategy generalization increase. Strategy-based actions directly influence the self-concept, attitudes about learning, and attributional beliefs about personal control. In turn, these personal-motivational states determine the course of new strategy acquisition and, more importantly, the likelihood of strategy transfer and the quality of self-understanding about the nature and function of mental processes. Borkowski and his collaborators (Borkowski et al., 1992) have developed a model of strategy-based intervention strongly linked to self-regulatory motivational and personality processes that has great relevance for both handicapped and nonhandicapped learners. This model provides a foundation and a new agenda for research on problem-solving acquisition and usage in persons who are mentally retarded. Most interesting is the view of Markus and her colleagues (Markus, Cross, & Wurf, 1990) and their theory of "possible selves," which are visions of the self in future states. In Borkowski's new theory (Borkowski et al., 1992), these "hoped-for" and "feared possible-selves" provide the impetus for achieving important short-term and long-term goals. In this way, the self-system takes on a futuristic perspective, providing incentives for the operation of the entire metacognitive system. I look forward to the further testing and refinement of these models for mentally retarded learners.

A major problem for mental retardation researchers who study motivational, personality, and self-system processes in mentally retarded and low mental-age persons has been the dearth of psychometric instruments and techniques with adequate construct validity. I have argued vigorously for the construct validity of the PCMS as a measure of intrinsic/extrinsic motivation in mentally retarded and low-mental age populations (Switzky & Heal, 1990), and I have documented the evidence to support these claims in this chapter. The Yale group has invented operational definitions for their major motivational constructs of positive reaction tendencies and overdependency, negative reaction tendencies and wariness, effectance motivation, expectancy of success, and outerdirectness by developing the EZYale Personality Questionnaire (see Chapter 9). Also promising is The Arc's Self-Determination Scale developed by Wehmeyer and Kelchner (1995). However, better measures of personality, self-regulatory, and motivational processes are needed to develop more fine-grained and refined theoretical models applicable to mentally retarded and low-mental age populations that are better integrated with motivational and personality theories of self-system processes derived from contemporary developmental psychology.

Nicholls (1989) has developed a set of instruments to measure task goal/learning goals in children that may have application to low mental-age and mentally retarded individuals. Bandura (1993) and his colleagues have developed new measures of self-efficacy that may also be very promising for mental retardation researchers. Deci and his collaborators (Deci & Ryan, 1985; Ryan, 1991) expanded their theory of self-determination by developing measures of an autonomous continuum of extrinsic/intrinsic motivation (e.g., external regulation, introjected regulation, identified regulation, and integrated regulation) related to how successfully an optimal self-regulatory style of intrinsic motivation has been internalized and integrated into the self. Ryan and Connell (1989) designed The Academic-Self-Regulation Questionnaire (ASRQ) for students in elementary and middle school. These measures of regulatory style may also be fruitfully adapted by mental retardation researchers for lower mental-age populations.

Motivational researchers need to develop a theoretical model of the ontology of personality and motivational self-system processes and their relationship to learning and achievement in persons with mental retardation. A social developmental theory and perspective needs to be developed and refined to ensure that every mentally retarded child and adult acquires and uses optimal problem-solving strategies and total fluid intelligences. A running start to achieve these goals has been made by both the Yale and Peabody–Vanderbilt Groups of mental retardation researchers. Future researchers building on the models of both contemporary developmental psychologists and developmental psychologists deriving from the mental retardation tradition are in a strong position to accelerate the integration of a psychology of mental retardation and an overall developmental psychology of individual differences in human growth and development applicable to both retarded and nonretarded individuals.

References

Bandura, A. (1976). Self-reinforcement: Theoretical and methodological considerations. *Behaviorism, 4,* 135–155.

(1978). The self-system in reciprocal determinism. *American Psychologist, 33,* 344–358.

(1986a). *Social foundations of thought and action: A social cognitive theory.* Englewood Cliffs, NJ: Prentice-Hall.

(1986b). From thought to action: Mechanisms of personal agency. *New Zealand Journal of Psychology, 15,* 1–17.

(1993). Perceived self-efficacy in cognitive development and functioning. *Educational Psychologist, 28*(2), 117–148.

(1997). *Self-efficacy: The exercise of control.* New York: W.H. Freeman and Company.

Bandura, A., & Perloff, B. (1967). Relative efficacy of self-monitored and externally imposed reinforcement systems. *Journal of Personality and Social Psychology, 7,* 111–116.

Borkowski, J.G., Carr, M., Rellinger, E., & Pressley, M. (1990). Self-regulated cognition: Interdependence of metacognition, attributions, and self-esteem. In B.F. Jones & L. Idol (eds.), *Dimensions of thinking and cognitive instruction* (pp. 53–92). Hillsdale, NJ: Erlbaum.

Borkowski, J.G., Day, J.D., Saenz, D., Dietmeyer, D., Estrada, T.M., & Groteluschen, A. (1992). Expanding the boundaries of cognitive interventions. In B.Y.L. Wong (ed.), *Contemporary intervention research in learning disabilities* (pp. 1–21). New York: Springer-Verlag.

Call, R.J. (1968). *Motivation-hygiene orientation as a function of socioeconomic status, grade, race, and sex.* Unpublished master's thesis, Tennessee State University, Nashville.

Carr, M., Borkowski, J.G., & Maxwell, S.E. (1991). Motivational components of underachievement. *Developmental Psychology, 27,* 108–118.

DeCharms, R. (1984). Motivating enhancement in educational settings. In R. Ames & C. Ames (eds.), *Research on motivation in education, Vol. 1: Student motivation* (pp. 275–310). Orlando, FL: Academic Press.

Deci, E.L., & Ryan, R.M. (1985). *Intrinsic motivation and self-determination in human behavior.* New York: Plenum.

Deci, E.L., & Ryan, R.M. (1991). A motivational approach to self: Integration in personality. In R. Dienstbier (ed.), *Nebraska Symposium on Motivation: Vol. 38, Perspectives on motivation* (pp. 237–288). Lincoln: University of Nebraska Press.

Dweck, C.S. (1986). Motivational processes affecting learning. *American Psychologist, 41,* 1040–1048.

Dweck, C.S., & Leggett, E.L. (1988). A social-cognitive approach to motivation and personality. *Psychological Review, 95,* 256–273.

Feuerstein, R., Klein, P.S., & Tannenbaum, A.J. (eds.). (1991). *Mediated learning experience (MLE): Theoretical, psychosocial and learning implications.* London: Freund Publishing House Ltd.

Feuerstein, R., Rand, Y., Hoffman, M.B., & Miller, R. (1980). *Instrumental enrichment: intervention program for cognitive modifiability.* Baltimore, MD: University Park Press.

Gambro, J.S., & Switzky, H.N. (1991). Motivational orientation and self-regulation in young children. *Early Child Development and Care, 70,* 45–51.

Haywood, H.C. (1968a). Motivational orientation of overachieving and underachieving elementary school children. *American Journal of Mental Deficiency, 72,* 662–667.

(1968b). Psychometric motivation and the efficiency of learning and performance in the mentally retarded. In B.W. Richards (ed.), *Proceedings of the First Congress of the International Association for the Scientific Study of Mental Deficiency* (pp. 276–283). Reigate, England: Michael Jackson.

(1977). A cognitive approach to the education of retarded children. *Peabody Journal of Education, 54,* 110–116.

(1992). The strange and wonderful symbiosis of motivation and cognition. *International Journal of Cognitive Education & Mediated Learning, 2,* 186–197.

Haywood, H.C., & Switzky, H.N. (1975). Use of contingent social reinforcement to change the verbal expression of motivation in children of differing motivational orientation. *Perceptual and Motor Skills, 86,* 356–365.

(1985). Work response of mildly mentally retarded adults to self versus external regulation as a function of motivational orientation. *American Journal of Mental Deficiency, 90,* 151–159.

(1986). Intrinsic motivation and behavioral effectiveness in retarded persons. In N. Ellis & N. Bray (eds.), *International review of research in mental retardation* (Vol. 14, pp. 1–46). New York: Academic Press.

(1992). Ability and modifiability: What, how and how much? In J.S. Carlson (ed.), *Advances in cognition and educational practice: Theoretical issues: Intelligence, cognition, and assessment.* (Vol. 1-Part A, pp. 25–85). Greenwich, CT: JAI Press.

Haywood, H.C., & Tzuriel, D. (eds.) (1992). *Interactive assessment.* New York: Springer-Verlag.

Haywood, H.C., & Wachs, T.D. (1966). Size discrimination learning as a function of motivation-hygiene orientation in adolescents. *Journal of Educational psychology, 57,* 279–286.

Haywood, H.C., & Weaver, S.J. (1967). Differential effects of motivational orientation and incentive conditions on motor performance in institutionalized retardates. *American Journal of Mental Deficiency, 72,* 459–467.

Haywood, H.C., Brooks, P., & Burns, S. (1986). Stimulating cognitive development at developmental level: A tested, non-remedial preschool curriculum for preschool and older retarded children. In M. Schwebel & C.A. Maher (eds.), *Facilitating cognitive development: Principles, practices, and programs* (pp. 127–147). New York: Haworth Press.

Herzberg, F. (1966). *Work and the nature of man.* Cleveland, OH: World.

Hodapp, R.M., Burack, J.A., & Zigler, E. (eds.). (1990). *Issues in the developmental approach to mental retardation.* New York: Cambridge University Press.

Hunt, J. McV. (1963). Motivation inherent in information processing and action. In O.J. Harvey (ed.), *Motivation and social interaction: Cognitive determinants* (pp. 35–94). New York: Ronald.

(1971). Toward a history of intrinsic motivation. In H.I. Day, D.E. Berlyne, & D.E. Hunt (eds.), *Intrinsic motivation: A new direction in education* (pp. 1–32). Toronto: Holt.

Kunca, D.F., & Haywood, N.P. (1969). The measurement of motivational orientation in low mental age subjects. *Peabody Papers in Human Development, 7* (Whole No. 2).

Lepper, M.R., & Hodell, M. (1989). Intrinsic motivation in the classroom. In C. Ames & R. Ames (eds.), *Research on motivation in education.* (Vol 3, pp. 73–105). San Diego, CA: Academic Press.

Lidz, C.S. (1991a). MLE components and their roots in theory and research. In R. Feuerstein, P.S. Klein, & A.J. Tannenbaum (eds.), *Mediated learning experience (MLE): Theoretical, psychosocial and learning implications* (pp. 271–291). London: Freund Publishing House Ltd.

(1991b). *Practitioner's guide to dynamic assessment.* New York: Guilford Press.

Markus, H., Cross, S., & Wurf, E. (1990). The role of the self-system in competence. In R.J. Sternberg & J. Kolligan, Jr. (eds.), *Competence considered* (pp. 205–225). New Haven, CT: Yale University Press.

McCombs, B.L. (1996). Alternative perspectives for motivation. In L. Baker, P. Afflerbach, & D. Reinking (eds.), *Developing engaged readers in school and home communities* (pp. 67–87). Hillsdale, NJ: Erlbaum.

McCombs, B.L., & Marzano, R.J. (1990). Putting the self in self-regulated learning: The self in regulating will and skill. *Educational Psychologist, 25,* 51–69.

McCombs, B.L., & Whisler, J.S. (1997). *The learner-centered classroom and school.* San Francisco, CA: Josey-Bass.

Maehr, M., Pintrich, P.R. (1991). *Advances in motivation and achievement: Goals and self-regulatory processes* (Vol. 7). Greenwich, CT: JAI.

Merighi, J., Edison, M., & Zigler, E. (1990). The role of motivational factors in the functioning of mentally retarded individuals. In R.M. Hodapp, J.A. Burack, & E. Zigler (eds.), *Issues in the developmental approach to mental retardation* (pp. 114–134). New York: Cambridge University Press.

Miller, M.B., Haywood, H.C., & Gimon, A.T. (1975). Motivational orientation of Puerto Rican children in Puerto Rico and the U.S. mainland. In G. Marin (ed.), *Proceedings of the 15th Interamerican Congress of Psychology.* Bogotà: Sociedad Interamericana de Psicologia.

Morgan, M. (1984). Reward-induced decrements and increments in intrinsic motivation. *Review of Educational Research, 54,* 5–30.

Nicholls, J.G. (1989). *The competitive ethos and democratic education.* Cambridge, MA: Harvard University Press.

Paris, S.G., & Newman, R.S. (1990). Developmental aspects of self-regulated learning. *Educational Psychologist, 25,* 87–102.

Pressley, M., Borkowski, J.G., & Schneider, W. (1990). Good information processing: What it is and how education can promote it. *International Journal of Educational Research, 2,* 857–867.

Pintrich, P.R., & Schrauben, B. (1992). Students' motivational beliefs and their cognitive engagement in classroom academic tasks. In D. Schunk & J. Meece (eds.), *Student perceptions in the classroom: Cause and consequences* (pp. 149–183). Hillsdale, NJ: Erlbaum.

Ryan, R.M. (1991). The nature of the self in autonomy and relatedness. In G.R. Goethals & J. Strauss (eds.), *Multidisciplinary perspectives on the self* (pp. 208–238). New York: Springer-Verlag.

Ryan, R., & Connell, J. (1989). Perceived locus of causality and internalization: Examining reasons for acting in two domains. *Journal of Personality and Social Psychology, 57,* 749–761.

Savell, J.M., Twohig, P.T., & Rachford, D.L. (1986). Empirical status of Feuerstein's "Instrumental Enrichment" (FIE) technique as a method of teaching thinking skills. *Review of Educational Research, 56*(4), 381–409.

Schultz, G.F., & Switzky, H.N. (1990). The development of intrinsic motivation in students with learning problems. *Preventing School Failure, 34,* 14–20.

    (1993). The academic achievement of elementary and junior high school students with behavior disorders and their nonhandicapped peers as a function of motivational orientation. *Learning & Individual Differences, 5,* 31–42.

Schunk, D.H. (1990). Goal setting and self-efficacy during self-regulated learning. *Educational Psychologist, 25*(1), 71–86.

Sternberg, R.J., & Berg, C.A. (eds.) (1992). *Intellectual development.* New York: Cambridge University Press.

Stevenson, H.W., & Zigler, E. (1958). Probability learning in children. *Journal of Experimental Psychology, 56*, 185–192.

Switzky, H.N. (1997). Individual differences in personality and motivational systems in persons with mental retardation. In W.E. MacLean, Jr. (ed.), *Ellis' Handbook of mental deficiency, psychological theory and research,* 3rd ed., pp. 343–377). Mahwah, NJ: Erlbaum.

Switzky, H.N., & Haywood, H.C. (1974). Motivational orientation and the relative efficacy of self-monitored and externally imposed reinforcement schedules. *Journal of Personality and Social Psychology, 30,* 360–366.

(1984). Bio-social ecological perspectives on mental retardation. In N.S. Endler & J. McV. Hunt (eds.), *Personality and the behavior disorders* (2nd ed., Vol 2, pp. 851–896). New York: Wiley.

(1991). Self-reinforcement schedules in persons with mild mental retardation: Effects of motivational orientation and instructional demands. *Journal of Mental Deficiency Research, 35,* 221–230.

(1992). Self-reinforcement schedules in young children: Effects of motivational orientation and instructional demands. *Learning & Individual Differences, 4,* 59–71.

Switzky, H.N., & Heal, L. (1990). Research methods in special education. In R. Gaylord-Ross (ed.), *Issues and research in special education* (Vol. 1, pp. 1–81). New York: Teachers College Press.

Switzky, H.N., & Schultz, G.F. (1988). Intrinsic motivation and learning performance implications for individual educational programming for the mildly handicapped. *Remedial & Special Education, 9,* 7–14.

Switzky, H.N., Haywood, H.C., & Isett, R. (1974). Exploration, curiosity, and play in young children: Effects of stimulus complexity. *Developmental Psychology, 10,* 321–329.

Switzky, H.N., Ludwig, L., & Haywood, H.C. (1979). Exploration, curiosity, and play in young children: Effects of object complexity and age. *American Journal of Mental Deficiency, 86,* 637–646.

Thoman, E.B. (1992). A mediated learning experience for very youngest: Premature infants. *International Journal of Cognitive Education & Mediated Learning, 2*(2), 117–129.

Tzuriel, D. (1991). Cognitive modifiability, mediated learning experience and affective motivational processes: A transactional approach. In R. Feuerstein, P.S. Klein, & A.J. Tannenbaum (eds.), *Mediated learning experience (MLE): Theoretical, psychosocial and learning implications* (pp. 95–120). London: Freund Publishing House Ltd.

Vye, N.J., Delclos, V.R., Burns, M.S., & Bransford, J.D. (1988). Teaching thinking and problem solving: Illustrations and issues. In R.J. Sternberg & E.E. Smith (eds.), *The psychology of human thought* (pp. 337–365). Cambridge: Cambridge University Press.

Wehmeyer, M., & Kelchner, K. (1995). *The Arc's Self-Determination Scale.* Arlington, TX: The Arc of the United States.

Weiner, B. (1990). History of motivational research in education. *Journal of Educational Psychology, 82,* 616–622.

Weisz, J.R. (1990). Cultural-familial mental retardation: A developmental perspective on cognitive performance and "helpless" behavior. In R.M. Hodapp, J.A. Burack, & E. Zigler (eds.), *Issues in the developmental approach to mental retardation* (pp. 137–168). New York: Cambridge University Press.

White, R.H. (1959). Motivation reconsidered: The concept of competence. *Psychological Review, 66,* 297–333.

Whitman, T.L. (1990). Self-regulation and mental retardation. *American Journal on Mental Retardation, 94,* 347–362.

Zewdie, A. (1995). *Work performances of Afro-American adults with mild and moderate mental retardation to self versus external regulation as a function of intrinsic versus extrinsic motivation.* Unpublished doctoral dissertation, Northern Illinois University, Dekalb, IL.

Zigler, E. (1971). The retarded child as a whole person. In H.E. Adams & W.K. Boardman, III (eds.), *Advances in experimental clinical psychology* (Vol. 1, pp. 47–121). New York: Pergamon Press.

Zigler, E., & Hodapp, R.M. (1991). Behavioral functioning in individuals with mental retardation. *Annual Review of Psychology, 42,* 29–50.

Zimmerman, B.J. (1990). Self-regulating academic learning and achievement: The emergence of a social cognitive perspective. *Educational Psychological Review, 2,* 173–201.

Zimmerman, B.J., & Schunk, D.H., (eds.), (1989). *Self-regulated learning and academic achievement.* New York: Springer-Verlag.

5   Motivation for Social Reinforcement: Positive- and Negative-Reaction Tendencies

Dianne Bennett-Gates
Edward Zigler

Positive-reaction tendency and negative-reaction tendency were among the first constructs to be identified in the personality-motivational functioning of individuals with mental retardation. Positive-reaction tendency refers to a heightened desire for social reinforcement, generally from a supportive adult; negative-reaction tendency reflects a wariness of and reluctance to interact with strangers. These behaviors, which may appear to be mutually exclusive, are observed in ambivalently attached infants (Ainsworth, 1973) who seek emotional and physical contact with their primary caregiver, but simultaneously reject the close interaction. An infant can be drawn to mother for comfort and nurturance, yet be fearful that these needs may not be met. Likewise, retarded individuals may hope to secure approval from significant adults (positive-reaction tendency) while being apprehensive about possible rejection or an aversive encounter (negative-reaction tendency).

Scientific understanding of the positive- and negative-reaction tendencies has evolved over the last fifty years from work on rigidity initially conducted by Lewin (1936). His view that individuals of low intelligence are inherently more rigid in their cognitive systems than those of normal intellect was one of the most significant formulations in the field of mental retardation, having considerable effect on care, treatment, and educational practices (Sarason & Gladwin, 1958). Lewin also suggested a motivational explanation for the more rigid behavior based on the inveterate failure experienced by individuals with mental retardation. Although he quickly dismissed this idea because of perceived inadequacies, he acknowledged the need to employ psychologically comparable situations when assessing differences in rigidity between retarded and nonretarded groups.

Interest in the rigidity position has waned over the years, but it has some staying power – attested to by the work of Dulaney and Ellis (1997). In fact, if stated in the current language of cognitive psychology, the rigidity formulation still makes a relevant contribution to our understanding of motivational differences between retarded and nonretarded individuals.

In this chapter, we present a historical overview of the theoretical and empirical work that led to identification of the positive- and negative-reaction tendency constructs. The early work by Lewin and Kounin is presented, followed by explanations of later work that revealed the role of social deprivation in the development of these tendencies. We also draw on attachment theory for its potential contribution to a more complete understanding of the positive- and negative-reaction traits.

Theoretical Beginnings

Rigidity Theory

The origins of the two interrelated constructs – positive- and negative-reaction tendencies – can be traced to the ideas of Lewin (1936) and Kounin (1939, 1941a, 1941b) about cognitive rigidity in individuals with mental retardation. In Lewin's original theory, all behavioral deficits associated with mental retardation were attributed to underlying cognitive impairments. Lewin argued that because of the very nature of development in mental retardation, affected individuals will think and behave more rigidly than those with normal intellectual development. Specifically, he viewed people with mental retardation as being cognitively less differentiated (i.e., having fewer regions in the cognitive structure) than nonretarded peers of the same CA, while also displaying a greater stiffness and diminished capacity for dynamic rearrangement of their cognitive systems.

Lewin's position was founded on a considerable amount of observational and anecdotal material as well as the results of one experimental study (1936). Lewin interpreted the finding of greater persistence on a drawing activity by 10-year-old retarded children (compared with CA-matched nonretarded children) as evidence of an association between rigidity and retardation. Although a lack of differentiation could lead to rigid behaviors (i.e., pedantry, fixation, stereotypy, inelasticity, and concreteness), Lewin clearly drew a distinction between degree of differentiation and rigidity. Whereas differentiation referred to the number and hierarchy of regions within the cognitive system, Lewin defined rigidity in terms of the fluidity between the regions.

His conclusions, however, were confounded. Because comparisons were made between groups having different mental ages, behavioral manifestations of rigidity could not be directly attributed to the degree of differentiation or to the permeability between regions of the cognitive system. Both aspects of cognition are presumably influenced by stage of development, and the development of the children with mental retardation lagged behind that of their nonretarded age-mates.

Despite being flawed, Lewin's work made a significant contribution to the formulation of mental retardation by identifying factors involved in the differential performance of retarded and nonretarded individuals. He summarized these factors as follows:

1. *Degree of differentiation.* Given a pair of individuals matched for CA, one retarded and one nonretarded, the retarded person will be less cognitively differentiated (i.e., have fewer regions). Because of the attenuated differentiation, the retarded individual will display more rigid behaviors over a wide range of tasks.
2. *Rigidity.* When an older retarded individual is matched to a younger nonretarded individual on the basis of cognitive differentiation (measured by MA), the boundaries between the regions in the one with mental retardation will be less permeable. This results in the total system being less fluid and more rigid. The behavior of the retarded individual will therefore be more rigid in most activities.
3. *Personal history.* Individuals who consistently encounter situations beyond their capacity and subsequently experience an inordinate amount of failure may become more rigid in their performance. Thus, their behavior may be the product of a unique history of inadequacy rather than the result of innate rigidity.
4. *The psychological situation.* For a meaningful comparison of the performance of retarded and nonretarded groups, care must be taken to ensure that the assessment situation is psychologically equivalent for the individuals being compared. If not, differences in the amount of rigid behavior may be confounded because the individuals are operating in phenomenally different situations.

Lewin–Kounin Formulation

Building on Lewin's work, Kounin adopted the view that rigidity was a positive, monotonic function of CA. Rather than referring to rigid behaviors per se, Kounin used rigidity to refer to properties of the functional boundaries between regions of the cognitive system that prevent communication between neighboring regions. With increasing CA, individuals become more differentiated (i.e., have more cognitive regions), which lowers the incidence of rigid behaviors. For individuals with mental retardation, however, permeability decreases with increasing CA, which results in characteristically rigid behaviors.

To verify his formulation, Kounin (1939, 1941a, 1941b, 1948) conducted a series of experiments in which he compared the performance of both older and younger institutionalized retarded groups with nonretarded individuals. The experimental manipulation involved switching tasks that required cognitive movement from one region to another, and provided measures of satiation (length of time on the first task), cosatiation (length of time on the second task), and error score (number of times the initial task was erroneously performed under the second stimulus). Kounin predicted that the permeability of the cognitive system in the nonretarded individuals would foster transfer effects between the two tasks, thereby shortening cosatiation, while the relative impermeability in the retarded group would limit transference. The potential confound in the degree of differentiation was controlled by equating on MA. Kounin also attempted to control for motivational factors, such as low expectancy of success and hesitance to enter unfamiliar rooms, by allowing the subjects to gain confidence by practicing the experimental tasks prior to the research session.

As predicted from the Lewin–Kounin hypothesis, the performance of the three groups differed on several experimental tasks (e.g., drawing cats until satiated and then drawing bugs until satiated; lowering a lever and then raising a lever to release marbles). The nonretarded individuals demonstrated the greatest degree of transfer effects – once satiation was reached on the first drawing task, less time was required to reach satiation on the subsequent drawing. In contrast, both younger and older retarded groups showed less transfer effects. Both spent more time on the second drawing, with the older group spending even more than the younger. Although Kounin had anticipated comparable satiation times for both parts of the task, he was not deterred by the findings of a longer satiation time on the second part. He held that his theory pertaining to the rigidity and consequent lack of transfer from one region to the next was confirmed because the retarded individuals did not reach satiation more quickly on the second task.

On the lever-pressing task, error scores were used to indicate transfer effects. The greatest number of errors (lowering rather than raising the lever on the second task) was made by the nonretarded group, the fewest number by the older retarded group, with the younger retarded group falling in between. Movement between regions would be more difficult for retarded than for nonretarded individuals; thus, the Lewin–Kounin formulation would anticipate fewer errors when retarded individuals are "psychologically" placed into a new region by following directions – for example, "push down; now push up."

The prediction that movement between regions would be more difficult for retarded than nonretarded individuals was confirmed in Kounin's concept-switching study. The task, which required participants to switch between sorting a deck of cards on the basis of either shape or color, proved to be easy for the nonretarded subjects. The older retarded group experienced the most difficulty, and the performance of the younger retarded group again fell in between. Kounin attributed the higher incidence of perseverative responses shown by the retarded individuals to difficulties in self-initiated movement across the less permeable boundaries between regions.

Kounin provided impressive experimental support for the view that with MA held constant, the behavior or older and/or more retarded individuals is characterized by greater rigidity in the boundaries between regions. Because he believed these results substantiated his theoretical predictions, Kounin did not pursue the unanticipated finding on his two-part tasks that retarded individuals took longer to reach satiation on the second half and spent a longer total time on the tasks than did the nonretarded groups.

Empirical Tests of the Lewin–Kounin Formulation

Subsequent investigations of the Lewin–Kounin formulation reported conflicting results. Some studies documented differences in perseverative behavior consistent with the general views of Lewin and Kounin. Kaufman and Peterson (1958), for example, found that retarded children, compared with nonretarded children, made a greater number of stimulus perseveration errors on a learning-set task. Greater perseveration by retarded children than nonretarded children was also found by Siegel and Foshee (1960). Using a task involving the selection of a button to turn on a light, nonretarded children demonstrated much greater variability in their selection of buttons than did retarded children. Perseveration was also observed by Terdal (1967) in visual attention to patterns projected alternately on the subject's right or left side. Retarded individuals, in contrast to nonretarded individuals, showed marked spatial preferences. Similarly, Penney, Croskery, and Allen (1962) found more perseveration in retarded children than nonretarded children on a habit-reversal task. Further evidence of rigidity in retarded individuals was found by Carkhuff (1962, 1966) in the perseveration of habit on drawing tasks.

Other research results failed to validate the Lewin–Kounin formulation. In a study by Plenderleith (1956), subjects first mastered discrimination tasks, and then had to reverse their response to the previously incorrect stimulus. The retarded children did not differ from the nonretarded children in ease of learning the original discrimination nor in reversal trials administered the next day.

Evidence from Stevenson and Zigler (1957) also failed to confirm the rigidity hypothesis. They investigated discrimination learning by measuring the relative incidence of perseverative responses followed by a change in task. They argued that continuing with the previously correct response is direct evidence of the subjects' remaining in a prior region rather than moving to a new region. As with the Kounin studies, three groups of MA-matched subjects were employed: younger and older retarded individuals and a nonretarded sample. Although the switching problem was more difficult than Plenderleith's reversal problem, the performance across the three groups on all measures (number of trials to learn the initial discrimination, number of correct choices on the reversal problem, number of subjects in each group who learned the reversal problem, and frequency of perseverative responding) was very similar. Replicating their procedure with a more difficult task, Stevenson and Zigler hypothesized that rigidity is a general behavior mechanism, and that the frequency of rigid behavior (perseverations) reflects the complexity of the task at hand. Their prediction of increased perseverations for both the retarded and nonretarded groups on the second, more difficult, experimental task was confirmed. Again, all three groups showed a similar number of such responses.

In a study designed to assess fluidity between cognitive regions, Kern (1967) compared the performance of retarded and nonretarded children on three tasks: sorting objects by shape, then by color, and finally by both shape and color. Because of the parallels between this series of tasks and the lever-pressing paradigm originally used by Kounin, Kern predicted that nonretarded children, in comparison with retarded children, would make more errors on the second and third sorting tasks as a result of greater negative transfer. The similarity in performance of the two groups, and the observation that the degree of negative transfer was related to MA rather than to IQ, failed to support the Lewin–Kounin formulation.

In another explicit test of the rigidity hypothesis (Corter & McKinney, 1968), performance across five tests of cognitive flexibility yielded equivocal results. Although nonretarded children were superior to retarded children on an object-sorting test reminiscent of Kounin's concept-switching task, no significant differences were found on the four other tasks. A similar study using five card-sorting tasks (Backer, 1966) also yielded inconsistent findings, with the majority of the results failing to support the rigidity hypothesis.

Zigler and Butterfield (1966) employed Kounin's original tasks (cosatiation of drawing, lever-pressing transfer-of-habit, and switching concepts in card-sorting) in an attempt to replicate his findings. These investigators compared the performance of three MA-matched groups: younger and older retarded individuals in two institutions and noninstitutionalized nonretarded individuals. Their results were inconsistent with those reported by Kounin. The drawing task yielded only one significant group difference, which was in the opposite direction of Kounin's results. The nonsignificant findings among groups on the lever-pressing tasks were contradictory to Kounin's rigidity formulation. The single finding consistent with Kounin's original work was that older retarded individuals experienced more trouble switching concepts than did the other groups. It was difficult to interpret this result as confirming the rigidity formulation, however, as there was an interaction with institutional setting. Those residing in the institution that had a relatively poor social climate did better on the concept-switching task than did those in the other institution that had a better social climate.

Social Deprivation and Positive-Reaction Tendency

As explained earlier, Lewin noted briefly that differences in personal history and feelings in the testing situation could contribute to retarded and nonretarded differences in performance. These suggestions inspired Stevenson and Zigler (1957) to direct their attention to subject characteristics over and above formal cognition that could influence behavior. In prior experimental work, the most readily apparent characteristic that differentiated the retarded from the nonretarded groups was institutionalization. Stevenson and Zigler theorized that the performance of retarded individuals could be ascribed, at least in part, to social deprivation experienced prior to and concomitant with institutionalization. Assuming that institutionalized children were relatively deprived of adult contact and approval, they would have a higher motivation to procure and maintain interactions with adults. This assumption was congruent with early views that even nonretarded individuals who reside in institutions exhibit an increased desire to interact with adult figures (Clark, 1933; Sarason, 1953; Skeels et al., 1938).

To explain the differences between their own and Kounin's findings, Stevenson and Zigler pointed out that the tasks they employed required minimal interaction with the experimenter, whereas Kounin's tasks involved following directions given by an adult. Consequently, Kounin's discovery of differences in rigid behavior between MA-matched retarded and nonretarded individuals may have arisen from their differential motivation for adult contact. To test this motivational hypothesis, Zigler, Hodgden, and Stevenson (1958) employed motor tasks comparable to Kounin's original satiation task. Each of the three tasks had two parts, allowing a measure of satiation, cosatiation, and error score. Modifications were made to Kounin's design by manipulating reinforcement conditions. In one condition, the experimenter maintained a nonsupportive role and did not comment on the subject's performance. In the second condition, the experimenter positively reinforced performance.

Using MA-matched retarded and nonretarded individuals, randomly assigned to support or nonsupport conditions, Zigler et al. obtained evidence that either fully or partially confirmed five of their six predictions:

1. Whereas retarded subjects spent a significantly greater amount of time on tasks with adult support than without adult support, nonretarded individuals did not.
2. Retarded individuals spent more time on the tasks than did nonretarded individuals in both supported and nonsupported conditions.
3. There was a significantly greater difference in the length of performance between support and nonsupport conditions for the retarded individuals than for the nonretarded individuals.
4. There was little difference in the cosatiation scores for nonretarded subjects between support and nonsupport conditions. For retarded individuals, however, adult support lowered cosatiation scores to the point where they became negative in value. That is, retarded individuals spent longer on the second part of the tasks than they did on the first part when their performance was positively reinforced.
5. Cosatiation effects were generally less for the retarded group under both support and nonsupport conditions.
6. The proportion of errors was not significantly different for retarded and nonretarded individuals.

To ascertain if the deprivation of supportive contacts with adults, both before and after institutionalization, influenced performance on cognitive tasks, Zigler (1961) observed retarded individuals playing an extremely boring and repetitive game. Participants dropped marbles of one color into one hole of a box and marbles of another color into a second hole. When satiated on the task, the color criteria were reversed, and the subjects again dropped marbles until satiated. The experimenter frequently smiled, nodded, and told participants that they were doing well. Reasoning that socially deprived individuals would be highly responsive to the adult attention and support, Zigler predicted that they would play longer on both parts of the task than those who were less deprived.

As expected, Zigler found that the subjects' histories of social deprivation prior to being institutionalized (determined from ratings by two experienced clinical psychologists) were related to task performance. Individuals who were rated as more deprived persevered longer on the marble-in-the-hole game than did their less-deprived peers. Thus, rather than being inherent to their cognitive functioning, the perseveration so frequently observed in the performance of retarded individuals appeared related to a lack of contact with supportive adults.

Another investigation of rigid behaviors and social deprivation was conducted by Green and Zigler (1962). They employed three MA-matched groups: institutionalized retarded, noninstitutionalized retarded, and nonretarded individuals. In this comparison, the Lewin–Kounin formulation would predict a similar level of performance for the two retarded groups, both of which would differ from the nonretarded group. Assuming that noninstitutionalized individuals with mental retardation would have experienced relatively less social deprivation, Green and Zigler contended that their performance would be similar to that of the nonretarded group. The findings were in accordance with this position, as only the institutionalized retarded group showed the perseverative behavior of relatively long satiation times.

Although this line of research demonstrated a relationship between institutionalization and desire for supportive social contact, institutionalization was an imprecise index of social deprivation. Zigler, Balla, and Butterfield (1968) therefore used a more objective measure – the Preinstitutional Social Deprivation Scale (Zigler, Butterfield, & Goff, 1966) – to document prior childhood experiences instead of relying on clinical opinions and de facto institutionalization. In this study, they compared the performance of organic and cultural-familial retarded individuals who had recently been placed into residential care, so that the results would not also reflect the deprivation inherent in institutional living. The findings, which were similar for both retarded groups, implicated low harmony and richness of the family and excessive desire by parents to institutionalize their child as heightening the motivation for social reinforcement.

The longevity of the effects of social deprivation was documented in a series of follow-ups of Zigler's (1961) previously mentioned study. Zigler and Williams (1963) found that after three additional years of institutional-ization, individuals became significantly more motivated to receive atten-tion and support from an amiable adult. The increase in motivation, how-ever, was related to the amount of preinstitutional deprivation. Individuals from relatively good homes showed a much greater increase in their moti-vation for social reinforcers – that is, they found institutionalization to be more socially depriving – than did individuals from more socially deprived homes. The effects of institutionalization thus depended on the individual's preinstitutional history. When studied at 7- and 10-year follow-ups (Zigler, Butterfield, & Capobianco, 1970), the effects of preinstitutional experience were still in evidence. Clearly, social deprivation is a phenomenon that is incorporated into a person's motivational structure and mediates subse-quent interactions with the environment.

In most of the studies supporting the motivational explanation for appar-ent rigidity, infrequent adult social reinforcement was interpreted as the underlying cause of the perseverative behaviors. Support for this view was provided by Harter and Zigler (1968), who found that an adult experimenter was a more effective social reinforcer than a peer experimenter for individ-uals with mental retardation living in institutional settings, but not for those residing in the community. Thus, the motivation to obtain social reinforce-ment appears to be very specific to the praise and attention dispensed by an adult, rather than a generalized desire for reinforcement from any social agent. Given the availability of peer contact in institutional settings noted by Balla (1967), it is not surprising that peer reinforcement was not as highly valued. Apparently, the willingness to perseverate on a dull monoto-nous task is dependent not only on a history of social deprivation but also on the valence of the social reinforcement available during the task.

Balla's (1967) observational study of both retarded and nonretarded children living either in their homes or in institutions provided direct evi-dence of the quality and quantity of adult interactions experienced in these settings. Within each setting, the experiences of both groups were compar-able. However, in the research comparison most often made in the litera-ture – that between institutionalized retarded children and their nonretarded peers living at home – the retarded children interacted with adults signifi-cantly less often. This difference helps to explain why institutionalized children with mental retardation choose, when given the opportunity, to remain in interactive social situations longer than noninstitutionalized chil-dren, who are more readily satiated on social reinforcers. Once thought to be inherent rigidity, perseveration can arise from the lack of supportive adult contact that leads to a positive-reaction tendency.

Social Deprivation and Negative-Reaction Tendency

Although an atypically high motivation for social reinforcement appears to be an important factor in the performance of institutionalized individuals with mental retardation, the opposite approach to adult encounters has long been observed (Hirsh, 1959; Sarason & Gladwin, 1958; Wellman, 1938; Woodward, 1960). That is, social deprivation can attenuate the effectiveness of social reinforcers, making retarded individuals reluctant to interact with adults. This orientation may underlie some of the differences in performance between retarded and nonretarded individuals that Kounin originally attributed to cognitive rigidity.

In the cosatiation task used by Kounin, the subjects performed a task until they wished to stop. They then performed a highly similar task until satiation was again reached. The cosatiation score was the measure of the degree to which performance on the first task influenced performance on the subsequent task. The prediction from the Lewin–Kounin formulation was that the absolute playing time of individuals with mental retardation would be comparable on both parts of the task. This position, however, could not explain the recurring finding (Kounin, 1941a; Zigler, 1958; Zigler et al., 1958) that under some conditions individuals with mental retardation perform longer on the second task than on the first one. Nonretarded individuals, in contrast, generally perform longer on the first task than on the second.

Whereas Kounin chose not to pursue this phenomenon, Zigler (1958) advanced the hypothesis that despite an increased motivation for adult contact (positive-reaction tendency), institutionalized individuals with mental retardation are cautious toward unfamiliar adults. This negative-reaction tendency, as Zigler termed the behavior, is due to the frequent aversive encounters with adults individuals with mental retardation commonly experience. Arguably, the institutionalized child learns during the first of Kounin's tasks that the experimenter is not like other strange adults who have initiated unpleasant experiences (physical examinations, vaccinations, etc.) with supportive comments. When no negative events occur, the situation is reappraised, and the child ceases to be as wary. When the tasks are switched, the child feels at liberty to maintain the adult contact, and plays for a longer period of time. Nonretarded children, on the other hand, begin the first task without the predisposing negative-reaction tendency. Positive-reaction tendency reduces over the first task, and through fatigue and satiation effects, these children demonstrate a briefer performance on the second task.

The view that cosatiation scores mirror motivational determinants, rather than inherent rigidity, was first tested by Shallenberger and Zigler (1961). Their study differed from others in that three experimental games preceded the two-part cosatiation task. The experimental games were given under two reinforcement conditions. In an appetitive reinforcement condition, the experimenter gave frequent verbal and nonverbal support, and all of the subject's responses met with success. The premise was that such reinforcement would reduce the negative-reaction tendency brought to the experimental session. In an adversive reinforcement condition, all of the subject's responses met with failure, and the lack of success was clearly noted by the experimenter. It was assumed that this experience would increase the negative-reaction tendency. The most striking finding in the comparisons of MA-matched retarded and nonretarded individuals was that both negatively reinforced groups spent more time on the second part of the cosatiation task than they did on the first; those who experienced the appetitive reinforcement engaged in the first task longer than they did the second. These findings support the position that cosatiation effects are the product of motivational variables such as positive- and negative-reaction tendencies rather than the outcome of inherent rigidity.

The study by Zigler, Balla, and Butterfield (1968) described earlier sought to identify the particular preinstitutional experiences that give rise to wariness and fearfulness of adults. Analyses of scores on the Preinstitutional Social Deprivation Scale revealed that the marital harmony factor was most related to the manifestation of negative-reaction tendency. Items subsumed in this factor include the nature of the marital relationship of the parents, and both the father's and the mother's mental health and general attitude toward the child.

The view that the genesis of negative-reaction tendency was to be found in early socially depriving experiences was central to a study by Harter and Zigler (1968). In this study, the performance of retarded individuals living at home and those in institutional care was compared across a two-part cosatiation task. Reinforcement was delivered by either an adult or a non-retarded child. Overall, the institutionalized children displayed a higher degree of negative-reaction tendency than did their noninstitutionalized peers, regardless of the reinforcement agent. These results suggested that institutionalized individuals with mental retardation suffer from a generalized wariness of strangers, whether the strangers are adults or children.

To ascertain whether negative-reaction tendency can arise from social deprivation that is not linked to institutionalization, Weaver (1966) studied the behavior of noninstitutionalized children with mental retardation who had extremely poor records of academic, social, and health adjustment. The children were asked to place felt shapes onto a long felt board. The experimenter sat at one end of the board and made either positive or negative comments about the child's performance, depending upon reinforcement condition. Instead of the timed cosatiation scores used in other studies, Weaver operationalized negative-reaction tendency as the physical distance the child maintained from the adult in placing the shapes. Over a series of trials, the children who received supportive comments moved toward the experimenter, whereas children receiving the negative comments moved away. Expanding the design to include comparisons between institutionalized and noninstitutionalized individuals with mental retardation as well as nonretarded children, Weaver, Balla, and Zigler (1971) found that only the institutionalized group of children with mental retardation reacted to the reinforcement conditions. Those who experienced the negative condition distanced themselves further from the experimenter, while those who experienced the positive condition placed themselves closer.

Findings from Balla, McCarthy, and Zigler (1971), whose sample was drawn from an institution with a structured program to ameliorate fear of strangers, found significant program effects. Individuals with mental retardation who were institutionalized at a younger age, and who therefore had longer exposure to the remedial program, were less circumspect in the presence of a strange adult than those who were institutionalized at an older age.

Other studies have documented the impact of primary caregiver arrangements on positive- and negative-reaction tendencies. Both Zigler (1971) and Balla (1967) found that retarded individuals who experienced frequent changes of primary caregiver before institutionalization were highly motivated to secure adult attention, yet, at the same time, were wary of doing so. Balla, Kossan, and Zigler (1980) found a relationship between type of institutional care and motivation for adult attention. Institutions with a large number of professional staff and an active volunteer program typically had residents with higher responsiveness to social reinforcement. On the other hand, poor-quality social interactions with caregiving staff heightened the negative-reaction tendency. Situations characterized by a larger number of residents in a living unit, high employee turnover, and a low proportion of aides to residents were associated with unpredictable caregiving and, consequently, a greater wariness of adults.

From this line of research, it is apparent that individuals with mental retardation often have particular social and family histories that can have a debilitating influence on their interactions with others. Both excessive desire to interact with adults and a wariness of doing so can undermine the quality of the retarded individual's performance in learning situations. Further, an atypically high negative-reaction tendency can motivate people with mental retardation to engage in behaviors – for example, withdrawal – that attenuate their social effectiveness. Harter and Zigler (1968) surmised that this negative approach was pervasive in the behavior of individuals with mental retardation, spilling over into their low expectancy of success (Chapter 6) in social and academic situations. These authors drew on Cromwell's (1963) observation of the failure-avoiding nature of retarded children's performance, a phenomenon that also indicates a certain wariness or fearfulness. Thus, a negative-reaction tendency would be anticipated on complex or challenging tasks, particularly those presented by adults. In this extension of the original theory, the negative-reaction tendency shown by individuals with mental retardation may be conceptualized as both the product of aversive experiences with social agents that engender a wariness of other human beings and the result of failure experiences on cognitive tasks that result in a cautious approach to intellectually demanding situations.

As the research described in this chapter shows, however, these behaviors are quite malleable. Excessive wariness, and indeed excessive dependency, are thus not inexorable consequences of either institutionalization or mental retardation. Both tendencies can be diminished by providing retarded individuals with more frequent positive social contacts and opportunities for success.

Thoughts on the Role of Attachment in the Reaction Tendencies

The developmental approach holds that most children with mental retardation traverse the same developmental stages as children of normal intellect. An early developmental task for all children is the formation of attachment to a primary caregiver. Attachment behavior has been studied extensively in nonretarded children, and this literature is readily generalizable to those at the lower end of the normal distribution of intelligence. In fact, retarded children's strong motivation for contact with adults, in conjunction with increased wariness of adults, have also been observed in research on attachment. This suggests that positive- and negative-reaction tendencies may have antecedents in attachment difficulties, and are not peculiar to mental retardation.

Attachment is the very close bond between the child and primary caregiver, typically the mother, that develops gradually during infancy. In their classic work, Ainsworth, Bell, and Stayton (1971) identified three patterns of childhood attachment. Some infants demonstrate a clear preference for being physically and emotionally close to their parents and a recognizable fear of strangers. These securely attached children will seek out their mother after a brief separation and maintain a relatively high degree of casual contact with her. Infants with anxious/avoidant attachment show little desire for contact, and generally ignore their mother after a brief absence. These children seem to maintain a psychological and/or physical distance from their parents by moving away from them, failing to cling when being put down, and avoiding direct eye contact. Anxious/resistant attachment infants might react quite violently to a mother's departure, yet show no sign of actively seeking her when she returns. These babies might cry to be picked up, but then struggle to be released, seeming to push away from mother while simultaneously attempting to maintain contact.

In studies of parenting styles, mothers of anxious/avoidant infants tended to reject their babies. These mothers engaged in parent-child interactions when they were inclined to do so, rather than when the infant indicated a need for attention (Smith & Pederson, 1988). Thus, infants may develop an anxious/avoidant pattern of behavior to avoid possible rebuff from people who have been unresponsive to their needs. Anxious/resistant attachment appears to stem from an inconsistent parenting style in which the mother is unreliable in meeting the infant's needs. Consequently, these children never know what to expect (Ainsworth et al., 1978). Secure attachment appears to develop when the parents are readily accessible, consistent, and responsive to their babies' needs.

The quality of early attachment is believed to be a significant precursor to the formation of adult relationships (Ainsworth, 1973; Maccoby & Masters, 1970; Martin, 1975; Schiller, 1980). The long-term influence of attachment on children's functioning was demonstrated in a longitudinal study from infancy to elementary school. At 5 years old, children who were securely attached as infants had better developed social skills with adults and peers than the children who had insecure (either anxious/avoidant or anxious/resistant) styles of attachment (Arend, Gove, & Sroufe, 1979). Two further studies showed that those with secure attachments maintained a higher level of social competence in second, third (Bergman, cited in Sroufe, 1985), and sixth grade (Estrada et al., 1987).

The relationship between attachment style and social competence may be mediated by other factors such as family stability and social deprivation (Lamb et al., 1984). Lamb et al. noted that predictions of future behavior based on attachment style were more likely to be correct for children from stable families. In particular, children with consistent child-care arrangements tended to have more secure attachments and appeared to be more successful in terms of their overall social-emotional development. On the other hand, indicators of social deprivation such as marital discord and inconsistencies in child-care arrangements were associated with insecure forms of attachment and poorer social-emotional development.

Research investigating the outcomes of extreme deprivation (Bowlby, 1951; Spitz, 1945; Spitz & Wolf, 1946) reported a high incidence of apathy and withdrawal in addition to a lack of responsivity among institutionalized children. Rheingold (1956) documented the importance of attachment to later social responsiveness in a comparison of previously institutionalized infants whom she mothered herself for two months while they were in residential care with infants who experienced a low level of socialization from a series of institutional caretakers. Even though the nurturing experience was brief, the mothered infants demonstrated more social responsiveness at a one-month follow up. Since this early work there have been numerous studies (e.g., Dennis, 1973; Rutter, 1974; Yarrow, Rubenstein, & Pederson, 1975) documenting the diminished social functioning arising from social deprivation and/or a disturbance in attachment.

The positive- and negative-reaction tendencies evidenced by socially deprived individuals with mental retardation appear similar to the behavior of children who had insecure forms of attachment in infancy. Individuals with either of these histories are motivated to seek and sustain adult interactions, but this occurs in conjunction with a fear and wariness that the adult will not be responsive. The effects of both insecure attachment and social deprivation are lasting, documented by longitudinal studies in both domains. These parallels beg the question of whether early social deprivation disrupts healthy attachment, which in turn leads to maladaptive positive- and negative-reaction tendencies. This hypothesis merits empirical scrutiny to further our understanding of the motivational/personality determinants of the behavior of individuals with mental retardation.

Remediating Positive- and Negative-Reaction Tendencies

The evidence reported thus far in this chapter has illustrated the susceptibility of individuals with mental retardation to the effects of social deprivation. Although these effects are profound and enduring, some studies have demonstrated that they can be ameliorated. For example, in a comparison of large residential schools with the same admission requirements, Butterfield and Zigler (1965) found that residents in more de-humanizing facilities showed significantly higher levels of behavior indicative of positive-reaction tendency. Supportive, more homelike environments reduced dependency on adult attention and approval. Zigler and Balla (1972) also found evidence that institutionalized children with mental retardation who maintained contact with their parental figures were more likely to display behavior similar to that of nonretarded children. Children who were visited by parents or went home for vacations were significantly less dependent on adults than were children with little or no parental contact.

In a study of residential facilities, Bjaanes and Butler (1974) observed residents' behavior in group homes (accommodating twenty-four to thirty individuals) and home-care facilities (housing four to six residents). They found more independent behavior in the individuals in group homes. (Note, however, that these facilities were larger than most of the group homes in operation today, which are more like the older home-care residences.) This finding was confirmed in a study by Landesman-Dwyer, Sackett, and Kleinman (1980), who also found that residents of group homes engaged in more appropriate social behavior and were more likely to have reciprocal friendships than were residents in smaller facilities. With their social needs being met through adequate adult interaction and appropriate peer relationships, individuals with mental retardation exhibit more trust of adults and less need to rely on them for social reinforcement.

In a study of receptive language in institutionalized retarded children, Gayton and Bassett (1972) found a relationship between quality of social reinforcement and positive-reaction tendency. Children who received frequent, but noncontingent, reinforcement learned the correct responses faster than either a group receiving minimal verbal reinforcement (experimenter saying "good" only after a correct response) or nonreinforcement (experimenter hidden behind a screen and ringing a bell after a correct response). The more rapid learning in the presence of maximum social reinforcement may indicate that saturation with positive interactions with an adult obviates dependent and wary behaviors that undermine the task at hand. This finding has obvious implications for practice, particularly in view of Balla's (1967) observation that institutionalized retarded children may use the classroom setting as a place to satisfy their social needs.

Further evidence that the effects of social deprivation are malleable is found in a study of nonretarded children. Gewirtz and Baer (1958) observed that exposure to brief periods of social deprivation immediately prior to task administration increased responsiveness to adult reinforcement in intellectually average children who lived with their families. Even though this study was designed to investigate the immediate effects of temporary deprivations, an important implication is that changes in responsivity are not peculiar to mental retardation.

Given the heightened motivation for social reinforcement, positive-reaction tendency may be a precursor to overdependency. Similarly, the wariness associated with negative-reaction tendency, exacerbated by chronic social rejection, may result in clinically significant anxiety problems in individuals with mental retardation. Yet, given a supportive environment, these individuals can display more adaptive behavior. Such findings signify the importance of providing individuals with mental retardation with a nurturing home environment, an educational curriculum that provides opportunities for success, and supportive clinical interventions.

Current Status

The evidence described in this chapter shows that a combined dependency on adults and a wariness of interacting with them leads to a general attenuation in retarded individuals' social and cognitive effectiveness. Their positive- and negative-reaction tendencies motivate them toward behaviors (e.g., overdependency and withdrawal) that are incompatible with optimal performance. Retarded individuals' poor performance on cognitive tasks must therefore be interpreted in view of their atypical motivational tendencies rather than ascribed to intellectual deficiencies alone. For example, behaviors previously thought to be indicative of cognitive rigidity (e.g., perseveration) appear to represent a strategic ploy to obtain highly desired social reinforcement when personality factors are taken into consideration.

Although the effects of social deprivation can persist for many years, they are not insurmountable. Research has shown that given a socially accepting environment both at home and at school, the behavior of individuals with mental retardation becomes commensurate with that of their nonretarded MA-matched peers. This scenario may become more common than it was at the time most of the research on positive- and negative-reaction tendencies was conducted. The prevalence of institutionalization has diminished, and residential care no longer isolates individuals to the extent that familiar adults become a respite from a solitary existence and unknown adults evoke fear. However, failure still pervades the experiences of individuals with mental retardation, and the majority of them are still of the cultural-familial type that is more prevalent in the lower socioeconomic class. They are thus still likely to be affected by social deprivation. The positive- and negative-reaction tendency constructs therefore remain valuable in understanding the behavior of individuals with mental retardation.

References

Ainsworth, M. (1973). The development of infant-mother attachment. In B.M. Caldwell & H.N. Riccuti (eds.), *Review of child development research* (Vol. 3). Chicago: University of Chicago Press.

Ainsworth, M., Bell, S., & Stayton, D. (1971). Individual differences in strange situation behavior of 1 yr olds. In H. Schaffer (ed.), *The origins of human social relations.* London: Academic Press.

Ainsworth, M., Blehar, M., Waters, E., & Wall, S. (1978). *Patterns of attachment: A psychological study of the strange situation.* New York: John Wiley.

Arend, R., Gove, F., & Sroufe, L. (1979). Continuity of individual adaptation from infancy to kindergarten: A predictable study of ego-resiliency and curiosity in preschoolers. *Child Development, 50,* 950–959.

Backer, H.M. (1966). An experimental investigation of the motivational hypothesis of rigidity in retardates: A comparison of retarded and normal performance on a series of card-sorting tasks. *Dissertation Abstracts, 26,* 4068–4069.

Balla, D. (1967). The verbal action of the environment on institutionalized and noninstitutionalized retardates and normal children of two social classes. Unpublished doctoral dissertation, Yale University, New Haven, CT.

Balla, D., McCarthy, E., & Zigler, E. (1971). Some correlates of negative reaction tendencies in institutionalized retarded children. *Journal of Psychology, 79,* 77–84.

Balla, D., Butterfield, E., & Zigler, E. (1974). Effects of institutionalization on retarded children: A longitudinal, cross-sectional investigation. *American Journal of Mental Deficiency, 78,* 530–549.

Balla, D., Kossan, N., & Zigler, E. (1980). Effects of preinstitutional history and institutionalization on the behavior of the retarded. Unpublished manuscript, Yale University, New Haven, CT.

Bjaanes, A.T., & Butler, E.W. (1974). Environmental variation in community care facilities for mentally retarded persons. *American Journal of Mental Deficiency, 78,* 429–439.

Bowlby, J. (1951). *Maternal care and mental health.* Geneva: WHO.

Butterfield, E., & Zigler, E. (1965). The influence of differing social climates on the effectiveness of social reinforcement in the mentally retarded. *American Journal of Mental Deficiency, 70,* 48–56.

(1970). Preinstitutional social deprivation and IQ changes among institutionalized retarded children. *Journal of Abnormal Psychology, 74,* 83–89.

Carkhuff, R.R. (1962). Perseveration of habit in drawing tasks as a characteristic distinguishing mental defectives from normals. *Journal of Clinical Psychology, 18,* 413–415.

(1966). Variations in performance of noninstitutionalized retardates. *Journal of Clinical Psychology, 22,* 168–170.

Clark, L. (1933). *The nature and treatment of amentia.* Baltimore: Wood.

Corter, H.M., & McKinney, J.D. (1968). Flexibility training with educable retarded and bright normal children. *American Journal of Mental Deficiency, 72,* 603–609.

Cromwell, R. (1963). A social learning approach to mental retardation. In N.R. Ellis (ed.), *Handbook of mental deficiency.* New York: McGraw-Hill.

Dennis, W. (1973). *Children of the Creche.* New York: Appleton-Century Crofts.

Dulaney, C., & Ellis, N. (1997). Rigidity in the behavior of mentally retarded persons. In W. MacLean, Jr. (ed.), *Ellis' handbook of mental deficiency, psychological theory, and research* (3rd ed., pp. 173–197). Mahwah, NJ: Erlbaum.

Estrada, P., Arsenio, W., Hess, R., & Holloway, S. (1987). Affective quality of the mother-child relationship: Longitudinal consequences for children's school-relevant cognitive functioning. *Developmental Psychology, 23,* 210–215.

Gayton, W., & Bassett, J. (1972). The effect of positive and negative reaction tendencies on receptive language development in mentally retarded children. *American Journal of Mental Deficiency, 76,* 499–508.

Green, C., & Zigler, E. (1962). Social deprivation and the performance of retarded and normal children on a satiation type task. *Child Development, 33,* 499–508.

Harter, S., & Zigler, E. (1968). Effectiveness of adult and peer reinforcement on the performance of institutionalized and noninstitutionalized retardates. *Journal of Abnormal Psychology, 73,* 144–149.

Hirsh, E. (1959). The adaptive significance of commonly described behavior of the mentally retarded. *American Journal of Mental Deficiency, 63,* 639–646.

Kaufman, M.E., & Peterson, W.W. (1958). Acquisition of a learning set by normal and mentally retarded children. *Journal of Comparative and Physiological Psychology, 51,* 619–621.

Kern, W. H. (1967). Negative transfer on sorting tasks, MA, and IQ in normal and retarded children. *American Journal of Mental Deficiency, 72,* 416–421.

Kounin, J. (1939). *Experimental studies of rigidity as a function of age and feeblemindedness.* Unpublished doctoral dissertation, State University of Iowa, Ames.

(1941a). Experimental studies of rigidity: I. The measurements of rigidity in normal and feeble-minded persons. *Character and Personality, 9,* 251–272.

(1941b). Experimental studies of Rigidity: II. The explanatory power of the concept of rigidity as applied to feeblemindedness. *Character and Personality, 9,* 273–282.

(1948). The meaning of rigidity: A reply to Heinz Werner. *Psychological Review,* *55,* 157–166.

Lewin, K. (1936). *A dynamic theory of personality.* New York: McGraw-Hill.

Lamb, M., Thompson, R., Gardner, W., Charnov, E., & Este, D. (1984). Security of infantile attachment as assessed by the "strange situation": Its study and biological interpretation. *The Brain and Behavioral Sciences, 7,* 127–171.

Landesman-Dwyer, S., Sackett, G., & Kleinman, J. (1980). Relationships of size to residential and staff behavior in small community residences. *American Journal of Mental Deficiency, 85,* 6–17.

Maccoby, E., & Masters, J. (1970). Attachment and dependency. In P. Mussen (ed.), *Carmicheal's manual of child psychology.* New York: John Wiley.

Martin, B. (1975). Parent-child relations. In F. Horowitz (ed.), *Review of child development research* (Vol. 4). Chicago: University of Chicago Press.

Penney, R.K., Croskery, J., & Allen, G. (1962). Effects of training schedules on rigidity as manifested by normal and mentally retarded children. *Psychological Reports, 10,* 243–249.

Plenderleith, M. (1956). Discrimination learning and discrimination reversal learning in normal and feebleminded children. *Journal of Genetic Psychology, 88,* 107–112.

Rheingold, H. (1956). The modification of social responsiveness in institutional babies. *Monographs of the Society for Research in Child Development* (Whole Number 63).

Rutter, M (1974). *The qualities of mothering.* New York: Jason Aronson.

Sarason, S. (1953). *Psychological problems in mental deficiency.* New York: Harper.

Sarason, S., & Gladwin, T. (1958). Psychological and cultural problems in mental subnormality: A review of the research. *Genetic Psychology Monographs, 57,* 3–290.

Schiller, J. (1980). *Child care alternatives and emotional well-being.* New York: Praeger.

Shallenberger, P., & Zigler, E. (1961). Rigidity, negative reaction tendencies, and cosatiation effects in normal and feebleminded children. *Journal of Abnormal and Social Psychology, 63,* 20–26.

Siegel, P.S., & Foshee, J.G. (1960). Molar variability in the mentally defective. *Journal of Abnormal and Social Psychology, 61,* 141–143.

Skeels, H., Updegraff, R., Wellman, B., & Williams, H. (1938). A study of environmental stimulation. *University of Iowa Study of Child Welfare, 15,* No. 4.

Smith, P., & Pederson, D. (1988). Maternal sensitivity and patterns of infant-mother attachment. *Child Development, 59,* 1097–1101.

Spitz, R. (1945). Hospitalism: An inquiry into the genesis of psychiatric conditions in early childhood. *Psychoanalytic Study of the Children, 2,* 113–117.

Spitz, R., & Wolfe, K. (1946). The smiling response: A contribution to the ontogenesis of social relations. *Genetic Psychology Monographs, 34,* 57–125.

Stevenson, H., & Zigler, E. (1957). Discrimination learning and rigidity in normal and feebleminded individuals. *Journal of Personality, 25,* 699–711.

Sroufe, L. (1985). Attachment classification from the perspective of infant-caregiver relationships and infant temperament. *Child Development, 56,* 1–14.

Terdal, L.G. (1967). Complexity and position of stimuli as determinants of looking behavior in retardates and normals. *American Journal of Mental Deficiency, 72,* 384–387.

Weaver, J. (1966). The effects of motivation-hygiene orientation and interpersonal reaction tendencies in intellectually subnormal children. Unpublished doctoral dissertation. George Peabody College for Teachers, Nashville, TN.

Weaver, S.J., Balla, D., & Zigler, E. (1971). Social approach and avoidance tendencies of institutionalized retarded and noninstitutionalized retarded and normal children. *Journal of Experimental Research in Personality, 5,* 98–110.

Wellman, B. (1938). Guiding mental development. *Childhood Education, 15,* 108–112.

Woodward, M. (1960). Early experiences and later social responses of severely subnormal children. *British Journal of Medical Psychology, 33,* 123–132.

Yarrow, L., Rubenstein, J., & Pederson, F. (1975). *Infant and environment.* New York: John Wiley.

Zigler, E. (1958). Social deprivation and rigidity in the performance of feebleminded children. Unpublished doctoral dissertation, University of Texas.

(1961). Social deprivation and rigidity in the performance of feebleminded children. *Journal of Abnormal and Social Psychology, 62,* 413–421.

(1971). The retarded child as a whole person. In H.E. Adams & W.K. Boardman (eds.). *Advances in experimental clinical psychology* (pp. 47–121). New York: Pergamon.

Zigler, E., & Balla, D. (1972). Developmental course of responsiveness to social reinforcement in normal children and institutionalized retarded children. *Developmental Psychology, 6,* 66–73.

Zigler, E., Balla, D., & Butterfield, E.C. (1968). A longitudinal investigation of the relationship between preinstitutional social deprivation and social motivation in institutionalized retardates. *Journal of Personality and Social Psychology, 10,* 437–445.

Zigler, E., & Butterfield, E.C. (1966). Rigidity in the retarded: A further test of the Lewin–Kounin formulation. *Journal of Abnormal Psychology, 71,* 224–231.

Zigler, E., Butterfield, E.C., & Capobianco, F. (1970). Institutionalization and the effectiveness of social reinforcement: A five- and eight-year follow-up study. *Developmental Psychology, 3,* 255–263.

Zigler, E., Butterfield, E.C., & Goff, G.A. (1966). A measure of preinstitutional social deprivation for institutionalized retardates. *American Journal of Mental Deficiency, 70,* 873–885.

Zigler, E., Hodgden, L., & Stevenson, H. (1958). The effect of support on the performance of normal and feebleminded children. *Journal of Abnormal Psychology, 26,* 106–122.

Zigler, E., & Williams, J. (1963). Institutionalization and the effectiveness of social reinforcement: A three year follow-up study. *Journal of Abnormal and Social Psychology, 66,* 197–205.

6   Expectancy of Success in Individuals with Mental Retardation

Dianne Bennett-Gates
Shulamith Kreitler

A commonly observed trait among individuals with mental retardation is a low expectancy of success, which undermines their performance. This discouraging outlook is viewed as an outgrowth of a lifetime characterized by frequent confrontations with tasks that are beyond their intellectual abilities (Zigler & Balla, 1982; Zigler & Hodapp, 1986). As attempts to complete tasks correctly result in failure, the expectation of success is gradually extinguished. The main motivation then becomes to avoid failure rather than to achieve success (Cromwell, 1963).

Although the effect of failure experiences, and the ensuing failure expectancies, has long been documented in individuals with average intellectual abilities (Atkinson, 1958a, 1958b; Katz, 1964; Rotter, 1954; Sarason et al., 1960), the initial comparisons with individuals with mental retardation were inconsistent. For example, Heber (1957) found that failure experiences prior to an experimental task had similar effects on the performance of retarded and nonretarded individuals, whereas Gardner (1958) reported differential effects. Further, Heber's finding that success experiences improved the performance of individuals with mental retardation more than that of nonretarded individuals was later contradicted by Kass and Stevenson (1961), who observed greater gains in the performance of individuals of average intelligence.

Butterfield and Zigler (1965) attributed these inconsistencies in part to individual differences in responsivity to adults (i.e., the desire to gain adult support and approval). Responsive nonretarded children react to failure experiences with increased effort. Among responsive individuals with mental retardation, the failure experience increases anxiety and lowers expectancy of success, which in turn hurts their performance. The reverse occurs for less responsive individuals, with failure undermining the performance of nonretarded individuals and improving the performance of individuals with mental retardation. Although responsivity, subsequently

130

termed positive-reaction tendency, was shown to be related to performance, it was not a sufficient explanation for the inconsistent findings.

Another factor contributing to the ambiguity in the research was that the experimental manipulations were generally very simple, circumscribed experiences of success or failure. Such brief setting conditions could not be analogous to the assumed history of failure experienced by individuals with mental retardation. In fact, under more representative conditions of prolonged failure, retarded individuals who had previously solved simple problems were no longer able to do so (Zeaman & House, 1960).

The criterion tasks were also problematic in that few studies had systematically compared retarded and nonretarded children on anything but very simple activities (Girardeau & Ellis, 1964; McManis, 1965; Prehm, 1966; Stevenson, 1965). Because the tasks involved only minimal learning and information processing (Weir, 1967), they lacked sufficient power to reveal potential group differences. With so many weaknesses, Butterfield and Zigler concluded that the early studies could not provide the unequivocal evidence necessary to validate the cognitive-developmental approach to mental retardation.

Probability Learning as a Measure of Expectancy of Success

In selecting an empirical task that would provide sufficient complexity, investigators shifted from simple information-processing to more difficult problem-solving tasks. Among these were discrimination tasks, which present a set of mutually exclusive and exhaustive responses and require a prediction of the "correct" response to obtain reinforcement. Predictability, and hence complexity, of the task can be manipulated by changing the probability of reinforcement and the range of alternative responses available (Miller & Frick, 1950).

Task Description

There are many forms of probability-learning tasks that can be traced to a paradigm used by Hamilton (1916: as cited in Ward, 1956) to study trial-and-error behavior in situations with no apparent solution. The typical research measures involve a choice between two or three stimuli and a manipulation of the reinforcement schedule. Because reinforcement is not given every time the correct stimulus is chosen (generally between 33 percent and 66 percent of the correct responses are rewarded depending on the study), these tasks can be very deceptive (Gardner, 1957). For the individual engaged in the task, the goal appears to be simply selecting the correct alternative on each trial. This leads to the presumption that for each trial there is a correct choice and that a solution yielding 100 percent reinforcement exists. The participant is unaware that reinforcement is delivered only for a specified percentage of correct responses and that there is no solution that will result in reinforcement every time. Furthermore, as the partial reinforcement schedule is randomized, whether reinforcement will be received or not cannot even be predicted. Despite this, the pervasive expectancy for a solution can be overwhelming. Hyman and Jenkins (1956), for example, encountered far more difficulty in trying to convince subjects that a sequence was random than in persuading them that it was structured.

Response Behaviors

Because there is no solution in the anticipated manner – in that it is impossible to obtain reinforcement on each trial – this task facilitates examination of problem-solving strategies over a series of trials (Stevenson & Weir, 1963; Weir, 1962, 1964). Some subjects appear to randomly vary their choices. This may reflect an unsophisticated hit-or-miss approach to the task, or a progression through different and often elaborate strategies based on complex hypotheses relating to the nature of the task and the reinforcement schedule. Others follow systematic patterns in their attempts to find the solution that results in 100 percent reinforcement. A common pattern among children is to choose the left, middle, and right (or right, middle, and left) stimuli.

Pattern frequency, which refers to the number of such instances of pattern-responding interrupted by nonpattern responses, provides a measure of two problem-solving strategies. In addition to reflecting a systematic search for the correct solution, it also captures the individual's tendencies toward active exploration and risk-taking by departing from a structured strategy (Luthar & Zigler, 1988). There are also individuals who seem to settle into a routine selection of a single alternative that is adequately, though not always, reinforced. Although this behavior does not meet the goal of 100 percent reinforcement, continual selection of this alternative actually provides the maximum reinforcement available in a probability-learning task, and is therefore referred to as maximization.

Factors Related to Performance

Two different types of determinants have been emphasized in explaining performance on probability-learning tasks. Some researchers have explored situational factors, whereas others have investigated characteristics the individual brings to the task. Although these interpretations are not mutually exclusive, research on these two types of determinants has generally been conducted independently of one another.

Situational Factors. Beginning with the work of Ward (1956) and Neimark (1956), considerable evidence has been presented that task-specific or situational factors influence an individual's performance on probability-learning tasks. Response choice has been found to be related to the number of alternatives available, as well as to the frequency, contingency, and relative worth of the reinforcement. Ward (1956) found that individuals are more likely to choose the more frequently rewarded alternative. On the other hand, increasing the amount of reward available on less frequently reinforced alternatives will increase their likelihood of selection, thereby mitigating the effect of the lower probability. Neimark (1964) found that selection of the correct response decreased in proportion to the number of "blank" trials in which no reinforcement was administered, as well as in the presence of noncontingent reinforcement.

Maximization is enhanced by several factors. Morse and Runquist (1960) reported that maximizing behavior increased when the series was perceived as being randomized but not when it was thought to follow a predetermined schedule. Both Edwards (1961) and Gruen and Weir (1964) confirmed these findings. Explicit training in the concepts of chance and risk (Keller, 1971; Ojemann, Maxey, & Snider, 1965a, 1965b) prior to participation in a probability-learning task has also been found to induce maximizing behavior.

The findings in terms of the amount of reward available are more ambiguous. Some studies (e.g., Brackill, Kappy, & Starr, 1962) found greater maximization associated with higher levels of reward. The opposite – lower reward leading to more maximization – occurred in other studies (e.g., Stevenson & Weir, 1959). One explanation attributed the differences to the number of choices available. Studies manipulating the number of choices, however, also had inconsistent results. Although Gardner (1957, 1958) initially found greater maximization as the number of choices increased, a subsequent study by Weir and Gruen (1965) found greater maximization with a two-choice task. Moran and McCullers (1979) tried to resolve the apparent conflict by investigating methodological differences in the reinforcement schedules used by various researchers. They found that under a probabilistic reinforcement schedule (when some reinforcement is received for choosing the less frequently rewarded stimulus), persistent choice of a single stimulus is less likely because it lowers the overall payoff. Partial reinforcement, in which only one stimulus is ever rewarded, is more conducive to maximization.

Behavior also changes as the number of trials increases (Edwards, 1961). In a two-choice situation, there is an initial tendency to engage in the gambler's fallacy. After a series of reinforcements is awarded for one alternative, participants are likely to perceive the other alternative as being "due" and therefore predict it on the next trial. Over the course of a large number of trials this reverses, and participants are more likely to choose the more frequently reinforced alternative. In a three-choice situation, individuals are more likely to display maximizing behavior as the number of trials increases (Detambel, 1955; Gardner, 1957). The presence of a distracting stimulus has also been shown to undermine attention, thereby strengthening maximization (Moran & McCullers, 1979; Straughn, 1956). Such complications arising from specific paradigm features highlight the fact that research on personality and motivation is not as straightforward as that on cognition. This is one reason why the latter has received far more empirical attention.

Cognitive-Developmental Factors. Research investigating individual characteristics that relate to performance on probability tasks has generally emphasized the role of cognitive functioning – particularly the individual's stage of cognitive development. Weir (1964) documented a U-shaped relationship between age and terminal level of correct response choice. Preschool age children and young adults demonstrate equally high levels of maximization by the end of the task, but for different reasons. Weir postulated that young children, who have little experience with formal problem-solving tasks, do not have preconceived expectations about a partial reinforcement schedule. This view is in accord with the work of Piaget and Inhelder (1951), who documented the observation that young children have little understanding of randomness or the concepts of chance and probability. Consequently, their behavior is governed by simple operant learning principles. Their choice of the correct stimulus is strengthened by reinforcement. Their responses to the incorrect alternatives are extinguished through nonreinforcement.

Young adults are distracted by their high expectations of success, and initially they engage in complex strategies to explore elaborate hypotheses about the solution. Given a large number of trials, they exhaust their strategies and realize that maximizing behavior provides the best level of reinforcement. The response of children in the middle-childhood years is characterized by highly stereotyped patterning rather than maximizing behavior. Children of this age group have either not developed the complex strategies to use when the simple ones are unsuccessful or they are not able to fully utilize the information available from their own responses.

Weir (1964) thus implicates children's information-processing ability in their probability task performance. His explanations have been supported by findings that memory and abstractive integration influence probability learning (Brainerd, 1981; Goulet & Goodwin, 1970; Gruen, Ottinger, & Zigler, 1970; Kreitler, Zigler, & Kreitler, 1983; Lewis, 1966; Offenbach, Gruen, & Caskey, 1984). Furthermore, similar U-shaped developmental trends have been obtained in studies operationalizing cognitive development as grade placement and achievement level (Alexander, 1980) and in those on the influence of incentives (Nation & McCullers, 1977). To explain the U-shaped developmental profile, Lewis, Wall, and Aronfreed (1963) suggested that the value of repeated external rewards diminishes with age and that intrinsic reinforcement of correct prediction holds greater sway with older children.

Motivational Factors. In addition to cognitive-developmental determinants, probability learning is also influenced by an individual's motivation. Goodnow's (1955) analysis of the determinants of choice behavior was the first to explicitly state that individuals who expect to succeed and eventually attain reinforcement on 100 percent of the trials are less likely to engage in maximizing behavior. He argued that maximization is manifested when individuals concede that complete success is unattainable and view a lower level of success as an acceptable outcome.

From this theoretical perspective, several studies have since documented the correlates of expectancy of success as manifested in probability learning. One correlate is socioeconomic status (SES). Assuming that a higher expectancy of success would be more prevalent in the middle-SES, Gruen and Zigler (1968) and Odom (1967) predicted that middle-SES children would exhibit less maximizing behavior than lower-SES children. Although these studies confirmed the prediction, Zigler and Child (1969) noted that SES per se was an incomplete explanation of maximizing behavior.

Going beyond variables of demographic, economic, or social class membership, Gruen and Zigler emphasized the incidence of success or failure experienced by children as underlying their probability-learning behavior. From this perspective, the expectancy of success hypothesis is predicated on individuals' confidence in their own abilities, which is derived from their personal experience. This view was supported by Luthar and Zigler (1988) in their finding that lower-SES children with an internal locus of control made fewer maximizing responses than their middle-SES counterparts.

By focusing on academic achievement rather than social class, Kier and Zigler (1969) were able to demonstrate a clearer relationship between a child's background of success and maximizing behavior. Consistent with the cognitive-developmental approach, these investigators found that independent of SES, children who had been ranked as being unsuccessful in school by their teachers were more likely to settle for a lower degree of success associated with the maximizing strategy than were students who were considered academically successful. Kier and Zigler also found a significant correlation between a direct measure of expectancy of success (see Diggory, 1966) and performance on the probability-learning task. Children with the lowest expectancy of success scores had higher scores on the three-choice probability-learning task (i.e., adopted a maximizing strategy) than did those with a higher expectancy of success. Gruen, Ottinger, and Zigler (1970) provided further direct evidence to support the cognitive-developmental approach with their findings that individuals with lower levels of aspiration showed more maximizing and less patterning than individuals with higher aspirations.

Negative relationships among curiosity, activity, and maximization have also been demonstrated (Kreitler, Zigler, & Kreitler, 1984). Although activity level was not related to curiosity, both variables exerted strong influences on probability learning. Curious or actively exploring children demonstrated less maximizing than those who were not as interested in their environment. Finally, Kreitler and Zigler (1989) found that children who were willing to postpone gratification demonstrated low levels of maximizing on a probability-learning task. Those who elected to receive immediate gratification – one book without delay rather than waiting six days to be given five books – used the maximizing strategy. Again, maximizing was evident when individuals focused on the immediacy of reinforcement, because that strategy provided instant reward.

Suitability of Probability-Learning Tasks

The evidence reviewed here clearly validates the use of probability-learning tasks to measure expectancy of success. In their most complex forms, they prove to be difficult tasks that induce a variety of problem-solving strategies. Probability learning also meets the criticisms that the tasks employed in early research only minimally involved learning and information processing. Features inherent in probability tasks are such that they also provide a common ground for research in the influence of learning, cognition, and motivation on performance.

Probability Learning in Individuals with Mental Retardation

A common observation among individuals with mental retardation is that they have a "failure set," often giving up before they even try in situations they perceive as challenging. By assuming that an inordinately high incidence of failure experiences produces a failure set, Stevenson and Zigler (1958) set up several experiments to see if they could manipulate success/failure expectancies. In one modification, they varied the frequency of reinforcement that the "correct" stimulus received on the three-choice probability-learning task. When the stimulus was reinforced 100 percent of the time, children with and without mental retardation learned equally well. When the reinforcement was less than 100 percent, nonretarded children maximized less. They apparently would not settle for the lower degree of success that satisfied their retarded peers.

Stevenson and Zigler then tried pretraining conditions in which non-retarded children played games that they won either all the time or very seldom. Children who experienced the prior failure were found to maximize their choice of the partially reinforced stimulus to a greater degree than those who had success experiences. Thus, evidence was provided that if nonretarded children receive the experimental analog of the real-life experiences of children with mental retardation (a low degree of success), their performance is likewise affected.

Such evidence gave firm support to the cognitive-development approach to mental retardation. Earlier interpretations of probability-learning behavior had been cast within the framework of the Lewin–Kounin rigidity formulation (Chapter 5). Maximization was viewed as indicative of perseverative, stereotyped behavior. The inherently rigid individual with mental retardation would therefore be expected to maximize more than the less rigid, nonretarded child of the same MA. The findings of Siegel and Foshee (1960) that children with mental retardation typically persisted in choosing the partially reinforced response, and that nonretarded children showed more patterning in their choices, were used to support the rigidity formulation.

In a study noted earlier, Gruen and Zigler (1968) reasoned that children from lower-SES homes appeared to have a background of both social and academic failure (see Gans, 1962) necessary to test the competing models of probability-task performance. According to the cognitive-developmental approach, if the lowered expectancy of success stemming from recurrent failure experiences caused maximizing behavior in children with mental retardation, then lower-SES children – who have also experienced considerable academic and social failure – should exhibit a similar behavior response. The rigidity model would predict instead that lower-SES children would perform like middle-SES peers of comparable intellectual levels.

Using MA-matched groups of middle- and lower-SES children of average intelligence and noninstitutionalized children with cultural-familial retardation, Gruen and Zigler manipulated the degree of success experienced prior to, and the consequences for incorrect responses during, a probability-learning task. They found that nonretarded middle-SES children showed the least maximizing and most patterning, and that nonretarded lower-SES children showed the most maximizing and least patterning. The performance of children with mental retardation fell between these two groups on both measures. Moreover, regardless of intellectual level or SES, those who experienced penalty conditions as opposed to nonpenalty conditions showed significantly more maximizing and less patterning.

In further examinations of performance across 100 trials, Gruen and Zigler found that during the early trials, all children relied heavily on a patterning strategy in their responses. Subsequently, several factors contributed to a child's willingness to abandon this cognitively congruent strategy for a maximizing strategy. Facing a penalty, such as giving up a previously earned reward after an incorrect response, children opted for a maximizing strategy rather than one of patterning. Independent of the penalty effects, however, the three groups differed in their tendency to make patterned responses, which in turn produced differences in maximizing responses.

Rather than supporting the rigidity formulation, these results appeared to be consistent with the expectancy-of-success hypothesis advanced in the cognitive-developmental approach. For middle-SES children, this expectancy was relatively high, and they were unwilling to settle for the lower level of success provided by the maximization response. In contrast, children with mental retardation, as well as those from lower-SES families, had a lower expectancy of success and more readily adopted a maximizing strategy. Gruen and Zigler attributed the tendency for low-SES children to make the least patterning and most maximizing responses to the fact that they attended school where they were continually competing with wealthier children. Their performance suggested that lower-SES children in the middle-SES oriented classroom may experience more failure than children with mental retardation who are in special education placements.

This line of research was followed in a study by Ollendick, Balla, and Zigler (1971), who utilized more intense and relatively enduring success and failure conditions. They found that for institutionalized children with cultural-familial mental retardation, failure experiences prior to probability-learning tasks increased failure-avoidance behavior (maximizing strategy indicative of a low expectancy of success), while success experiences led to a success-striving pattern (lose-shift strategy indicative of a high expectancy of success). Since the entire sample was comprised of children with mental retardation, these data provide further evidence that the degree of maximizing behavior was motivationally based and not an artifact of cognitive rigidity.

In another study, Gruen, Ottinger, and Ollendick (1974) explored whether the success-failure findings obtained in experimental settings could be replicated in the natural school environment. They found that children with mental retardation placed in regular classes, where they presumably encountered repeated social and academic failures, had higher expectancies of failure than their peers in the more nurturing environment (relatively high degree of success) of special education classes. Another important finding was that children with mental retardation in special education classes demonstrated a pattern of responding similar to that of MA-matched children of average intelligence. This is consistent with the previous findings of Ollendick, Balla, and Zigler (1971) that maximizing behavior is a function of repeated failure in school and not a defining feature of mental retardation. It should be noted, however, that the anticipated relationship between length of time in a mainstreamed setting and maximization was not found. In a comparison of children in partial or total mainstreaming, Carparulo (1979) observed no systematic differences in expectancy of success. The increased academic failure encountered in an inclusive classroom may be equivalent to the social failure children experience by being withdrawn from the mainstreamed class to complete their day in a special education setting.

Conclusions

The use of probability-learning tasks helped to establish the role of expectancy of success in understanding behavior of individuals with mental retardation. Studies have clearly documented that motivational factors arising from experiential events interact with cognitive, developmental, and situational factors to determine maximizing behavior. Individuals who believe they can succeed are willing to abandon certain – but smaller – amounts of reinforcement in favor of searching for a more successful strategy. Individuals who do not share such a high expectancy of success, and who also have little confidence in their own resourcefulness, are much more likely to continue with the lower level of reinforcement obtained with the maximizing strategy. The findings also indicate that maximizing behavior is not limited to individuals with mental retardation. Instead, it seems to be related to a history of repeated failure in academic and social settings. The fact that success experiences have been found to be effective in preventing low expectancy of success has practical implications that should be addressed in the education of children with mental retardation.

Although the evidence is not yet definitive, it does provide an indication of the important interplay between motivational and cognitive factors in determining the behavior of individuals with mental retardation, and can help clarify ambiguous research findings. Knowledge of what motivates individuals with mental retardation can be of assistance in day-to-day activities at home, school, work, and clinical settings. The cognitive-developmental approach draws attention to the individuality of people with mental retardation and the need for appropriate motivational incentives, based on unique social and intellectual histories, to facilitate their cognitive, social, emotional, and educational development.

References

Alexander, K. (1980). Cognitive and motivational aspects of probability learning as a function of grade, gender, and achievement level. Doctoral dissertation, New York University. *Dissertation Abstracts International, 41/07B,* 2800.

Atkinson, J. (1958a). Motivational determinants of risk taking behavior. In J.W. Atkinson (ed.), *Motives in fantasy, action, and society.* Princeton: Van Nostrand.

(1958b). Towards experimental analysis of human motives in terms of motives, expectancies, and incentives. In J.W. Atkinson (ed.), *Motives in fantasy, action, and society.* Princeton: Van Nostrand.

Brackill, Y., Kappy, M., & Starr, R. (1962). Magnitude of reward and probability learning. *Journal of Experimental Psychology, 63,* 32–35.

Brainerd, C.J. (1981). Working memory and the developmental analysis of probability judgement. *Psychological Review, 88,* 463–502.

Butterfield, E., & Zigler, E. (1965). The effects of success and failure on the discrimination learning of normal and retarded children. *Journal of Abnormal Psychology, 70,* 25–31.

Carparulo, B. K. (1979). Mainstreaming and teachers' attitudes toward mainstreaming: Their influence on the behavior of mildly retarded children. Unpublished manuscript, Yale University.

Cromwell, R. (1963). A social learning approach to mental retardation. In N.R. Ellis (ed.), *Handbook of mental deficiency.* New York: McGraw-Hill.

Detambel, M.H. (1955). A test of a model for multiple choice behavior. *Journal of Experimental Psychology, 49,* 97–104.

Diggory, J. (1966). *Self-evaluation: Concepts and studies.* New York: John Wiley.

Edwards, W. (1961). Probability learning in 1000 trials. *Journal of Experimental Psychology, 62,* 385–394.

Gans, H. (1962). *The urban villagers.* New York: Free Press.

Gardner, R. (1957). Probability learning with two and three choices. *American Journal of Psychology, 70,* 174–185.

Gardner, W. (1958). Reactions of intellectually normal and retarded boys after experimentally induced failure: A social learning theory interpretation. Unpublished doctoral dissertation. Nashville, TN: George Peabody College for Teachers.

Girardeau, F.L., & Ellis, N.R. (1964). Rote verbal learning by normal and mentally retarded children. *American Journal of Mental Deficiency, 68,* 525–532.

Goodnow, J.J. (1955). Determinants of choice-distribution in two-choice situations. *American Journal of Psychology, 68,* 106–116.

Goulet, L.R., & Goodwin, K.S. (1970). Development of choice behavior in probabilistic and problem-solving tasks. In H.W. Reese & L.P. Lipsett (eds.), *Advances in child development and behavior* (Vol. 5). New York: Academic Press.

Gruen, G., Ottinger, D., & Ollendick, T. (1974). Probability learning in retarded children with differing histories of success and failure in school. *American Journal of Mental Deficiency, 79,* 417–423.

Gruen, G., Ottinger, D., & Zigler, E. (1970). Level of aspiration and the probability learning of middle- and lower-class children. *Developmental Psychology, 3,* 133–142.

Gruen, G.E., & Weir, M.W. (1964). Effect of instruction, penalty, and age on probability learning. *Child Development, 35,* 265–273.

Gruen, G., & Zigler, E. (1968). Expectancy of success and the probability learning of middle-class, lower-class, and retarded children. *Journal of Abnormal Psychology, 73,* 343–352.

Heber, R. (1957). Expectancy and expectancy changes in normal and mentally retarded boys. Unpublished doctoral dissertation. Nashville, TN: George Peabody College for Teachers.

Hyman, R., & Jenkins, N.W. (1956). Involvement and set as determinants of behavior stereotypy. *Psychological Reports, 2,* 131–146.

Kass, N., & Stevenson, H. (1961). The effect of pretraining reinforcement conditions on learning by normal and retarded children. *American Journal of Mental Deficiency, 66,* 76–80.

Katz, I. (1964). Review of evidence relating to effects of desegregation on the intellectual performance of Negroes. *American Psychologist, 19,* 381–99.

Keller, H.R. (1971). Children's acquisition and reversal behavior in a probability learning situation as a function of programmed instruction, internal-external control, and schedules of reinforcement. *Journal of Experimental Child Psychology, 2,* 281–295.

Kier, R.J., Styfco, S.J., & Zigler, E. (1977). Success expectancies and the probability learning of children of low and middle socioeconomic status. *Developmental Psychology, 13,* 444–449.

Kier, R.J., & Zigler, E. (1969). Probability learning strategies of lower- and middle-class children and the expectancy of success hypothesis. Unpublished manuscript, Yale University.

Kreitler, S., & Zigler, E. (1989). Motivational determinants of children's probability learning. *Journal of Genetic Psychology, 151,* 301–316.

Kreitler, S., Zigler, E., & Kreitler, H. (1983). The effects of memory and abstractive integration in children's probability learning. *Child Development, 56,* 1487–1496.

(1984). Curiosity and demographic factors as determinants of children's probability learning. *Journal of Genetic Psychology, 145,* 61–75.

(1989). Probability learning and Piagetian probability conceptions in children 5–12 yrs old. *Genetic, Social, and General Psychology Monographs, 114,* 505–533.

Lewin, K. (1936). *A dynamic theory of personality.* New York: McGraw-Hill.

Lewis, M. (1966). Probability learning in young children: The binary choice paradigm. *Journal of Genetic Psychology, 108,* 43–48.

Lewis, M., Wall, A., & Aronfreed, J. (1963). Developmental changes in the relative value of social and nonsocial reinforcement. *Journal of Experimental Psychology, 66,* 133–138.

Luthar, S., & Zigler, E. (1988). Motivational factors, school atmosphere, and SES: Determinants of children's probability task performance. *Journal of Applied Developmental Psychology, 9,* 477–494.

McManis, D. (1965). Relative errors with serial lists of different lengths. *American Journal of Mental Deficiency, 70,* 125–128.

Miller, G.A., & Frick, F.C. (1950). Statistical behavioristic sequences of responses. *Psychological Review, 59,* 311–324.

Moran, J.D., & McCullers, J.C. (1979). Reward and number of choices in children's probability learning: An attempt to reconcile conflicting findings. *Journal of Experimental Child Psychology, 27,* 527–532.

Morse, E., & Runquist, W.N. (1960). Probability learning with an unscheduled random sequence. *American Journal of Psychology, 73,* 603–607.

Nation, J.R., & McCullers, J.C. (1977). An expectancy model for estimating the effects of age and incentive in probability learning. *American Journal of Psychology, 90,* 103–119.

Neimark, E. (1956). Effects and type of nonreinforcement and number of alterna tive responses in two verbal conditioning situations. *Journal of Experimental Psychology, 52,* 207–220.

Odom, R. (1967). Problem-solving strategies as a function of age and socio-economic level. *Child Development, 38,* 753–764.

Offenbach, S., Gruen, G., & Caskey, B. (1984). Development of proportional response strategies. *Child Development, 55,* 1487–1496.

Ojemann, R., Maxey, E., & Snider, B. (1965a). Effects of guided learning experience in developing probability concepts at the fifth grade level. *Perceptual and Motor Skills, 21,* 415–427.

(1965b). The effect of a program of guided learning experience in developing probability concepts at the third grade level. *Journal of Experimental Education, 33,* 321–335.

Ollendick, T., Balla, D., & Zigler, E. (1971). Expectancy of success and the probability learning of retarded children. *Journal of Abnormal Psychology, 77,* 275–281.

Piaget, J., & Inhelder, B. (1951). *La genèse de l'idée de hasard chez l'enfant* [The development of the idea of chance in the child]. Paris: Presses Universitaires de France.

Prehm, J. (1966). Retention in retarded and normal children as a function of task difficulty, meaningfulness, and degree of original learning. *Journal of Mental Deficiency, 10,* 221–229.

Rotter, J. (1954). *Social learning and clinical psychology.* Englewood Cliffs, NJ: Prentice Hall.

Sarason, S., Davidson, K., Lighthall, F., Waites, R., & Ruebush, B. (1960). *Anxiety in elementary school children.* New York: Wiley.

Siegel, P.S., & Foshee, J.G. (1960). Molar variability in the mentally defective. *Journal of Abnormal and Social Psychology, 61,* 141–143.

Stevenson, H.W. (1965). Social reinforcement of children's behavior. In L.P. Lipsett & C. Spiker (eds.), *Advances in child development* (Vol. 2). New York: Academic Press.

Stevenson, H., & Weir, M. (1959). Variables affecting children's performance in a probability learning task. *Journal of Experimental Psychology, 57,* 403–412.

(1963). The role of age and verbalization in probability learning. *American Journal of Psychology, 76,* 299–305.

Stevenson, H.W., & Zigler, E. (1958). Probability learning in children. *Journal of Experimental Psychology, 56,* 185–192.

Straughn, J.H. (1956). Human escape learning in relation to reinforcement variables and intertrial conditions. *Journal of Experimental Psychology, 52,* 1–8.

Ward, E. (1956). Reward probability, amount, and information as determiners of sequential two-alternative decisions. *Journal of Experimental Psychology, 52,* 177–188.

Weir, M.W. (1962). Effects of age and instruction on children's probability learning. *Child Development, 33,* 729–735.

(1964). Developmental changes in problem-solving strategies. *Psychological Review, 71,* 473–490.

(1967). Mental retardation. *Science, 157,* 576–578.

Zeaman, D., & House, B.J. (1960). Approach and avoidance in the discrimination learning of retardates. In D. Zeaman et al., *Learning and transfer in mental defectives.* Progress Report No. 2, NIMH, USPHS, Res. Grant M-1099 to University of Connecticut.

Zigler, E. (1958). Social deprivation and rigidity in the performance of feebleminded children. Unpublished doctoral dissertation, University of Texas.

Zigler, E., & Balla, D. (1982). Issues in personality motivation in mentally retarded persons. In M.J. Begab, H.D. Haywood, & H. Garber (eds.), *Psychosocial influences in retarded performance* (Vol. 1, pp. 197–218). Baltimore: University Park Press.

Zigler, E., & Child, I.L. (1969). Socialization. In G. Lindzey & E. Aronson (eds.), *Handbook of social psychology* (2nd ed., pp. 450–589). Reading, MA: Addison-Wesley.

Zigler, E., & Hodapp, R. (1986). Conceptualizing the effects of "out of home" environments on the development of mentally retarded and nonretarded children. *Paedovita, 1,* 38–44.

7 Effectance Motivation and the Performance of Individuals with Mental Retardation

Dianne Bennett-Gates
Edward Zigler

Socialization of children into functioning adults hinges on parents, teachers, and others encouraging the young to adopt the values and norms of their culture (e.g., Denham et al., 1997). Although various cultures may differentially promote individual identity or group solidarity, most emphasize strong personal attributes such as self-reliance, responsibility, and diligence (Fyans et al., 1983). In the course of socialization, most children therefore are urged to pursue important goals, take pride in their accomplishments, and try to succeed in the tasks they undertake. Given the encouragement to perform to their highest abilities, most children become achievement oriented, seeking opportunities that present novel stimuli and challenging problems. This motivation to have an effect on the environment and master the challenges it presents – termed effectance motivation – is readily apparent when children approach tasks eagerly, don't shirk from difficult or complex problems, and find joy in a job well done.

Whereas children of average intelligence are typically motivated to attempt new problems with concentrated effort, individuals with mental retardation are not always inclined to do so. Past institutional practices deprived many retarded citizens of the challenges and social interactions that enhance effectance motivation (Zigler & Hodapp, 1986). Despite the current trend for home and home-like placements, children with mental retardation still fail to become achievement oriented. Daily life provides repeated exposure to demands that exceed their intellectual abilities, which leads to personality and motivational traits – such as high dependency on adults, low expectancy of success, and a reliance on external cues in problem-solving situations – that bring attention to their inadequacies and further undermine performance. Thus, situations and tasks that provide nonretarded children with feelings of accomplishment will often engender feelings of incompetence in a child with mental retardation (Merighi, Edison, & Zigler, 1990).

This becomes a significant problem when effectance motivation is so

145

low that the prospect of a new task generates anxiety, inattention, and lack of effort that inhibit learning and performance. In this chapter, we explore factors related to the socialization of children with mental retardation as they gain mastery over their environment. We discuss the effect of experience on the development of effectance motivation and explain its value in understanding the behavior of individuals with mental retardation. Finally, we identify classroom practices that may facilitate feelings of efficacy.

Defining Effectance Motivation

This pervasive need for achievement has been explained using a variety of theoretical perspectives. One early theory, advanced by McClelland and his colleagues, conceptualized the need for achievement as a learned motive to compete and strive for success whenever there is an opportunity to be evaluated against a standard of excellence (McClelland et al., 1953). Parents' behavior toward their children in challenging situations was thought to shape the development of achievement motivation. Hence, those with high achievement needs had been taught to take pride in their ability to meet or exceed high standards. The ensuing sense of self-fulfillment then becomes a motivator to work hard, to be successful, and to outperform others (McClelland, 1961, 1971).

Bandura (1977a, 1977b, 1986) described parents as having a very significant role in the acquisition of behaviors indicative of effectance motivation. From his vantage point, parents have control of the powerful effects of reinforcement and punishment that can be used to introduce, increase, decrease, and/or remove behaviors. According to his social-cognitive theory, children's cognitions are able to mediate the effects of punishment and reward by filtering behavioral consequences through personal memory, perceived attributions, and individual biases. Instead of passively experiencing the parents' reinforcement contingencies, children are believed to actively process environmental information and generate expectations about the likelihood of reinforcement. This was demonstrated in the classic study of vicarious learning in which children adopted aggressive behavior they had witnessed in an adult model (Bandura, 1965).

The psychoanalytic interpretation proposed by White (1959) traced achievement behavior to innate motivation. Using Piaget's (1952) beliefs in an intrinsic motivation to adapt to the environment, White's explanation holds that children not only seek to adapt to, but also to exert control over, their environment. White observed that humans, unlike other species, are born with very few competencies and must learn to deal with their surroundings. Being equipped with an innate disposition to develop one's abilities would have considerable adaptive value. White believed this inherent motivation is revealed in the tendency children have to "effect" various acts that will enable them to cope with the demands of both the environment and the people encountered within it. As children practice their new skills and feel some sense of control, they experience positive emotions that White termed a "feeling of efficacy." Thus, even with very little or no parental prompting, children will display their "effectance motivation" in tackling and solving problems from their own initiatives.

Another perspective portrays humans as information processors, predisposed to derive pleasure from creating, processing, or investigating stimuli that are somewhat incongruous and/or discrepant to the anticipated situation (Berlyne, 1966; Hunt, 1965; Kagan, 1972). Activities and events that are similar do not arouse interest, while those that are far removed from an individual's expectations are either ignored or a source of anxiety. This approach is compatible with the concept of effectance motivation advanced by White (1959) in that both assume individuals will actively seek, and find pleasure in, the successful completion of challenging tasks.

Using a developmental perspective, Zigler (1971) views effectance motivation as inherent and central to the human organism yet different from such primary drives as hunger and thirst. If these basic physiological needs are not met, the individuals dies. This is hardly the case with the need to be effective or, more specifically, to utilize one's cognitive resources to the fullest. To note that cognitive mastery is not life-preserving does not mean that it is automatically expelled from the area of primary needs. To demonstrate this, Zigler (1971) draws an analogy between effectance motivation and the sex drive, whose satisfaction is also not life-preserving to the individual. Conceptualizing both sexual and effectance needs as life-fulfilling ones is easy when such fulfillment is defined in terms of the successful perpetuation and evolution of the species. A species would cease to exist if procreation stopped. By the same token, the adaptive aspects of effectance motivation in the face of a continually changing environment are important to the successful evolution of the species. Given this, Zigler argues that it would not be surprising to find the human organism at the biological level preprogrammed with such needs as sexual activity and cognitive mastery.

Such species programming, however, does not guarantee that every member of the species will at all times be highly motivated by such self-fulfilling needs. Forgoing circumstances of more elevated sexual abstinence, there are examples of individuals whose life experiences have resulted in frigidity or impotence. In terms of some hierarchy of motives, their sexual motive has dropped from its normal place toward the top to some place near the bottom. Zigler contends that the same could happen with the motive for cognitive mastery. This could occur from experiences that either specifically extinguish the effectance motive or elevate/emphasize other motives that are more important to physiological or psychological self-preservation.

In the case of individuals with mental retardation, whose efforts to attain cognitive mastery so frequently meet with failure, challenging tasks could easily become associated with anxiety. Accordingly, the retarded individual would then be more motivated to escape the painful anxiety associated with cognitive effort (which has become a highly placed negative reinforcer) than to try to gratify the cognitive mastery motive (which has dropped to a lower position on the hierarchy). Such processes may explain the considerable evidence that children with mental retardation are more motivated to avoid failure that to achieve success (Cromwell, 1963).

The model suggested by Harter (1981) combines elements from several theories, and builds on the research that will be presented in this chapter. In Harter's view, children's attempts to achieve are attributed to either internal or external factors, depending on the particular circumstances. In some situations, children may be driven to satisfy their own needs for competence or mastery for intrinsic reasons similar to both White's achievement motivation and Zigler's effectance motivation. In other circumstances, their goal may be to obtain external incentives such as grades, prizes, or social approval. Irrespective of the basic conceptualization, there is a consensus that experiences in childhood play a significant role in achievement situations, the development of effectance motivation, and the relative strength of this motive – that is, its position in the child's reinforcer hierarchy.

The Reinforcer Hierarchy

The concept of a reinforcer hierarchy was first applied to mental retardation when Zigler pondered the inconsistencies between his findings and those of Kounin (1941a, 1941b) on concept-switching tasks. Although positive-reaction tendency, negative-reaction tendency, and expectancy of success (described in Chapters 5 and 6) were able to explain many of the differences in performance found between retarded and nonretarded individuals, Zigler realized that these constructs could not parsimoniously handle the finding that individuals with mental retardation evidenced greater difficulty switching concepts. Early in the debate, Zigler (1958) relied heavily on positive-reaction tendency, arguing that the heightened motivation to interact with an adult would result in greater compliance when it increases the degree of social interaction. For situations such as Kounin's card-sorting task, however, the motivation for adult approval may not necessarily elicit compliance when complying would have the opposite effect of ending the interaction. Institutionalized retarded individuals thus faced the dilemma of (a) making an appropriate response that would terminate the social contact, or (b) making an incorrect response that would continue the pleasurable interaction. Since nonretarded children would not experience such a high degree of conflict, their performance would be superior on the concept-switching task.

Though this was a plausible argument at the time, Zigler (1971) eventually felt it could not satisfactorily explain the sizeable difference in concept-switching between retarded and nonretarded individuals. The explanation was flawed in its basic assumption that all of Kounin's subjects were aware that resorting the cards (a correct response) would terminate the social interaction with the adult. Since this was unlikely, Zigler looked for other ways the testing situation might not be "psychologically equivalent" for the retarded and nonretarded participants. One difference was the relative importance of the specific reinforcer used in the experimental design. In studies by Plenderleith (1956) and Stevenson and Zigler (1957), institutionalized individuals with cultural-familial retardation were found to be no more rigid than nonretarded individuals of the same mental age on a discrimination reversal-learning task when tangible reinforcers were given.

Further reflection on the nature of the concept-switching task led Zigler to deemphasize the role of positive-reaction tendency and focus instead on the relative weakness of Kounin's reinforcer to motivate retarded children. The only reinforcer obtained by Kounin's subjects for correctly switching concepts was the inherent reinforcement of being correct. Being correct was probably more reinforcing for nonretarded children, while the social interaction and adult attention were probably more valued for the retarded participants. Following this line of reasoning, Zigler (1971) suggested that if equally effective reinforcers were dispensed to retarded and nonretarded children of the same MA, no difference in their ability to switch concepts would be found.

This explanation is predicated on the assumption that the positions of various reinforcers in the reinforcer hierarchies of retarded and nonretarded children differ. Within each group, individual differences are also to be expected. Thus, each person has his or her own reinforcer hierarchy. The position of a given reinforcer for a given person is determined by a complex interaction of developmental level, past experience, availability of the reinforcer, and whether or not it has acquired the properties of a higher-order reinforcer.

SES and Reinforcer Hierarchy

Considerable evidence is available to support the existence of different reinforcer hierarchies, with much of the experimental work focusing on the relevance of tangible and intangible reinforcement (Havinghurst, 1970). Several studies have documented the fact that children from middle socio-economic status (SES) families are more motivated to be correct for the sheer sake of correctness than are lower-SES children (Cameron & Storm, 1965; Davis, 1944; Douvan, 1956; Ericson, 1947; Terrell, Durkin, & Wiesley, 1959; Zigler & Kanzer, 1962). Specifically, it has been noted that the pairing of this intangible reinforcer with other primary and secondary reinforcers is mainly a practice in middle-SES families (Davis, 1941, 1943, 1944; Douvan, 1956; Ericson, 1947). Both Terrell et al. (1959) and Cameron and Storm (1965), for example, found that middle-SES children performed better on a discrimination-learning task when an intangible reinforcer was used. Lower-SES children demonstrated superior performance with the reinforcer was tangible.

Such findings appeared pertinent to much of the early research on Kounin's hypothesis. Many of those studies compared institutionalized individuals with cultural-familial retardation – individuals drawn predominantly from the lowest segments of the lower-SES (Zigler, 1961) – with middle-SES nonretarded children. While Kounin attributed the poor performance of the retarded participants to cognitive rigidity, his findings could have reflected socioeconomic differences in the value of the intangible reward (being correct) provided by the task. This reinforcer simply held more valence for children from a middle-SES background. If the lower-SES children were rewarded with more optimal reinforcers (i.e., ones higher on their hierarchy), their performance might improve to the level of their middle-SES peers.

These predictions were tested by Zigler and deLabry (1962), who presented Kounin's concept-switching task to three groups: institutionalized retarded children, nonretarded children from the lower-SES, and nonretarded children with middle-SES backgrounds. Half of the children in each group received Kounin's original reinforcer (the reinforcement that inheres in a correct response) for switching from one concept (form or color) to the other. The other half received a tangible reward (a small toy).

The reinforcement hypothesis and the ensuing predictions were supported by the findings. The children with mental retardation and the non-retarded lower-SES children needed fewer trials to switch concepts (indicating superior performance) in the tangible condition. This was reversed with the middle-SES nonretarded group, who performed slightly better in the intangible condition. Comparisons among the three groups who received intangible reinforcers were reminiscent of Kounin's results in that the middle-SES nonretarded children outperformed both the retarded and lower-SES nonretarded children. However, when tangible reinforcement was used, there were no significant differences among the three groups. Furthermore, no differences were demonstrated among the groups who received what was assumed to be their optimal reinforcer (retarded, tangible; lower-SES, tangible; and middle-SES, intangible). Interestingly, in another analysis, both retarded and upper-SES children were found to switch concepts more readily in a tangible than in an intangible reinforcement condition (Zigler & Unell, 1962).

Social Deprivation and Reinforcer Hierarchy

These studies by Zigler and his colleagues highlight an erroneous assumption underlying standard classroom practices – that children are uniformly responsive to the same types of reinforcement. The evidence indicates that children with mental retardation as a group, like lower-SES children as a group, may value being correct less than do middle-SES children as a group. Yet even this generalization may not hold true for any given child. The crucial determining factor does not appear to be membership in a particular social or intelligence grouping, but rather the particular social learning experiences of the child.

This point is aptly underlined in a study by Byck (1968), who compared institutionalized individuals with either Down syndrome or cultural-familial retardation. The groups were matched on MA, CA, IQ, and length of institutionalization. Using the same design as Zigler and deLabry (1962), Byck found superior concept-switching for the children with Down syndrome in the intangible condition compared with the tangible condition. The reverse pattern was found for the children with cultural-familial retardation. These results are consistent with the literature on social class and reinforcer effectiveness: Individuals with cultural-familial retardation are generally from a lower-SES background, while children with Down syndrome are just as likely to be from middle- and upper-SES homes.

The enhanced effectiveness of tangible reinforcers for lower-SES and institutionalized cultural-familial retarded children would appear to be due partly to the relative deprivation of treats such as toys and candy in their environments. In addition, a history of frequent failure may undermine their responsiveness to intangible reinforcement. For example, because individuals with mental retardation frequently face challenges beyond their intellectual abilities, they may acquire an aversion to the intangible feedback of constantly being incorrect. Eventually they may come to ignore or avoid intangible reinforcement altogether.

Awareness of variations in the reinforcer hierarchy can assist both scholarly and practical efforts. For example, in interpreting findings derived from comparisons of retarded and nonretarded individuals, it is important to realize that any performance differences may be confounded by the relative value of the reinforcer for each group. Individuals with mental retardation, who may not find intangible reinforcers to be salient, might perform differently with reinforcers they value more highly.

The variability in the reinforcer hierarchy also has practical significance because intangible reinforcement, such as information that a response is correct or a job is well done, is the most immediate and frequent reward dispensed in real-life tasks. Yet some children who are retarded or from impoverished homes may be unresponsive to this type of motivator and appear to be poor learners. They might well be able to master the tasks given other types of rewards.

Internal versus External Motivation

The concept of reinforcer hierarchy served to focus attention on how particular reinforcers (e.g., a small toy or verbal praise), dispensed by some agent external to the child, acquired their effectiveness as a consequence of the child's general cognitive-developmental level and/or social learning experiences. This line of research was limited, however, in that it did not tap the possibility that children are active participants and might generate their own internal reinforcement. Within the developmental model of mental retardation, individuals with cultural-familial retardation represent the lower portion of the Gaussian distribution of intelligence. They follow the same developmental pattern, and at any given MA their cognitive structure should resemble that of nonretarded individuals. Thus, they are subject to the innate and permeating nature of the effectance motive, just like their nonretarded peers. With the movement toward viewing an individual with mental retardation as a whole person (discussed in Chapter 1), attention shifted from external aspects of a task that influence performance to the role that intrinsic reinforcement might play in the behavior of retarded persons.

Competing Motive Sources

Whether or not one accepts White's (1959) or Zigler's (1971) view that the individual's needs for effectance or mastery parallel other basic needs or primary drives, there is little question that the effectance concept provides a rubric for a variety of behaviors that appear across the lifespan (e.g., the desire for optimal levels of sensory stimulation, manipulation, exploration, and curiosity). In a series of studies (Shultz & Zigler, 1970; Zigler, 1966a, 1966b; Zigler, Levine, & Gould, 1967), conducted primarily with non-retarded middle-SES children, support was gained for the view that using one's own cognitive resources to their utmost is intrinsically gratifying, and thus motivating. However, it also became apparent that few tasks appeal purely to the effectance motive. Instead, as active participants in their environments, individuals may experience both intrinsic and extrinsic motives in the situation in which the task is presented. Rather than responding to one or the other, the presence of both types of reinforcement often seems to generate conflict.

Several studies have, in fact, documented how intrinsic and extrinsic reinforcers vie for supremacy on the reinforcer hierarchy. Deci (1971), for example, found that university students who were offered a tangible reward (money) for time spent on a task devoted more time to it than those who were not offered an extrinsic reinforcer. In a subsequent session in which no external reinforcement was offered, those who had previously received a tangible reward spent less time engaged with the task than students who had only experienced intrinsic reinforcement. Intrinsic motivation could, therefore, not maintain the behavior in the absence of the extrinsic reinforcer.

In a similar study involving preschoolers, Lepper, Greene, and Nisbett (1973) confirmed these results. They also found that in addition to a decline in the frequency of the behavior when rewards were withheld, the quality of behavior also diminished. The finding that external rewards undermine intrinsic motivation has since been documented in almost eighty studies using similar paradigms. (See Morgan, 1984, for a review.)

Two complementary explanations for this phenomenon are based on cognitive processes. Self-attribution theorists (e.g., Festinger, 1957) contend that even though an individual may initially be intrinsically motivated to perform a task, when a reward is offered it comes to be perceived as the reason for engaging in the activity. In terms of reinforcer hierarchy, even though the intrinsic reinforcer was originally in a high position, after the extrinsic reinforcer became available it quickly moved to a higher place in the hierarchy.

The discounting principle offers another explanation for why an activity originally rewarded externally diminishes when the reward is withdrawn (Stipek, 1993). According to this principle, the salience of the extrinsic reinforcer overshadows or dismisses the intrinsic reasons for engaging in the behavior. Once dismissed in a given situation, an intrinsic reinforcer cannot regain a position of supremacy.

Discounting offers some insight into why retarded and nonretarded individuals performed differently in the studies discussed earlier in this chapter. Individuals with mental retardation may tentatively approach a task with some intrinsic interest. However, the presence of external rewards such as social interaction with an adult or tangible gifts – rewards that are more salient because of histories of social or economic deprivation – displaces potential intrinsic motivators. For nonretarded children, the rewards of pride in conquering a challenge and feelings of competence remain high in the reinforcer hierarchy because the external rewards are not appealing enough to discount them.

Motivational Orientation

Since the work by Zigler and his colleagues, the concept of effectance motivation has advanced on several fronts. Haywood, for example, has conducted a line of research with his associates investigating a personality trait – referred to as "motivational orientation" – that is probably learned and therefore modifiable. Within this framework, individuals are described in terms of the sources of incentives that are effective in motivating their behavior. Those who typically seek satisfaction from task-intrinsic factors (e.g., responsibility, challenge, and creativity) are referred to as intrinsically motivated (IM). The avoidance of dissatisfaction by concentrating on the ease, comfort, and practical aspects of the environment, which are task-extrinsic factors, characterizes those who are extrinsically motivated (EM). (See Chapter 4 and Haywood & Switzky, 1985.)

IM orientation, which is comparable to a high degree of effectance motivation, is associated with greater task persistence (Haywood & Weaver, 1967); learning in laboratory tasks that is more effective and more resistant to extinction (Haywood & Wachs, 1966); higher school achievement (Dobbs, 1967; Haywood, 1968a, 1968b; Woolridge, 1966); and preference for self-monitored rather than externally imposed control of performance and reinforcement (Haywood & Switzky, 1985; Switzky & Haywood, 1974). Haywood (1966a, 1966b) contends that IM orientation is a function of increasing CA and MA, and that individuals with mental retardation are generally less intrinsically motivated than their nonretarded peers.

Self-Efficacy

Whereas Haywood explored the incentive for effectance motivation, Bandura (1986) focused on individuals' appraisal of their effectiveness in accomplishing a specific task or goal. His model of self-efficacy does not include a competence motive, but he does acknowledge that efficacy beliefs play a central role in the self-regulation of motivation (Bandura, 1995). He identified four main sources of information for efficacy beliefs: mastery experience (past successes and failures), vicarious experience (observational learning), verbal persuasion (feedback from a significant person), and physiological arousal (self-monitoring of bodily responses). This information is mediated by cognitive judgments to form opinions of self-efficacy in a specific situation.

Perceptions of self-efficacy influence which tasks people attempt and their ability to concentrate on those tasks (Bandura, 1981). Those who see themselves as having a high degree of self-efficacy are confident in their abilities and are more likely to concentrate on problem-solving strategies, thereby increasing the probability of being successful. Success brings positive emotional experiences, which in turn foster future feelings of self-efficacy (Bandura, 1986). Individuals with lower levels of self-efficacy tend to believe that the challenge of a task exceeds their abilities. They often fail to completely engage in the task, which undermines their problem-solving strategies and negates the possibility of success. The subsequent failure exacerbates feelings of inadequacy and perpetuates the expectancy of failure.

Several researchers have confirmed the important role of self-efficacy on achievement behavior in nonretarded individuals. Collins (1982), for example, demonstrated that regardless of basic skill in a specific subject, students with higher self-efficacy worked more diligently and more correctly than students low in self-efficacy. Similarly, independent of actual ability, students with higher self-efficacy made more attempts to link assigned textbook readings with their classroom instruction (Locke et al., 1984).

Learning versus Performance Goals

The research investigating extrinsic and intrinsic reinforcement is almost parallel to that examining learning and performance goals (also known as task and ego goals). According to Dweck (1986) and Nicholls (1983), individuals who are learning-oriented focus on their own efforts in response to a task. Thus, they might concentrate on understanding the material at hand or finding the solution to a problem. Those who are performance-oriented are concerned with external evaluations and winning approval. By emphasizing either the benefits of learning or the importance of being correct, Elliot and Dweck (1988) experimentally induced learning- or performance-orientation in children prior to giving them problem-solving tasks. Self-confidence was also manipulated in the pretraining session by telling some of the children that their performance was inadequate, while others were led to believe that they had outstanding abilities.

The problem-solving strategies of performance-oriented children with low self-confidence deteriorated when they encountered difficult tasks. This was not seen in the high-confidence children. The strategies of the learning-oriented children were unaffected by their level of confidence. Their persistence may relate to the finding that learning-oriented individuals experience greater pleasure and more emotional involvement with task situations than do performance-oriented individuals (Ames & Archer, 1988). This evidence is reminiscent of the research on intrinsic and extrinsic forms of reinforcement.

These three lines of research indicate the advantages of intrinsic motivational factors in task performance. Those who are oriented to intrinsic reinforcers approach a task with different goals, engage in more relevant problem-solving strategies, and find more enjoyment in their performance than do individuals who focus on extrinsic factors. Although this research is based on nonretarded individuals, it is consistent with previous findings with retarded persons and gives rise to many testable hypotheses. Given a lower level of effectance motivation, children with cultural-familial retardation should prove to be extrinsically oriented. This approach, coupled with low perceptions of self-efficacy, should lead them to focus on performance goals. Studies exploring these tendencies, and possible ways to ameliorate them, are the topics of the next section.

Strengthening Effectance Motivation in Retarded Children

Like responsiveness to intangible reinforcers, the strength of the effectance motive may be different for retarded and nonretarded individuals. Evidence on this point was provided by Harter and Zigler (1974), who constructed several measures of effectance motivation, including variation seeking, curiosity, mastery for the sake of competence, and preference for challenging tasks. They presented these measures in a game format to MA-matched groups of nonretarded and retarded children who lived at home or in an institution. Confirming the earlier research on reinforcer hierarchy, non-retarded children generally selected a nontangible reward (a "good player" certificate) over a tangible prize (candy) more frequently than did either group of children with mental retardation. Furthermore, the nonretarded children demonstrated the greatest desire to master a problem for the sake of mastery itself, chose the more challenging tasks, and showed the greatest curiosity and exploratory behavior – all behaviors indicative of effectance motivation. The children with mental retardation living at home showed less of these elements of effectance motivation, and in most cases the institutionalized children with mental retardation displayed the least.

In addition to documenting the differences between retarded and non-retarded groups, these findings provided support for the pervasive influence of social deprivation on the performance of individuals with mental retardation. Because the groups were matched on intellectual functioning, the differences in effectance motivation between the institutionalized and non-institutionalized retarded individuals could be attributed to their differing life experiences.

Another study by Harter (1977) explored the influence of task difficulty and type of reinforcement on effectance motivation. Retarded and non-retarded children were given the opportunity to work with puzzles of differing levels of difficulty in a situation with or without an extrinsic social reinforcer. In measuring the amount of smiling at task completion, Harter found that nonretarded children showed more enjoyment of their success in the presence of extrinsic social reinforcement. Children with mental retardation in the same situation showed less pleasure at the completion of their task. In the absence of the social reinforcement, nonretarded children expressed more pleasure solving difficult puzzles than easy puzzles. The reverse was found when children with mental retardation worked without an extrinsic reinforcer. These children displayed less pleasure with their effort on the difficult task and more enjoyment on the easier one.

While these findings demonstrate that children with mental retardation experience effectance motivation, they do so in ways that offer the security of assured success. They appear to be satisfied with the affirmation of their existing capabilities. The potential for failure in performing a challenging task abrogates the possibility of enjoyment.

Facilitating Effectance Motivation

Children's beliefs in themselves, whether founded on reality or not, have a profound influence on their learning and achievement. Research presented in this book attests to the impact of social and academic failure. From an early age, children compare themselves with their peers and quickly become aware of any deficiencies. Children who lack self-confidence in their academic ability and are socially rejected do not perform to their full potential, and they come to avoid situations that could expose their limitations. Because of the potential for negative evaluations, they put greater effort into maintaining their self-image than into problem-solving strategies.

Like all children, children with mental retardation need to feel efficacious – that they have the competence to learn and to successfully complete assigned tasks. To achieve this feeling, anxieties must be allayed, strategies to focus on the task acquired, and self-evaluations must shift to concept mastery rather than comparisons with peers. Research by Nicholls et al. (1989) suggests that using this type of approach will increase effectance motivation in children who are functioning at a very low level in relation to their classmates.

Considering the research showing that children do not feel efficacious when faced with overly easy or extremely difficult tasks (Harter 1978a, 1978b), the assigned tasks should be within their abilities to complete, yet challenging enough to offer pride in accomplishment. Because help-seeking behavior may be evidence of their incompetence, children who need assistance are sometimes the least likely to request any (Karabenick & Knapp, 1988; Newman, 1991). Tasks should therefore be sequenced with small increases in difficulty to foster a sense of mastery through continued success (Bandura, 1981; Schunk, 1991). Necessary assistance should be offered to enable children to complete the task on their own without undermining mastery or fostering dependency (Nelson-Le Gall, 1981, 1990). Moreover, as shown in studies of children with learning disabilities, inclusion in the goal-setting process raises perceptions of self-efficacy (Schunk, 1985) and improves performance (Hom & Murphy, 1985).

Undifferentiated classrooms in which all students work at the same level may be problematic for children with mental retardation. Such classroom structure promotes evaluative comparisons with other students (Simpson & Rosenholtz, 1986). Whole-class instruction is typically dominated by self-confident, high-achieving children, which increases the likelihood of comparative judgments among the students (Bossert, 1979). Multidimensional classrooms tend to provide an environment that enhances effectance motivation. The only contrary evidence has been found in classes in which grades were heavily emphasized (MacIver, 1987, 1988). Informative feedback assessing mastery, identifying strengths and weaknesses, and commenting on how to focus future effort has been shown to be most beneficial to low-achieving students (Connell, 1985).

Reflections on Effectance Motivation

Evidence clearly demonstrates that most people, whether retarded or with greater intellectual endowment, do not enjoy confronting tasks that produce only feelings of incompetence and inadequacy. Such tasks are frequent in the lives of children with mental retardation. In their attempts to avoid failure and gain some degree of success, these children come to prefer tasks that are well within their abilities and easily accomplished. Although this strategy may be effective in the short term for avoiding the distress of confirming their lack of ability, in the long term it may undermine learning and performance.

Although effectance motivation was one of the last personality factors identified by Zigler and his colleagues, it may well be the most important for understanding and improving the performance of children with mental retardation. From a developmental perspective, the growing body of empirical evidence clearly indicates the presence of an innate predisposition to achieve that develops in response to environmental experiences. The degree of success attained in achievement situations is the result of complex interactions between the individual's cognitive abilities and motivational variables associated with the situation, such as perceived task difficulty, type of reinforcement available, and the individual's goals. In the day-to-day experience of encountering tasks they believe they cannot do, or will do less well than their nonretarded peers, children with mental retardation acquire maladaptive but face-saving strategies that inhibit their functioning. A lack of effectance motivation may be the predisposing factor in the development of outerdirected problem-solving strategies (discussed in Chapter 8) and the overdependence on adult reinforcers seen in the positive-reaction tendency (Chapter 5).

Because of the centrality of effectance motivation to all areas of performance, a strong research effort is justified. By mapping the development of this and other personality and motivational factors, and exploring how they operate in combination, better instructional strategies can be designed to facilitate the socialization of retarded individuals as functioning adult members of society.

References

Ames, C., & Archer, J. (1988). Achievement goals in the classroom: Students' learning strategies and motivation processes. *Journal of Educational Psychology, 80,* 260–267.

Bandura, A. (1965). Influence of models' reinforcement contingencies on the acquisition of imitative responses. *Journal of Personality and Social Psychology, 50,* 35–46.

(1977a). Self-efficacy: Toward a unifying theory of behavioural change. *Psychological Review, 84,* 191–215.

(1977b). *Social learning theory.* Englewood Cliffs, NJ: Prentice Hall.

(1981). Self-referent thought. A developmental analysis of self-efficacy. In J. Flavell & L. Ross (eds.), *Social cognitive development: Frontiers and possible futures.* Cambridge: Cambridge University Press.

(1986). *Social foundations of thought and action: Social cognitive theory.* Englewood Cliffs, NJ: Prentice Hall.

(1995). Exercise of personal and collective efficacy in changing societies. In A. Bandura (ed.) *Self-efficacy in changing societies.* New York: Cambridge University Press.

Berlyne, D. (1966). Curiosity and exploration. *Science, 153,* 25–33.

Bossert, S. (1979). *Tasks and social relationships in classrooms.* (The Arnold and Caroline Rose Monograph Series of the American Sociological Association.) Cambridge: Cambridge University Press.

Byck, M. (1968). Cognitive differences among diagnostic groups of retardates. *American Journal of Abnormal Psychology, 70,* 97–101.

Cameron, A., & Storm, T. (1965). Achievement motivation in Canadian Indian middle- and working-class children. *Psychological Reports, 16,* 459–463.

Collins, J. (1982, March). *Self-efficacy and ability in achievement behavior.* Paper presented at the annual meeting of the American Educational Research Association.

Connell, J. (1985). A new multidimensional measure of children's perceptions of control. *Child Development, 56,* 1018–1041.

Cromwell, R. (1963). A social learning approach to mental retardation. In N.R. Ellis (ed.), *Handbook of mental deficiency.* New York: McGraw-Hill.

Davis, A. (1941). American status systems and the socialization of the child. *American Sociological Review, 6,* 234–254.

(1943). Child training and social class. In R. Barker, J. Kounin, & M. Wright (eds.), *Child behavior and development.* New York: McGraw-Hill.

(1944). Socialization and adolescent personality. In *Adolescence. National Society for the Study of Education,* Part 1. Chicago: National Society for the Study of Education.

Deci, E. (1971). The effects of externally mediated rewards on intrinsic motivation. *Journal of Personality and Social Behavior, 18,* 105–115.

Denham, S., Mitchell-Copeland, J., Strandberg, K., Auerbach, S., & Blair, K. (1997). Parental contributions to preschoolers' emotional competence: Direct and indirect effects. *Motivation and Emotion, 21,* 65–86.

Dobbs, V. (1967). *Motivational orientation and programmed instruction achievement gains of educable mentally retarded adolescents.* Unpublished doctoral dissertation. George Peabody College, Nashville, TN.

Douvan, E. (1956). Social status and success striving. *Journal of Abnormal and Social Psychology, 52,* 219–223.

Dweck, C. (1986). Motivational processes affecting learning. *American Psychologist, 41,* 1040–1048.

Elliot, E., & Dweck, C. (1988). Goals: An approach to motivation and achievement. *Journal of Personality and Social Psychology, 54,* 5–12.

Ericson, M. (1947). Social status and child rearing practices. In T. M. Newcomb & E. L. Hartley (eds.), *Readings in social psychology.* New York: Holt, Rinehart, & Winston.

Festinger, L. (1957). *A theory of cognitive dissonance.* Stanford: Stanford University Press.

Fyans, L.J., Jr., Salili, F., Maehr, M.I., & Desai, K.A. (1983). A cross-cultural exploration into the meaning of achievement. *Journal of Personality and Social Psychology, 44,* 1000–1013.

Harter, S. (1977). The effects of social reinforcement and task difficulty level on the pleasure derived by normal and retarded children from cognitive challenge and mastery. *Journal of Experimental Child Psychology, 24,* 476–494.

Harter, S. (1978a). Effectance motivation reconsidered: Toward a developmental model. *Human Development, 21,* 34–64.

(1978b). Pleasure derived from challenge and effects of receiving grades on children's difficulty level choice. *Child Development, 49,* 788–799.

(1981). A new self-report scale of intrinsic versus extrinsic orientation in the classroom: Motivational and informational components. *Developmental Psychology, 17,* 300–312.

Harter, S., & Zigler, E. (1974). The assessment of effectance motivation in normal and retarded children. *Developmental Psychology, 10,* 169–180.

Havinghurst, F.J. (1970). Minority subcultures and the law of effect. *American Psychologist, 25,* 313–322.

Haywood, H.C. (1968a). Motivational orientation of overachieving and underachieving elementary school children. *American Journal of Mental Deficiency, 72,* 662–667.

(1968b). Psychometric motivation and the efficiency of learning and performance in the mentally retarded. In B.W. Richards (ed.), *Proceedings of the First Congress of the International Association for the Scientific Study of Mental Deficiency.* Reigate, England: Michael Jackson.

Haywood, H.C., & Switzky, H.N. (1985). Work response of mildly mentally retarded adults to self versus external regulation as a function of motivational orientation. *American Journal of Mental Deficiency, 90,* 151–159.

Haywood, H.C., & Wachs, T. D. (1966). Size discrimination learning as a function of motivation-hygiene orientation in adolescents. *Journal of Educational Psychology, 57,* 279–286.

Haywood, H.C., & Weaver, S.J. (1967). Differential effects of motivational orientation and incentive conditions on motor performance in institutionalized retardates. *American Journal of Mental Deficiency, 72,* 459–467.

Hom, H., & Murphy, M. (1985). Low-need achievers' performance: The positive impact of a self-determined goal. *Personality and Social Psychology Bulletin, 11,* 275–285.

Hunt, J. McV. (1965). Intrinsic motivation and its role in psychological development. In D. Levine (ed.), *Nebraska Symposium on Motivation* (Vol. 13). Lincoln, NE: University of Nebraska Press.

Kagan, J. (1972). Motives and development. *Journal of Personality and Social Psychology, 22,* 51–66.

Karabenick, S., & Knapp, J. (1988). Help-seeking and the need for academic assistance. *Journal of Educational Psychology, 80,* 406–408.

Kounin, J. (1941a). Experimental studies of rigidity: I. The measurements of rigidity in normal and feeble-minded persons. *Character and Personality, 9,* 251–272.

(1941b). Experimental studies of Rigidity: II. The explanatory power of the concept of rigidity as applied to feeblemindedness. *Character and Personality, 9,* 273–282.

Lepper, M., Greene, D., & Nisbett, R. (1973). Undermining children's intrinsic interest with intrinsic rewards: A test of the overjustification hypothesis. *Journal of Personality and Social Psychology, 28,* 129–137.

Locke, E., Frederick, E., Lee, C., & Bobko, P. (1984). Effects of self-efficacy, goals, and task strategies on task performance. *Journal of Applied Psychology, 69,* 241–251.

MacIver, D. (1987). Classroom factors and student characteristics predicting students' use of achievement standards during ability self-assessment. *Child Development, 58,* 1258–1271.

(1988). Classroom environments and the stratification of pupils' ability perceptions. *Journal of Educational Psychology, 80,* 495–505.

McClelland, D.C. (1961). *The achieving society.* New York: Free Press.

(1971). *Motivational trends in society.* New York: General Learning Press.

McClelland, D.C., Atkinson, J.W., Clark, R.A., & Lowell, E.L. (1953). *The achievement motive.* New York: Appleton-Century-Crofts.

Merighi, J., Edison, M., & Zigler, E. (1990). The role of motivational factors in the functioning of mentally retarded individuals. In R. Hodapp, J. Burack, & E. Zigler (eds.), *Issues in the developmental approach to mental retardation.* New York: Cambridge University Press.

Morgan, M. (1984). Reward-induced decrements and increments in intrinsic motivation. *Review of Educational Research, 54,* 5–30.

Nelson-Le Gall, S. (1981). Help-seeking: An understudied problem-solving skill in children. *Developmental Review, 1,* 224–246.

(1990). Classroom help-seeking behavior of African-American children. *Education and Urban Society, 24,* 27–40.

Newman, R. (1991). Goals and self-regulated learning: What motivates children to seek academic help? In M. Maehr & P. Pintrich (eds.), *Advances in motivation and achievement* (Vol. 7). Greenwich, CT: JAI Press.

Nicholls, J. (1983). Conception of ability and achievement motivation: A theory and its implications for education. In S. Paris, G. Olson, & H. Stevenson (eds.), *Learning and motivation in the classroom.* Hillsdale, NJ: Erlbaum.

Nicholls, J., Cheung, P., Lauer, J., & Patashnick, M. (1989). Individual differences in academic motivation: Perceived ability, goals, beliefs, and values. *Learning and Individual Differences, 1,* 63–84.

Piaget, J. (1952). *The origins of intelligence in children.* New York: Norton.

Plenderleith, M. (1956). Discrimination learning and discrimination reversal learning in normal and feebleminded children. *Journal of Genetic Psychology, 88,* 107–112.

Shultz, T., & Zigler, E. (1970). Emotional concomitants of visual mastery in infants: The effects of stimulus movement on smiling and vocalizing. *Journal of Experimental Child Psychology, 10,* 390–402.

Schunk, D. (1985). Participation in goal setting: Effects on self-efficacy and skills of learning-disabled children. *Journal of Special Education, 19,* 307–317.

(1991). Goal setting and self-evaluation: A social cognitive perspective on self-regulation. In M. Maehr & P. Pintrich (eds.), *Advances in motivation and achievement* (Vol. 7). Greenwich, CT: JAI Press.

Simpson, C., & Rosenholtz, S. (1986). Classroom structure and the social construction of ability. In J. Richardson (ed.), *Handbook of theory and research for the sociology of education.* New York: Greenwood Press.

Stevenson, H.W., & Zigler, E. (1957). Discrimination learning and rigidity in normal and feebleminded individuals. *Journal of Personality, 25,* 699–711.

Stipek, D. (1993). *Motivation to learn: From theory to practice* (2nd ed.). Needham Heights, MA: Allyn and Bacon.

Switzky, H.N., & Haywood, H.C. (1974). Motivational orientation and the relative efficacy of self-monitored and externally imposed reinforcements schedules. *Journal of Personality and Social Psychology, 30,* 360–366.

Terrell, G., Jr., Durkin, K., & Wiesley, M. (1959). Social class and the nature of incentive in discrimination learning. *Journal of Abnormal and Social Psychology, 59,* 270–272.

White, R. (1959). Motivation reconsidered: The concept of competence. *Psychological Review, 66,* 297–333.

Woolridge, R. (1966). *Motivation-hygiene orientation and school achievement in mentally subnormal children.* Unpublished E.D. study, George Peabody College, Nashville, TN.

Zigler, E. (1958). *Social deprivation and rigidity in the performance of feebleminded children.* Unpublished doctoral dissertation, University of Texas.

(1961). Social deprivation and rigidity in the performance of feebleminded children. *Journal of Abnormal and Social Psychology, 62,* 413–421.

(1966a). Mental retardation: Current issues and approaches. In L.W. Hoffman & M.L. Hoffman (eds.), *Review of child development research* (Vol. 2). New York: Russell Sage.

(1966b). Motivational determinants in the performance of feebleminded children. *American Journal of Orthopsychiatry, 36,* 848–856.

(1971). The retarded child as a whole person. In H.E. Adams & W.K. Boardman (eds.), *Advances in experimental clinical psychology.* New York: Pergamon Press.

Zigler, E., & deLabry, J. (1962). Concept-switching in middle-class, lower-class, and retarded children. *Journal of Abnormal and Social Psychology, 65,* 267–273.

Zigler, E., & Hodapp, R. (1986). *Understanding mental retardation.* New York: Cambridge University Press.

Zigler, E., & Kanzer, P. (1962). The effectance of two classes of verbal reinforcers on the performance of middle- and lower-class children. *Journal of Personality, 30,* 157–163.

Zigler, E., Levine, J., & Gould, L. (1967). Cognitive challenge as a factor in children's humor appreciation. *Journal of Personality and Social Psychology, 6,* 332–336.

Zigler, E., & Unell, E. (1962). Concept-switching in normal and feebleminded children as a function of reinforcement. *American Journal of Mental Deficiency, 66,* 651–657.

8   Outerdirectedness in Individuals with and without Mental Retardation: A Review

Jane Bybee
Edward Zigler

Imagine teaching a class:

> You ask the children what is the capital of the United States. You call on a
> student in the front row. "New York," the child responds. "No," you reply.
> "Can someone else tell me what is the capital of the United States?" A
> student in the back waves his hand frantically and blurts out, "New York."
> "No, that's incorrect. What is the capital of the United States?" You call
> upon a third child, who without batting an eyelid, replies, "New York."

Reports from the classroom such as the one described here captivated the
attention of Edward Zigler more than three decades ago. Why would mentally retarded students in this class repeat a response they knew to be
incorrect rather than attempt to offer a new solution, which at least stood a
chance of being correct? Could this phenomenon be captured in scientific
study?

> The adolescent boy was seated in front of a large wooden box. Like
> curtains on a stage, the door in front was pulled up to reveal a stage of
> sorts with different sized squares on the floor. Above the squares on the
> right, left, and center of the back wall were light bulbs. Each time the door
> lifted, the squares were in a different position and/or the bulb that was lit
> changed. Again and again, the boy chose whichever square was under the
> light even though every time the answer under the light was wrong. Ten
> wrong answers in a row. Twenty. The experimenter had been testing
> students with mental retardation since early that morning at their school,
> and had now moved into a room in the residence areas where she con-
> tinued testing into the evening. Again and again, she observed students

Portions of this chapter were adapted from Bybee, J., & Zigler, E. (1998). Outerdirectedness in individuals with and without mental retardation: A review. In J.
Burack, R. Hodapp, & E. Zigler (eds.), *Handbook of mental retardation and
development* (pp. 434–461). New York: Cambridge University Press.

choosing the cued or light response until they reached the ceiling of seventy times in a row in each of two conditions. Her back was aching from reaching over to raise and lower the heavy guillotine door hundreds upon hundreds of times. Thirty wrong answers in a row. Why, she wondered, would Eric never try the correct answer (the small square)? Only minutes earlier, he had been very articulate in responding to a questionnaire, and later spoke intelligently about his sticker pictures. Forty wrong answers in a row. What if she explained the instructions again in excruciating detail to make absolutely sure he understood the task? If he solved it, though, she would have to throw out his data as tainted. Fifty wrong answers in a row. She could stand it no longer. "Eric, you know the purpose of this task is to figure out which one of these different sized boxes is the right answer. One size is right and the other two sizes are wrong." "Yes, I know," Eric said quietly. "And, you understand, I tell you if you pick the right box. I ring the bell like this and I say, 'Good Eric. That box is correct." "Yes," said Eric looking up, "I know." The experimenter lifted the door. Eric picked the correct answer. "Yes!" The experimenter said with great enthusiasm, ringing the bell, "That's good. That's great. You got the right answer. You figured it out." She opened the door again. Eric chose the box under the light. Again. And again. And again. Sixty wrong. Seventy wrong. End.

When presented with an unfamiliar situation or problem, individuals such as Eric in this true story sometimes choose to imitate others or utilize templates, cues, and examples rather than attempting to solve the problem on their own. This phenomenon is called outerdirectedness. Research findings over the last three decades indicate that mentally retarded individuals are consistently more outerdirected than nonretarded individuals (Achenbach & Zigler, 1968; Balla, Styfco, & Zigler, 1971; Bybee, LeDuc, & Zigler, 1998; Bybee & Zigler, 1992; Cohen & Heller, 1975; Drotar, 1972; Lustman & Zigler, 1982; MacMillan & Cauffiel, 1977; Sanders, Zigler, & Butterfield, 1968; Turnure & Zigler, 1964; Yando & Zigler, 1971).

One factor that has hampered the study of outerdirectedness in past research is that the measures traditionally used to assess it have been time-consuming and/or costly. The discrimination task that Eric completed, for example, takes up to twenty-five minutes to complete and requires a special apparatus calling for skills in carpentry and electrical wiring to construct. We begin our review by distinguishing outerdirectedness from like concepts, and by examining measures of outerdirectedness, giving special attention to a newly developed teacher report that may be completed quickly and at less cost.

Why do mentally retarded individuals such as Eric have a heightened proclivity for outerdirectedness? Empirical findings indicate that the predisposition is not the result of a permanent or irreversible deficit (such as rigidity or lack of creativity) in cognitive reasoning skills. Indeed, mentally retarded children are no more outerdirected than nonretarded children under certain experimental conditions (Bybee & Zigler, 1992). Turnure and Zigler (1964) suggest that mentally retarded children have a heightened proclivity for outerdirectedness because of a history of failure in independent problem solving. Repeated failures are said to undermine their confidence in self-generated solutions to problems, leading them to turn instead to external cues as guides to action. Considerable empirical evidence has now been amassed to support this viewpoint. An alternate possibility is that mentally retarded individuals are less interested in solving the task than in sustaining the interaction with the experimenter. Mentally retarded children, compared with children of average intellect, are not as well-liked by and are more often rejected by their nonretarded peers (Gresham, 1982; Zigler & Hodapp, 1986). Ostracism and social deprivation may result in a heightened motivation to interact with supportive adults. Zigler and Hodapp (1986) note that this motivation to interact with an approving adult may be so strong that it competes with attention given to task performance. Eric, for example, clearly knew the correct answer. Perhaps he continued to choose the incorrect answer to prolong the session and receive more individual attention from a friendly adult. We explore reasons for the high outerdirectedness of mentally retarded children in our review of individual differences.

Individuals with mental retardation are not uniform in their proclivity for outerdirectedness. The etiology of the mental retardation – whether it results from an organic cause such as Down syndrome or a cultural-familial condition – affects level of outerdirectedness. Living conditions – such as whether the individual resides at home or, like Eric, in an institution – also affect level of outerdirectedness. Moreover, age affects outerdirectedness and its usefulness for the person. These and other individual difference variables will be reviewed.

Next, we review effects of experimental manipulations such as type of external cue, characteristics of the model, and variations in the task on levels of outerdirectedness shown by mentally retarded and nonretarded participants. Following this, we review correlations of outerdirectedness with indices of personal competence.

Finally, the important question of whether outerdirectedness is useful or harmful to the individual will be considered. Researchers at first adopted a noncommittal position on this question, noting that there is nothing inherently useful or destructive in utilizing external cues. Manipulations utilized in the research on outerdirectedness have now reached a critical mass that makes it possible to draw the following conclusions: Outerdirectedness is generally used in a strategic and beneficial manner by children without mental retardation. Mentally retarded children, in contrast, often use external cues in a harmful and indiscriminate manner. As in the example of Eric's behavior on the discrimination task, it is not unusual for children with mental retardation to choose the incorrect response seventy times in a row! We review the relationship of outerdirectedness not only to problem-solving success and social rewards in experimental settings, but to indicators of cognitive and social competence in everyday life.

Distinguishing Outerdirectedness from Related Constructs

Outerdirectedness occurs when an individual is presented with an ambiguous or novel task to be solved or dealt with. The individual then relies on external cues rather than on his or her internal cognitive abilities to solve a task or problem. Cues that may be used in problem solving must be available, and an element of free choice must be present.

Imitation

Unlike outerdirectedness, imitation need not involve a problem. Infants mimicking adults' facial expressions, comedians aping someone's gait and speech style, and teenagers following the latest body-piercing fad are all imitating someone. None of these examples involves outerdirectedness, as no problem, however loosely defined, is involved.

Outerdirectedness and imitation overlap in problem-solving situations when a model or modeled action is available. For example, if students are given a choice of any topic for an art project and choose the same topic as their friends do, they are imitating and they are being outerdirected.

Outerdirectedness, but not imitation, may occur in problem-solving situations in the absence of a human model or modeled act. In outerdirectedness, few restrictions are placed on the type of cue. Cues may be helpful, irrelevant, or misleading. Cues may be provided by other people or by machines, but unlike imitation, may also take the form of written instructions, auditory cues, or visual prompts. A child who opens the third of three doors because it is the one with the star on the front is being outerdirected, but is not imitating because there is no one or nothing to model.

Obedience

An element of choice in whether to utilize cues or rely on internal cognitive resources is a necessary precondition for outerdirectedness. If the only way of solving the problem is to employ external cues, or if the person is explicitly directed or required to employ external cues, utilization of the cues would be obedience or compliance rather than outerdirectedness. Whether or not a person obeys orders seemingly has little to do with whether he or she is outerdirected. Outerdirectedness and obedience are only weakly related among mentally retarded individuals, $r = .22$ for both teacher reports and experimental measures of outerdirectedness (Zigler, Bennett-Gates, & Hodapp, Chapter 9).

Creativity

Outerdirectedness is not the lack of creativity. Indeed, it is possible to be both outerdirected and creative. Consider, for example, schools of art such as impressionism or abstract expressionism. Artists representing a particular school use certain common features. Impressionists generally shun the color black, choose topics that show the effects of sunlight, avoid highlighting borders, favor bright or pastel colors, and do not hide their brushstrokes. Monet, Renoir, van Gogh, and Gaugin were outerdirected in following these guidelines, yet all were creative geniuses. External cues or guidelines may be employed in new and interesting ways. On a small stage, children's work on the sticker game can show both creativity and outerdirectedness. Children may copy the "rocket ship" design in perfect detail, but then add stars, constellations, and sister satellites, or copy the idea of "kitty cat," but construct a family of cats bearing little similarity to the original.

In practice, children who copy show somewhat less originality. Creativity shows a moderate inverse correlation with teacher reports of outerdirectedness, $r = -.31$, and a nonsignificant inverse correlation with experimental measures, $r = -.15$ (Zigler et al., Chapter 9).

New Directions in the Assessment of Outerdirectedness

Experimental Measures

Six of the most commonly used measures of outerdirectedness are described here.

1. *Discrimination task,* or the cued-learning task (Achenbach & Zigler, 1968; Bybee & Zigler, 1989; Massari & Mansfield, 1973; Ruble & Naka-

mura, 1972; Sanders et al., 1968; Yando & Zigler, 1971). This task employs a three-choice (small, medium, large) size-discrimination problem. The apparatus used is a large box with a sliding door in front that opens to reveal three light bulbs on the base, spaced so that each square is under a bulb. One size square, chosen in advance by the experimenter, is the correct answer for all trials. For each trial, a light appears over one of the squares, and the positions of the squares and the light are changed between trials. As explained in the instructions, the object of the task is to choose the correct square, and correct responses are followed by a bell. The trials continue until five consecutive correct responses are made, or to a maximum of seventy trials. In some studies, the light always appears over the correct response (Achenbach & Zigler, 1968; Massari & Mansfield, 1973), whereas in others, the light always appears over one of the two incorrect squares (Bybee & Zigler, 1989; Yando & Zigler, 1971).

Two main scoring approaches have been used. The first, used when the correct square is cued, compares the cue present condition with a control condition where no cues are available. The dependent variable is the mean number of trials to criterion (Achenbach & Zigler, 1968). Differences in the cue condition compared with the no-cue condition are said to reflect effects of outerdirectedness. The second approach, used when incorrect responses are cued (Yando & Zigler, 1974), employs only the experimental condition, comparing cued errors (responses to the light) with uncued errors (responses not cued by the light). A greater number of cued than uncued errors is said to reflect greater outerdirectedness.

2. *Sticker Game* (Achenbach & Zigler, 1968; Balla, Butterfield, & Zigler, 1974; Bybee & Zigler, 1989; Gordon & MacLean, 1977; Leahy, Balla, & Zigler, 1982; Lustman & Zigler, 1982; MacMillan & Cauffiel, 1977; Maguire, 1976; Turnure & Zigler, 1964; Yando & Zigler, 1971). The materials used for this task include stickers sorted by color and shape, construction paper, and a sponge for wetting the stickers. The experimenter makes one of a series of predetermined pictures using five stickers uniform in color, and labels it with a two-part name such as "little person." The experimenter then places the picture in full view of the child and instructs the child to make a picture and give it a name. Before making the next predetermined picture, the experimenter removes both completed pictures from view. The scoring system awards points to each of the child's pictures on the basis of its similarity in name, form, sticker color, and background sheet to that of the experimenter. Interjudge reliability for this scoring system is high, $r = .93$ (Leahy et al., 1982).

3. *Glancing.* Two types of tasks have typically been employed in mea-

sures of glancing. For each task, greater glancing – at the experimenter, the experimenter's task, or around the room – is said to reflect greater outer-directedness.

(i) *Oddity Problem* (Turnure, 1973; Turnure, Larsen, & Thurlow, 1976). For this task, children are instructed to select the odd one of three figures displayed in three stimulus response windows. Correct responses are rein-forced by a red reward light. The correct response never appears in the middle window, and its position (right or left) is selected randomly. Behind the apparatus containing the response windows is a one-way mirror. In the relevant cue condition, the experimenter sits a foot or two behind the subject and alternatively looks at a clipboard containing the correct answers and at the correct response on the apparatus, tilting his head sharply to the left or right in the process. The subject can clearly see the experimenter in the mirror or by turning around slightly. In the no-cue (not-in) condition, the experimenter merely sits in the back of the room. The observer behind the one-way mirror records the number of glances and the amount of time spent glancing. As the experimenter cues are always correct, glancing provides a measure of reliance on task-relevant cues.

(ii) *WISC Items* (Drotar, 1972; Gordon & MacLean, 1977; MacMillan & Cauffiel, 1977; Ruble & Nakamura, 1972, 1973; Turnure & Zigler, 1964). Ruble and Nakamura (1973) employed two different tasks adapted from the WISC: (a) object assembly problems, specifically puzzles adapted from the face and automobile items, and (b) block design items of varying difficulty in which children are given two minutes to copy each design with blocks. Experimenters behind a screen record the number of times partici-pants glance away from the task. As there are no external cues – task-relevant or misleading – apart from the task, glancing may be said to reflect reliance on incidental cues. In another variation (Drotar, 1972; Ruble & Nakamura, 1972; Turnure & Zigler, 1964), the experimenter solves puzzle 2 while the child works on puzzle 1. The child is then asked to complete puzzle 2. Children's glances during both time periods are examined. Greater outerdirectedness is assumed to hurt task 1 performance (because cues are not relevant) and enhance task 2 performance (because cues pro-vided during the first task are relevant to the second task).

4. *Preference Tasks* (Lustman & Zigler, 1982; Thelen et al., 1983). The subject and the experimenter (or confederate) are shown a set of four photographs of people's faces. For each set, the people depicted are of the same sex and similar age. Subjects are asked to pick the face they judge to be most attractive (or most intelligent or most likable). The procedure is repeated for additional sets of pictures. To provide a measure of imitation,

matches between the model's and the subject's responses are scored as an index of imitativeness.

5. *Vertical Aspiration Board* (Becker & Glidden, 1979; Strichart, 1974). The vertical aspiration board consists of a platform that can be raised along a vertical board using a wire pulley. The purpose of the task is to score a high number of points by raising the platform as high as possible without dropping a steel ball off the platform. Unbeknown to the subjects, a hidden electromagnet holds the ball in place, and the experimenter can break the contact at any time, causing the ball to fall off the platform. In demonstrating how to play the game, the experimenter models four variations such as holding the handle at waist level, rotating the handle so that the wire wraps around it, standing off to one side, and standing with feet apart. The experimenter receives either a good score (defined as above 70) or a poor score (below 40). The subject then completes ten to twelve trials. Greater use of the modeled variations is scored as greater imitativeness. Becker and Glidden (1979) report high interscorer agreement between two "blind" raters, who disagreed on only 1.9 percent of the ratings.

6. *Sorting Task, Pegboard, Feltboard, & Abacus* (Yando, Seitz, & Zigler, 1978, 1989). For each of these tasks, the experimenter demonstrates predetermined strategies that lead to successful completion of the task, and predetermined task-irrelevant behaviors such as sitting in an unusual position or walking in a circle around the table. The child is then asked to complete the task. The child's performance is scored using a checklist on which the presence or absence of each relevant and irrelevant behavior modeled by the experimenter is recorded.

Commonalities. These six experimental measures assess different behaviors that are all indicative of outerdirectedness. In the sticker game, outerdirectedness is indexed by copying a model. In the discrimination task, outerdirectedness is tapped by reliance on a problem-solving cue provided by a machine. The more often individuals choose responses cued by a light, the more outerdirected they are said to be.

Greater glancing has also been used as an index of outerdirectedness. For some of these tasks, participants are given the opportunity to ignore or to look at the correct response to a task. In others, participants may look at the experimenter, who solves a puzzle that is the same or different than their own. Greater outerdirectedness is measured by the length and frequency of glancing at the cues.

In the preference-for-faces tasks, individuals are asked to choose the most attractive, intelligent, or likable of four people depicted in photos after someone else has voiced an opinion. Matches between the participants' and modeled choices are taken as a reflection of outerdirectedness. Finally, for the vertical aspiration board and the sorting and similar tasks, the experimenter models relevant and irrelevant problem-solving strategies. Individuals who utilize the modeled behaviors score higher on outerdirectedness.

Critical components are present in all of these measures of outerdirectedness: They have a task component, they offer external cues, and they involve an element of free choice. One striking difference across measures is that some, such as the discrimination tasks, assess reliance on misleading cues, whereas others, such as the sticker game, assess reliance on task-relevant or incidental cues. As discussed later, different measures are generally intercorrelated for mentally retarded individuals, but seemingly tap different underlying constructs among individuals of average intellect.

Questionnaire Measures

Until recently, no existing questionnaire was available to assess outerdirectedness. The time required for administration of experimental tasks, the expense of equipment and materials, and problems with order effects hampered researchers in their efforts to examine outerdirectedness and other personality-motivational constructs of interest to researchers in the field of mental retardation. The EZ-Yale Questionnaire, described in Chapter 9, is a thirty-seven-item inventory that taps outerdirectedness, effectance motivation, expectancy of success, negative-reaction tendency (wariness), positive-reaction tendency (clinginess), creativity, and obedience. Items are rated by teachers on a 1–5 scale, where higher numbers represent a higher degree or greater presence of each construct. In a sample of 661 mentally retarded individuals, the items formed distinct factors, with acceptable factor loadings for the constituent subscale items. The seven outerdirectedness items – imitates others' work, is a follower, likes to be given a lot of direction, does what others say regardless of the consequences, does something just because social custom dictates, is apt to pass up something he or she wants to do when others feel it isn't worth doing, observes what others are doing to guide his/her own actions – demonstrate good construct validity. The item on imitation, for example, clearly specifies copying others' work, thereby tapping the one situation in which imitation and outerdirectedness overlap. Other items indicative of outerdirectedness but not imitation are included (e.g., likes direction). Items emphasize using external cues as guides to action. Items tapping obedience/compliance and creativity load on two factors that are only weakly related to outerdirectedness. From a theoretical and psychometric standpoint, then, the measure does an excellent job in distinguishing outerdirectedness from like concepts.

Among mentally retarded individuals, the outerdirectedness scale evidences no problems with restriction in range and has good split-half reliability, $r = .74$, good internal consistency as indicated by Cronbach's alpha (.83), and good test – retest reliability over a three-month period, $r = .81$. Moreover, among mentally retarded individuals, the outerdirectedness subscale correlates well, $r = .71$, with scores on the sticker game, a widely used experimental measure, attesting to the external validity of the scale. Finally, mentally retarded children score higher on the outerdirectedness subscale than nonretarded children (Turner, 1998; Zigler et al., Chapter 9), a finding consistent with research using experimental measures.

Among fourth-graders of normal intellect, the teacher report of outerdirectedness has a Cronbach's alpha of .76 (Sussman, 1998). The teacher report is not correlated with scores on the sticker game or discrimination learning task. (Sussman notes that the experimental measures were limited by restricted range in her sample.)

Comparison of Teacher and Experimental Measures

The type of model and type of cue are less explicit for the teacher than for the experimental measures. The teacher report of outerdirectedness assesses utilization of cues provided by *peers* (e.g., "is a follower"), *teachers* (e.g., "likes to be given a lot of direction"), and *social norms* (e.g., "does something just because social custom dictates"). The experimental measures of outerdirectedness, in contrast, generally assess utilization of cues provided by a *strange adult* (the experimenter). Researchers report cues from different sources (for example, humans versus machines) are treated differently (Balla, Styfco, & Zigler, 1971; Yando & Zigler, 1971; Zigler & Yando, 1972). In addition, whether the type of cue is helpful, incidental, or misleading is clear for the different experimental tasks. The type of cue is more ambiguous for the teacher report as it taps reliance on both helpful cues (e.g., "likes to be given a lot of direction") and potentially harmful cues (e.g., "does what others say regardless of the consequences"). The teacher report may thus be tapping a more general proclivity than the individual experimental measures.

As noted in an earlier review (Bybee & Zigler, 1998), a limitation of studies to date is that adults and peers previously unknown to the child have been used as models rather than models whom the students more typically encounter, such as family members, teachers, and classmates. Indeed, the experimental measures may not be easily used to assess imitation of anyone except individuals serving as experimenter or confederate. In contrast, the teacher report could be easily adapted to assess utilization of cues provided by peers, teachers, parents, or siblings. Such an adaptation could open up previously unexplored areas of investigation.

The Origins of Outerdirectedness

Why are mentally retarded individuals especially prone to outerdirectedness? The best explanation is that outerdirectedness results from a history of failure in independent problem-solving and, perhaps, from social deprivation. We consider these explanations in turn.

A History of Failure in Problem-Solving Increases Outerdirectedness

The greater history of failure that mentally retarded children experience in applying their own solutions to problems has repeatedly been offered as the primary explanation for the high levels of outerdirectedness they show compared with children of normal intellect (Achenbach & Zigler, 1968; Lustman & Zigler, 1982; Turnure & Zigler, 1964). A history of failure experiences is said to lower children's self-confidence and to lead them to distrust their own solutions to problems, increasing outerdirectedness. Evidence to support this position is now overwhelming.

Experimental Studies Demonstrate Outerdirectedness Increases after Failure Experiences. Experiences of success and failure affect outerdirectedness on subsequent similar tasks. Outerdirectedness is greater after experiences of failure than after experiences of success among both mentally retarded and nonretarded children (Bybee & Zigler, 1992; MacMillan & Wright, 1974; Turnure & Zigler, 1964). Likewise, Strichart (1974) reports that experimental participants, mentally retarded as well as nonretarded, who were led to believe that they had performed poorly on a previous task were more outerdirected on the criterion task than participants who were led to believe they performed well.

Evidence showing generalization would provide stronger support for the hypothesis that repeated failure experiences may result in a permanently higher predisposition for outerdirectedness. Repeated failure experiences should theoretically lead outerdirectedness to become a crystallized and stable predisposition shown on a range of dissimilar tasks (Turnure &

Zigler, 1964). Bybee and Zigler (1992) provided experimental evidence that students who are given a task that most fail to solve are more outer-directed on a later dissimilar task. Similarly, Greenberg (1979) in his study of children of normal intellect, and Marburg, Houston, and Holmes (1976) in their examination of individuals with mental retardation, found that success or failure in independent problem-solving may generalize to different situations. Experimental participants given positive verbal reinforcement for imitating (but not for independent problem-solving) showed elevated levels of imitation on different tasks, with different models, and at later testing sessions.

Correlational Studies Link Outerdirectedness with Personality Traits that Would be Expected to Result from Repeated Failure. Individuals, both mentally retarded and of average intellect, who have lower self-confidence and worse self-esteem show more outerdirectedness (Leahy et al., 1982; Ruble & Nakamura, 1973). Those with low expectancies of success and low ideal self-images also score higher on outerdirectedness. (In studies by Leahy et al., 1982, and Turner, 1998, correlations are reported for the total sample with no report of interactions with mental retardation status. Findings from Zigler et al., Chapter 9, are for mentally retarded children only; findings from Ruble & Nakamura, 1973, are for nonretarded children only.) Moreover, Ruble and Nakamura (1973) found that in a sample of children of normal intellect, those with worse academic achievement scored higher on outerdirectedness.

Developmental Findings Also Support the History of Failure Interpretation. In their original theoretical formulation of outerdirectedness, Turnure and Zigler (1964) hypothesized that the lower the cognitive-developmental level of the child, the higher the level of outerdirectedness will be, because reliance on external cues is more conducive to problem-solving success than reliance on poorly developed cognitive skills. At higher mental age levels, as internal problem-solving skills become more refined and effective, external cues provide increasingly less marginal utility. Moreover, children (such as those of average intellect) who experience repeated success in independent problem-solving may come to favor inner-directed approaches. In contrast, mentally retarded children may meet with repeated failure experiences over a long period of time in their problem-solving efforts. As their history of failure becomes ever longer, they may increasingly learn to distrust internally generated solutions to problems and become more outerdirected. This is precisely what is found: With development during childhood and adolescence, nonretarded children show *decreases* (or no change) in levels of outerdirectedness, whereas mentally retarded children show *increases* (or no change) in levels of outerdirectedness. Mentally retarded children are seemingly more outerdirected on tasks that contain an element of success or failure than on nonthreatening tasks, a distinction that becomes more pronounced with development. We now review the results of the studies summarized here.

An overwhelming preponderance of evidence indicates that for children of normal intellect, beyond infancy outerdirectedness declines with development. Researchers report declines at higher MA levels in outerdirectedness as assessed by glancing (MacMillan & Cauffiel, 1977; MacMillan & Wright, 1974; Nottelmann & Hill, 1977; Ruble & Nakamura, 1973), reliance on task-relevant and incidental cues from the sticker game (Balla, Styfco, & Zigler, 1971; Bybee, LeDuc, & Zigler, 1993; Yando & Zigler, 1971), reliance on incidental cues when selecting marbles (Zigler & Yando, 1972), and teacher reports (Bybee, LeDuc, & Zigler, 1993). Additional studies report developmental declines that do not reach significance on the discrimination task (Achenbach & Zigler, 1968; Bybee, LeDuc, & Zigler, 1993; Bybee & Zigler, 1992; Yando & Zigler, 1971) and the sticker game (Bybee & Zigler, 1992; Lustman & Zigler, 1982). Few studies report no changes in outerdirectedness with development (MacMillan & Cauffiel, 1977, on the sticker game; Lustman & Zigler, 1982, on the preference for-faces task). (Achenbach and Zigler, 1968, used task-relevant cues instead of misleading cues in the discrimination task, and ceiling effects may have contributed to findings of no developmental effects.)

For mentally retarded individuals, effects of development vary by task. In the sticker game, there are no right or wrong answers, and the task – that of making a picture with stickers – may be familiar and nontaxing. The cues are either task-relevant or incidental. The sticker game is not threatening to the child; for this reason, in fact, researchers have used this task as a preface to intelligence tests to set the child at ease and optimize performance (e.g., Zigler, Abelson, & Seitz, 1973). With development, outerdirectedness as assessed by the sticker game declines for mentally retarded children (Bybee, Ennis, & Zigler, 1989; incidental cues only from Bybee, LeDuc, & Zigler, 1993; Gordon & MacLean, 1977), or shows no change (task-relevant cues from Bybee, LeDuc, & Zigler, 1993; MacMillan & Cauffiel, 1977). Declines with development are consistently reported for glancing tasks in which incidental and task-relevant cues are provided (Gordon &

MacLean, 1977; MacMillan & Cauffiel, 1977). No changes with development have been found for a teacher report of outerdirectedness (Bybee, LeDuc, & Zigler, 1993).

A strong success/failure component is associated with the discrimination task. Researchers have suggested that the discrimination task may be perceived as threatening by many children as there are definite correct and incorrect responses that are immediately reinforced or not reinforced by a bell (Bybee, Ennis, & Zigler, 1989). An additional factor that may prove disconcerting to the children is that all cues provided for this task are misleading. Both of these factors may raise failure concerns, and hence outerdirectedness. For mentally retarded children (who as a group may be especially sensitive to failure because of their more frequent experiences of being presented with problems outside their ability to solve), outerdirectedness on threatening tasks such as the discrimination task increases (Bybee, LeDuc, & Zigler, 1993) or shows no changes (Achenbach & Zigler, 1968) with development. An increase in outerdirectedness with development has also been reported for the preference for faces task (Lustman & Zigler, 1982). (Institutionalization interacts with effects of development, as described in the individual differences section.)

Social Factors Affecting the Development of Outerdirectedness

In problem-solving settings, children may look to others for social interaction as well as task solution purposes (Turnure, Larson, & Thurlow, 1976; Zigler & Hodapp, 1986). Imitation may be used to sustain social interactions and strengthen social bonds with parents and other adults (Kucyznski, Zahn-Waxler, & Radke-Yarrow, 1987). Individuals may react favorably to being imitated by their peers when the imitation is not overly blatant (Thelen et al., 1983).

We revisit a vignette from the introduction to this chapter. Eric clearly knew the correct answer, but preferred to choose the wrong answer dozens of times. Why? If his motive was to correctly solve the task, his behavior makes no sense at all. But if his motive, as a child institutionalized and starved for individual adult attention, was to sustain a social interaction with a supportive adult, his actions become understandable. We offer two theoretical tenets. First, we hypothesize that outerdirectedness will be highest among children who are most in need of adult attention. Conversely, we predict outerdirectedness will be lowest among children who are wary of other people and suspicious of cues they offer.

Among children of average intellect, experimental evidence provides support for the tenet that outerdirectedness is highest when need for social interaction is greatest. Nonretarded children with higher need for social approval are more imitative (Brannigan & Duchnowski, 1976). Moreover, children of average intellect who put comparatively more importance on interactions with adults than on schoolwork are more outerdirected even though the cues offered are misleading (Bybee, LeDuc, & Zigler, 1998).

Among nonretarded children, developmental studies are also in accord with the tenet that outerdirectedness is greatest among those who most desire interaction with adults. Younger children spend more time than older children interacting with parents (Hunter & Youiss, 1982). Young children appear to be more responsive to social reinforcement as opposed to nonsocial reinforcement (Ruble & Nakamura, 1973), a dichotomy akin to praise-versus performance-oriented behavior discussed by Zigler and Kanzer (1962). Young children may put the social benefits that imitation provides through ingratiation and establishment of a rapport above the rewards of mastery provided by independent problem-solving. A decreased need for social approval with age parallels developmental declines in outerdirectedness among children of normal intellect.

Experimental studies of nonretarded children support the tenet that outerdirectedness is lowest when wariness and distrust of adults are highest. Nonretarded students who place high comparative importance on social interactions accepted external cues when they had reason to be trusting (following an offering of helpful cues), but rejected external cues when they had reason to be wary (after they were offered misleading cues) (Bybee, LeDuc, & Zigler, 1998).

Individual Differences in Outerdirectedness

Effects of Abuse and Neglect

Results of studies of effects of abuse and neglect among children of average intellect are consistent with the tenet that outerdirectedness is low when wariness and distrust of adults are high. Yando and Zigler (1971) hypothesized that life experiences that lead to suspiciousness and wariness of others may lead children to distrust and avoid utilizing cues provided by adults. These researchers reported that children who had been abused or neglected by their parents were less outerdirected than children who were not from abusive environments.

Bybee, McGrath, and Quiles (1998) argued that important distinctions may be made between abuse and neglect. They compared children removed from their homes for abuse with children removed for reasons of neglect. (Children who had been both abused and neglected were excluded from the study.) Because abused children have been physically assaulted by adults in the past, they may be fearful of adults and distrusting of the cues they offer. Bybee et al. hypothesized that abused children would be very low on outerdirectedness. Because neglected children have been ignored and/or abandoned by caregivers, they may crave the social approval gained through imitation. Bybee et al. predicted that neglected children, because of their emotional neediness, would be more outerdirected. Consistent with predictions, abused children were less outerdirected than neglected children in two repetitions of the discrimination task. Indeed, abused children's scores on outerdirectedness, measured on both the discrimination task and sticker game (as assessed by Bybee et al.), were strikingly lower than scores found among nonmaltreated children (as assessed by Bybee & Zigler, 1992).

Effects of Socioeconomic Status (SES)

Baumrind's (1971) work on parenting styles indicates that parents from lower socioeconomic classes often employ authoritarian parenting styles. According to Baumrind, authoritarian parents discourage children from questioning rules and demand obedience and compliance. As parents from lower SES backgrounds are not often self-employed, they themselves may have to answer to other people on the job and may see compliance as essential in keeping their jobs (Baumrind, 1971). Children in families from low SES backgrounds may be encouraged by their parents to adopt an unquestioning, compliant, and outerdirected approach in new situations.

Individuals of low social status, such as women, are more reliant on and more skilled at interpreting nonverbal cues. LaFrance and Henley (1994) observed that females are consistently better than males at decoding facial expression, body language, and other nonverbal cues. They hypothesized that this difference may result from women's low social status and the accompanying need to anticipate and cater to the needs of higher status males.

Individuals from the lower SES have a greater expectancy of failure (Gruen & Zigler, 1968; Turner, 1988). A greater expectancy of failure in turn is correlated with greater outerdirectedness among both mentally retarded (Zigler et al., 1988) and nonretarded (Sussman, Bennett-Gates, & Zigler, 1998) individuals. Again, these findings would lead to the prediction that higher SES is inversely related to outerdirectedness.

Based on the aforementioned empirical and theoretical work, individuals from lower SES backgrounds would be expected to be more outerdirected than individuals from higher SES backgrounds. Turner (1988) confirmed that consistent with expectations, individuals from the lower SES score higher on teacher reports of outerdirectedness.

Effects of Mental Retardation

Perhaps no finding in the outerdirectedness literature is stronger or more consistent than the finding that mentally retarded children are more outerdirected than children of average intellect. Mentally retarded children may continually be confronted with behaviors and tasks more appropriate to their CA than their MA level. Ensuing failure to perform these tasks may lead mentally retarded children to become distrustful of their own solutions to problems and look to others for cues (Turnure & Zigler, 1964). The history of failure hypothesis to date provides the most convincing explanation of the greater outerdirectedness of mentally retarded children relative to nonretarded children (see earlier review by Bybee & Zigler, 1998).

In research efforts spanning three decades, investigators have examined the use of outerdirectedness by individuals of average intellect and by those with mental retardation. Mentally retarded individuals have consistently been found to be more outerdirected on various measures. Only two studies failed to find a significant difference between these groups on at least one measure of outerdirectedness (Leahy, Balla, & Zigler, 1982; Maguire, 1976). In no studies have individuals of average intellect scored higher on outerdirectedness. Differences across groups have been found on virtually every measure of outerdirectedness in use.

Differences between mentally retarded and nonretarded children in outerdirectedness cannot be attributed to differences in problem-solving abilities because subjects are typically matched on MA. Neither may these differences be attributed to the workings of the brain, its chemistry, or its physiology. Many studies do not show differences between mentally retarded and nonretarded children on outerdirectedness measures when an external cue is not available (e.g., Achenbach & Zigler, 1968; Sanders, Zigler, & Butterfield, 1968). The children also do not differ after experimentally constructed success experiences (Bybee & Zigler, 1992). The ease with which group differences may be eliminated suggests that the high levels of outerdirectedness shown by mentally retarded individuals are not a result of some permanent, irreversible, intellectual and/or physical deficit. Nor does the answer seem to lie in some unchangeable cognitive limitation such as a deficit in creative reasoning. Outerdirectedness and lack of creativity are only moderately related among mentally retarded individuals (Zigler et al., Chapter 9). Further, evidence that differences in outerdirectedness across groups may not be attributed to distractibility is provided by Cohen and Heller (1975).

Effects of Etiology. Within mentally retarded samples, organically retarded individuals (whose mental retardation may be attributed to some biological or physiological factor) have been distinguished from familial retarded individuals (who have no known organic impairment, who typically come from the lower SES, and who have family members who are similarly retarded). We previously offered two explanations for differences across groups (see Bybee & Zigler, 1998): (a) organically retarded children objectively fail more because they are more likely to be presented with situations geared toward their high-achieving family members, and (b) organically retarded children, who more typically live in middle-class homes surrounded by educated parents and intellectually achieving siblings, are more likely to perceive themselves as less competent than are familial retarded children, who have parents and siblings whose intellectual attainments are also low.

In this chapter, we offer a third explanation. When mental retardation is due to organic factors (e.g., prenatal exposure to toxins, perinatal insults such as anoxia, or a chromosomal abnormality), physical and motor deficiencies are often present as well. Cerebral palsy would be among the most extreme examples of this. Bybee, Quiles, and Zigler (1998) found that deficiencies in gross and fine motor skills were strongly correlated with outerdirectedness on the sticker game. Organically and familial retarded individuals may both be subject to a history of failure in problem-solving, but organically retarded individuals alone would be expected to have a greater history of failure in tasks requiring motor skills and coordination, a history that may serve to increase reliance on external cues. In accordance with predictions, organically retarded children have consistently been found to be more outerdirected than familial retarded children (Balla, Styfco, & Zigler, 1971; Sanders, Zigler, & Butterfield, 1968; Yando, Seitz, & Zigler, 1989; Yando & Zigler, 1971).

Familial retarded individuals, then, more closely resemble nonretarded individuals in their reliance on external cues. Studies comparing familial retarded students with nonretarded students have reported no differences across groups in outerdirectedness (Balla, Styfco, & Zigler, 1971; Maguire, 1976; Sanders, Zigler, & Butterfield, 1968). Turner (1998) found that familial retarded and nonretarded low SES children did not differ on outer-directedness. In summary, the few exceptions to the rule that mentally retarded children are more outerdirected than nonretarded children involve familial retarded children.

Effects of Institutionalization

The influences of abuse, socioeconomic class, mental retardation and its etiology, and development all must be understood to interpret the effects of institutionalization.

Researchers studying children of average intellect who have been institutionalized report that many had an early life filled with abuse and maltreatment and had been removed from their homes for this reason (Yando & Zigler, 1971; Zigler & Yando, 1972). The relatively high outerdirectedness shown by nonretarded children who have been institutionalized likely has to do with their preinstitutional life. Early experiences of maltreatment may lead to feelings of suspiciousness and wariness toward adults, and in turn to a reluctance to employ cues offered by them (Yando & Zigler, 1971). Among children of average intellect, institutionalized children are less outerdirected than noninstitutionalized children (Yando & Zigler, 1971; Zigler & Yando, 1972).

The effects of institutionalization for mentally retarded individuals are dependent on the etiology of the mental retardation. Among organically retarded children, institutionalized children are less outerdirected than non-institutionalized children (Yando & Zigler, 1971). Organically retarded children are more likely than familial retarded children to come from higher socioeconomic classes and more highly educated families. These children may be particularly vulnerable to feelings of failure and inadequacy in their home environment and to rely on cues from others as guides to action. For organically retarded children who live outside institutions, the world may be filled with experiences that trigger feelings of inadequacy and failure. Peers and siblings are likely to be more competent than themselves. Parental and societal expectations may be more geared to mentally retarded children's CA than their MA, and opportunities for imitating more competent models may be abundant. Children with forms of organic retardation who are in institutions would be spared from unfavorable comparisons with siblings and failure to meet high parental expectations. Indeed, they may compare themselves with other mentally retarded residents, and may have no trouble meeting the limited expectations of paid caregivers. Organically retarded children living in "real-life" settings may experience more objective failure and hence be more outerdirected than their counterparts living a relatively protected and isolated life in institutions.

Among the familial retarded group, institutionalized children are more outerdirected than noninstitutionalized children (Lustman & Zigler, 1982; Zigler & Yando, 1972). Familial retarded children generally have families who are similar to them in intellectual ability, leaving them less subject to repeated failures in "measuring up" at home. As reviewed earlier, familial versus organic retarded children are low on outerdirectedness in noninstitutional samples. There is plenty of room, then, for institutionalization to result in upward movement in outerdirectedness scores. We consider, next, characteristics of the institution that apparently serve over time to foment and encourage outerdirectedness among familial retarded children.

Institutionalized children become progressively more outerdirected relative to noninstitutionalized children with development (as indexed by mental age, Achenbach & Zigler, 1968; Bybee, Ennis, & Zigler, 1989; Zigler & Yando, 1972). Likewise, Bybee, Ennis, and Zigler (1989) found that among mentally retarded individuals, institutionalized children compared with noninstitutionalized children were progressively more outerdirected at higher CA and IQ levels.

It is not clear whether outerdirectedness increases with development among institutionalized individuals in an absolute sense. Among mentally retarded children who are institutionalized, one group of investigators reported a decline (on the sticker game, Balla, Butterfield, & Zigler, 1974). In contrast, Bybee, Ennis, and Zigler (1989) reported no change on this measure with development. For the discrimination task, studies found no age-related changes (Achenbach & Zigler, 1968; Massari & Mansfield, 1973) or increases (Bybee, Ennis, & Zigler, 1989).

The observed comparative increases in outerdirectedness may result from the infantalizing quality of life in an institution, a quality that leads residents to forgo their autonomy and the dangers associated with independent problem-solving (Lustman & Zigler, 1982). According to Bybee, Ennis, & Zigler (1989), successful adaptation to the social milieu of an institution may require that residents be highly sensitive to directions or subtle cues provided by their adult caregivers. In addition, there may be a higher premium placed on expediency than on independent mastery in the institutional environment compared with the home.

Further, institutionalized children may have fewer and more superficial social interactions with adults than do children who live with their parents. Imitation may provide one of the few methods available to these children for establishing a social rapport with an adult. Compared with noninstitutionalized children, those who live in institutions may place a higher value on the social rewards of outerdirectedness, and they may utilize outer-directed approaches more often as a result. Evidence to support this interpretation comes from findings that institutionalized mentally retarded children are more responsive to adult social reinforcement than to peer social reinforcement, in contrast to their noninstitutionalized counterparts who display the reverse pattern (Harter & Zigler, 1968). These studies provide further empirical support for the hypothesis that a history of social deprivation and interpersonal neglect increases outerdirectedness.

As mentioned earlier in this section, MA or IQ of the child correlates with institutionalization status. Institutionalized children who are brighter or at higher MA levels may be better able to discern caregiver cues and utilize them, and to recognize the social benefits of imitation. Attempts to tease apart the effects of MA, IQ, and CA suggest that the three variables may have similar effects.

High- and low-quality institutions do not differ in the extent to which they promote or stifle independent problem-solving. A study by Balla, Butterfield, and Zigler (1974) examined whether objective features of four institutions, such as size and cost, were related to reliance on outerdirected approaches by mentally retarded children. Quality of the institution was unrelated to outerdirectedness.

Summary of Effects of Institutionalization. In sum, institutionalized retarded children are less outerdirected than noninstitutionalized children or children of average intellect (Yando & Zigler, 1971; Zigler & Yando, 1972) and those with organic forms of mental retardation (Yando & Zigler, 1971), whereas the reverse is true for familial retarded children (Lustman & Zigler, 1982; Zigler & Yando, 1972). And institutionalized children become progressively more outerdirected relative to noninstitutionalized children with development (Achenbach & Zigler, 1968; Bybee, Ennis, & Zigler, 1989; Zigler & Yando, 1972).

Males and Females Do Not Differ on Measures of Outerdirectedness

Studies consistently report no gender differences in experimental measures of outerdirectedness (Achenbach & Zigler, 1968; Anderson & Willis, 1976; Balla et al., 1974; Balla et al., 1971; Bybee, Ennis, & Zigler, 1989; Bybee, Quiles, & Zigler, 1998; Bybee & Zigler, 1992; Gordon & MacLean, 1977; Lustman & Zigler, 1987; Massari & Mansfield, 1973; Ruble &

Nakamura, 1972, 1973; Turnure & Zigler, 1964; Yando, Seitz, & Zigler, 1989; Zigler & Yando, 1972). Moreover, no gender differences in teacher reports of outerdirectedness have been found (Bybee, Quiles, & Zigler, 1998; Sussman, 1998; Turner, 1998; Zigler et al., Chapter 9). Nottelmann and Hill (1977) reported that compared with females, males directed more comments and questions to the experimenter while completing a task, though no gender differences were found on six measures of outerdirectedness. Neither were gender differences found in studies of both mentally retarded and nonretarded children and of institutionalized as well as noninstitutionalized children. The lack of gender differences in over a dozen studies of outerdirectedness is impressive and is consistent with reviews that report no gender differences in imitation when the modeled behavior is not sex-typed (Maccoby & Jacklin, 1975).

Researchers have reported no same-sex or cross-sex effects of experimenter on outerdirectedness (Balla, Styfco, & Zigler, 1971; Bybee & Zigler, 1992). Turnure, Larson, and Thurlow (1976) reported no sex of child, sex of experimenter, or interaction effects for glancing, their measure of outerdirectedness. Likewise, Turnure (1973) found no gender differences in glancing (outerdirectedness).

MacMillan and Wright (1974) found no main effect of sex on outerdirectedness, but they did report that girls were more outerdirected than males in a success condition, and that males were more outerdirected than females in a failure condition. Other studies reported that after success versus failure experiences, males and females showed similar levels of outerdirectedness (Achenbach & Zigler, 1968; Bybee & Zigler, 1992). The majority of studies, however, did not assess gender differences (e.g., Cohen & Heller, 1975; Drotar, 1972; Harnick, 1978; Kuczynski, Zahn-Waxler, & Radke-Yarrow, 1987; Kuhn, 1972; Leahy, Balla, & Zigler, 1982; Maguire, 1976; Sanders, Zigler, & Butterfield, 1968; Silverstein et al., 1979; Strichart, 1974; Turnure, 1970).

Individual Differences in Field Dependence

On a series of experimental tasks administered to mentally retarded and nonretarded children, field-dependent subjects glanced more compared with field-independent subjects, and they had greater difficulty giving up formerly relevant cues (Massari & Mansfield, 1973). Ruble and Nakamura (1972) reported that field-dependent subjects compared with field-independent subjects of average intellect glanced more and had worse performance on the experimental tasks.

Effects of Characteristics of the External Cue on Outerdirectedness

Usefulness of the External Cue

Children of average intellect utilize relevant external cues more often than irrelevant or misleading ones. Yando, Seitz, and Zigler (1978) reported that older age groups (7-, 10-, and 13-year-olds) utilized relevant cues more than irrelevant cues, though for very young children (4-year-olds), differences in reliance on relevant and irrelevant cues were not significant. In a similar vein, Bybee and Zigler (1992) found that nonretarded children increased their use of relevant cues on hard compared to easy tasks, but did not increase their reliance on incidental cues on hard problems.

Mentally retarded children do not always utilize external cues in a strategic manner (Bybee & Zigler, 1992). Whereas Yando, Seitz, and Zigler (1989) reported that these children use relevant cues more than irrelevant cues, Turnure (1973) found them to spend the same amount of time glancing at both types of cues. In addition, misleading cues hurt the performance of mentally retarded children relative to nonretarded children more. Mentally retarded children had worse task performance than children of average intellect when external cues were irrelevant or misleading (Drotar, 1972; Sanders, Zigler, & Butterfield, 1968; Turnure & Zigler, 1964). When external cues were helpful, one study (Turnure & Zigler, 1964) found mentally retarded children to perform better than children of average intellect, whereas other studies (Drotar, 1972; Sanders, Zigler, & Butterfield, 1968) indicated they did not.

Nonhuman Cues Compared with Human Cues

In a number of studies, utilization of cues provided by a human model has been compared with utilization of cues provided by a machine (Yando & Zigler, 1971; Zigler & Yando, 1972), a light (Sanders, Zigler, & Butterfield, 1968; Yando & Zigler, 1971), or markers of a certain color or size (Balla, Styfco, & Zigler, 1971). Three studies, using a variety of experimental tasks and prompts, reported that the nonhuman model produces more outerdirectedness than the human model, a finding that apparently holds true for both nonretarded children (Balla, Styfco, & Zigler, 1971; Yando & Zigler, 1971; Zigler & Yando, 1972) and mentally retarded children (Balla, Styfco, & Zigler, 1971; Yando & Zigler, 1971). One study failed to find differences between a human and a nonhuman model (Sanders, Zigler, & Butterfield, 1968), though the authors noted that their operationalization of the human cue – an outline of a human finger on a card – may not have been an optimal one.

Nonhuman cues may possess two characteristics, novelty and credibility, that serve to increase outerdirectedness (Zigler & Yando, 1972). Lights, physical markers, and machines that provide cues to problem-solving may draw the child's attention, increasing the opportunity for imitation. In addition, children may believe that machines are less fallible than humans, and are thus a more trustworthy guide to action. Conversely, some children may actively reject the human cues. For children who have been abused or who are distrustful of adults or their peers for other reasons, the preference for machine cues versus human cues may be heightened (Zigler & Yando, 1972). Bybee, LeDuc, and Zigler (1993) suggested that mentally retarded children who have been rejected by their peers, or subjects who have been previously misled by the experimenter, may be especially wary of cues offered by other people.

Novel and/or Salient Cues

Simple exposure to a set of cues provides no assurance that the observer will closely attend to or utilize them (Bandura, 1977). Properties of the stimuli, such as intensity, vividness, novelty, complexity, and movement (Bandura, 1977; Drotar, 1972), may affect attention and hence outerdirectedness. In addition, for familiar tasks compared with novel tasks, cues, and situations, children may already have well-rehearsed problem-solving strategies that decrease the need for reliance on external cues. Evidence that children use human cues less often than those provided by a machine has been interpreted as reflecting the greater tendency of children to rely on novel or attention-drawing cues (Yando & Zigler, 1971, Zigler & Yando, 1972). Similarly, findings that children of average intelligence are more outerdirected on ambiguous tasks than on simple tasks (Bybee & Zigler, 1992) fit well with hypotheses that novelty increases outerdirectedness.

Effects of Characteristics of the Model on Outerdirectedness

Competence of Models

Competent models are imitated more than incompetent models. Strichart (1974) reported that mentally retarded children imitate peers who competently perform a task more than peers who perform the task incompetently. Likewise, Turnure, Larson, and Thurlow (1976) found that mentally retarded children glance more at a model who is providing relevant cues than at a model who is providing irrelevant cues. In a third study, also with mentally retarded children as subjects, Becker and Glidden (1979) reported more on-task and off-task imitation of both adults and peers who were higher in competence. In all cases, children appeared to use outerdirected approaches in a way that would maximize their problem-solving success.

Nurturing Models

Strichart (1974) reported that employing a nurturant model has no effect on observed levels of imitation. In this study, nonretarded peers identified in pretesting as liked by the mentally retarded target child were used as nurturant models, and those identified as disliked were used as nonnurturant models. Popularity and nurturance may not be interchangeable constructs, and a different operationalization of nurturance may have produced different findings.

Dominant Models

Teacher ratings and observations during play time were used to rate 4- and 5-year-olds (who were all of average intellect) on dominance (Anderson & Willis, 1976). According to observer ratings, children glanced more often at dominant classmates over the course of ten daily free-play periods.

Peer Models Compared with Adult Models

Results from Lustman and Zigler (1982) indicate more imitation of peers than adults on the preference-for-faces task for both mentally retarded and nonretarded children. There were no model effects for the sticker game. In a sample of fifth graders of average intellect, Brannigan and Duchinowski (1976) found no differences for adult models versus peer models. Becker and Glidden (1979) reported that among mentally retarded children, peers were imitated more than adults for off-task behaviors, but there were no differences between adults versus peers for on-task cues.

Effects of Task Characteristics on Outerdirectedness

Difficulty of the Task

If children use outerdirected approaches in a manner that optimizes their problem-solving success, we would expect children to utilize external cues more on tasks that are difficult for them to complete independently than on tasks that are within their problem-solving abilities. Studies by Bybee and Zigler (1992), Harnick (1978), Kuhn (1972), and Ruble and Nakamura (1973) all concluded that children of average intellect are more outer-directed on difficult tasks than on easy ones. When the difficulty of the task is very great compared with the child's MA level, however, external cues may be of little use as the child may lack the skills necessary to conceptualize task requirements and to identify, remember, and employ external cues in problem solution (Yando, Seitz, & Zigler, 1989). Consistent with this hypothesis, Kuhn (1972) reported that children were less outerdirected on tasks two levels above their current level of problem-solving skills than on tasks at or slightly above their abilities. The only study to examine the effects of task difficulty among mentally retarded children (Bybee & Zigler, 1992) found no relation between difficulty and outerdirectedness for this group.

Perceived Difficulty of the Task

A number of studies have examined the effect of experimental variations in children's expectancy of difficulty with the problem (Ruble & Nakamura, 1973; Yando et al., 1978, 1989; Zigler & Yando, 1972). The experimenter told the children that (a) they were going to be completing an easy task or playing a game, or (b) they were going to be completing a very difficult task, or one with right and wrong answers, on which they would be evaluated. In actuality, the same task was employed for both conditions. Among mentally retarded children, perceived difficulty of the task was unrelated to outerdirectedness (Yando, Seitz, & Zigler, 1989). All three studies that used this task manipulation among children who were not mentally retarded or institutionalized found that children were more outerdirected when told the task was going to be difficult than when told the task would be easy (Ruble & Nakamura, 1973; Yando, Seitz, & Zigler, 1978; Zigler & Yando, 1972).

This effect may be most pronounced among older children. Yando, Seitz, and Zigler (1978) found an increased reliance on external cues in the problem condition compared with the no-problem condition for their older age groups (7-, 10-, and 13-year-olds), though not for the youngest age group (4-year-olds). Similarly, among noninstitutionalized children examined in a study by Zigler and Yando (1972), older children (mean MA = 11.61) were more outerdirected in the problem condition than in the no-problem condition, whereas younger children (mean MA = 7.08) showed a relatively small difference across conditions.

Perceived Personal Competence

In a study by Strichart (1974), a hidden magnet was used to assure that the subject either performed well or poorly at an experimental task. Task performance thus had no relation to actual competence. Subjects, both mentally retarded and not retarded, were more outerdirected when they were led to believe they were incompetent at the task than when they thought they were competent.

Success or Failure on Preceding Task

Central to the theoretical formulation of outerdirectedness is the hypothesis that a history of failure leads to greater outerdirectedness. Several attempts have been made to assess whether experimental manipulations of success or failure affect outerdirectedness on subsequent tasks. Two of these studies appear to have had difficulty with floor effects (Achenbach & Zigler, 1968; Maguire, 1976). These studies reported no effects of condition (success vs. failure), no effects of type of subject (mentally retarded vs. nonretarded), and no appreciable levels of outerdirectedness for any group or condition.

The remaining studies all provide evidence that outerdirectedness is greater following failure than following success experiences (Bybee & Zigler, 1992; MacMillan & Wright, 1974; Turnure & Zigler, 1964), though the effects vary according to the sample. Bybee and Zigler (1992) found that compared with children of average intellect, mentally retarded children are apparently more affected by the task manipulation. Achenbach and Zigler (1968) reported that the condition by type of subject (mentally retarded vs. nonretarded) interaction was not significant, whereas Turnure and Zigler (1964) reported a marginal interaction whose source was not discussed. Success/failure manipulations have been found to affect similar subsequent tasks, whereas for dissimilar subsequent tasks, changes in outerdirectedness as a result of the experimental manipulation were not as pronounced (Bybee & Zigler, 1992) or were not significant (MacMillan & Wright, 1974).

Performance Anxiety and Time Constraints

Nottelmann and Hill (1977) suggested that anxiety may distract children and prevent them from concentrating fully on the problem at hand. Compared with low-anxious children, these authors maintained that anxious children may pay less attention to the problem itself and spend more time glancing at models, at external cues, and elsewhere around the room. In a sample of elementary school children of average intellect, Nottelmann and Hill confirmed that high-anxious children engage in more off-task glancing than do children with lower anxiety levels.

In addition, situational factors that increase anxiety also seem to increase outerdirectedness. Reports (reviewed in an earlier section) that outerdirectedness increases among children of average intellect when a task is described as difficult are consistent with the position that anxiety increases outerdirectedness. Tight time constraints may not only increase anxiety, but may also restrict the time available for independent problem-solving. Studies are needed to examine the role of time limitations.

Outerdirectedness and Personal Competence

IQ

Among students who are not mentally retarded, a lower IQ is correlated with greater outerdirectedness on experimental (Leahy, Balla, & Zigler, 1982) and teacher (Sussman, 1998) measures. Bybee, Ennis, and Zigler (1990) found no relation between IQ and outerdirectedness for noninstitutionalized mentally retarded individuals. Among institutionalized mentally retarded individuals, they found that a higher IQ was associated with greater outerdirectedness as assessed by both the sticker game and the discrimination task.

Academic Achievement

Among intellectually average individuals, those with lower academic achievement have been found to be more outerdirected according to teacher reports (Ruble & Nakamura, 1973; Sussman, 1998). Poor academic performance was also related to greater outerdirectedness among both mentally retarded and nonretarded students in a study by Bybee, Quiles, and Zigler (1998), although the effect did not reach significance for all indices of outerdirectedness.

Expectancy of Success

Among nonretarded students, teacher reports of expectancy of success were inversely correlated with outerdirectedness (Ruble & Nakamura,

1973; Sussman, 1998). Among mentally retarded individuals, those with low expectancies of success scored higher on teacher reports but not on experimental measures of outerdirectedness (Zigler et al., Chapter 9).

Effectance Motivation

Among children of average intellect, Ruble and Nakamura (1973) found that compared with children who are not outerdirected, outerdirected children want to do fewer things by themselves, engage in more help-seeking behavior, and are less persistent. These investigators also reported that outerdirected children express less pride after completing an experimental task, even though there was no actual performance difference between the two groups. Among mentally retarded individuals, effectance motivation was inversely correlated with outerdirectedness using a variety of experimental tasks and teacher reports (Zigler et al., Chapter 9).

Self-Esteem

Greater outerdirectedness correlated with low self-esteem and a low ideal self-image in a sample of nonretarded and mentally retarded individuals (Leahy, Balla, & Zigler, 1982; correlations were reported for the total sample, with no report of interactions with mental retardation status). Consistent with these findings, Ruble and Nakamura (1973) found that among nonretarded children, those who were outerdirected had lower self-confidence than those who were not outerdirected. Sussman (1988) found no correlation between self-esteem in the academic competence domain and outerdirectedness among children of average intellect.

Shyness and Anxiety

Among nonretarded children, greater outerdirectedness has been related to greater shy-anxious behavior, lack of assertive social skills, and greater trait-anxiety (Bybee, Quiles, & Zigler, 1998; Nottelmann & Hill, 1977). Outerdirectedness was not related to shyness in a study by Ruble and Nakamura (1973). Bybee, Quiles, and Zigler (1998) found evidence that patterns for younger (compared with older) children were weaker or reversed. Among mentally retarded students, they found that outerdirectedness was sporadically correlated with lack of assertive social skills and was unrelated to shy-anxious behavior.

Communication, Daily Living, and Social Skills

Among nonretarded children, greater outerdirectedness appears to be correlated with better communication, daily living, and social skills among younger children, but is inversely correlated with these skills among older children. Correlations, however, were weak to moderate in strength and generally did not reach significance. Among mentally retarded individuals, greater outerdirectedness was strongly correlated with worse communication, daily living, and social skills (Bybee, Quiles, & Zigler, 1998). Maladaptive correlations were more pronounced and consistently significant among the older students.

The longer the history of failure, the more damaging its effects should become. Findings that outerdirectedness shows stronger and more numerous correlations among older children are certainly consistent with this interpretation. An alternate explanation is that imitation is more beneficial for younger children because they have a more limited arsenal of problem-solving skills. As independent problem-solving skills improve and diversify with age, imitation would be expected to compete with and prevent the use of more efficacious methods.

Coping

In a study of fourth graders of average intellect, Sussman (1998) examined the relationship of outerdirectedness to four types of coping: positive coping (e.g., attempting to solve the perceived cause of the problem), denial, anxiety amplification/self-blame, and projection (e.g., blaming others). No correlations reached significance. The age range employed in the study is relevant in interpreting the results. As reported in the following section, Bybee, Quiles, and Zigler (1998) found outerdirectedness related to better coping for younger children, $r = .43$, but worse coping for older children, $r = -.34$. Given the developmental changes in directionality of relationships, studies examining an age range near the crossover point may not find relationships. Bybee et al., did find outerdirectedness correlates with worse coping among mentally retarded children.

Maladaptive Behavior

For older nonretarded students, greater outerdirectedness as assessed by teachers is very strongly related to more maladaptive behavior (e.g., thumb-sucking, sexual problems) as assessed by the Vineland, and greater acting-out, *rs* = .69 and .60, respectively (Bybee, Quiles, & Zigler, 1998). The results are remarkable not only for their strength, but for providing one of the rare cases where outerdirectedness exhibits a maladaptive relationship among children of average intellect. Perhaps adolescents who imitate the misbehavior of their peers are more likely to get into trouble. No clear effects emerged for younger or mentally retarded participants.

Motor Skills

Among mentally retarded individuals, worse gross and fine motor skills were strongly related to use of both task-relevant and incidental cues on the sticker game (Bybee, Quiles, & Zigler, 1998). Correlations were not significant for nonretarded students. The sticker game requires motor coordination to manipulate small objects. The findings suggest that outerdirectedness may result not only from a history of failure in problem-solving, but from a history of failure in performing motor tasks. Findings that up to one-quarter of the variance in the sticker game may be explained by poor motor dexterity are remarkably strong.

The relationship of motor skills to indices of outerdirectedness that do not involve manual dexterity are a bit more complicated. According to teacher reports, among both mentally retarded and nonretarded individuals with poor motor skills younger students utilize external cues less, whereas older students utilize external cues more. Perhaps young, poorly coordinated individuals are not skilled enough to imitate well or at all. With a greater history of failure at motor tasks, older poorly coordinated students may feel more of a need to imitate and may develop over time the minimal skills necessary to be able to copy.

Is Outerdirectedness Harmful or Beneficial?

1. *Mentally retarded individuals rely more heavily on all types of external cues, misleading as well as task-relevant.* Mentally retarded individuals are more outerdirected than nonretarded individuals when cues are helpful or neutral. Most studies report that retarded children utilize more helpful and incidental cues on the sticker game (Achenbach & Zigler, 1968; Bybee, LeDuc, & Zigler, 1993 – relevant cues only; Bybee & Zigler, 1992; Lustman & Zigler, 1982; MacMillan & Cauffiel, 1977; Turnure & Zigler, 1964; Yando & Zigler, 1971) and glance more while solving a puzzle (Cohen & Heller, 1975; Drotar, 1972; Turnure & Zigler, 1964). (Several studies report no differences across groups: on the sticker game, according to Leahy,

Balla, & Zigler, 1982, and Maguire, 1976; on glancing, according to Mac-Millan & Cauffiel, 1977.) If the mentally retarded individual's heightened reliance on external cues were only evident when cues were helpful, this heightened proclivity might be interpreted as a helpful one. Findings indicate, however, that mentally retarded individuals are also more likely to employ misleading cues (on the discrimination task, from Balla, Styfco, & Zigler, 1971; Bybee & Zigler, 1992; Sanders, Zigler, & Butterfield, 1968; Yando & Zigler, 1971; but no group differences were found for the discrimination task by Bybee, LeDuc, & Zigler, 1993).

2. *Outerdirectedness is used indiscriminately by mentally retarded individuals, but in a strategic manner by nonretarded individuals.* Nonretarded individuals use external cues in a very strategic, situation-specific, and circumscribed manner. Less than 5 percent of nonretarded children compared with 25 percent of mentally retarded children displayed outerdirectedness on dissimilar tasks (Bybee & Zigler, 1992). Dissimilar tasks or types of cues were not generally intercorrelated for nonretarded individuals. In contrast, different indices were intercorrelated for mentally retarded individuals (Bybee, LeDuc, & Zigler, 1993; Bybee & Zigler, 1992; Gordon & MacLean, 1977; Lustman & Zigler, 1982; Strichart, 1974). Details of these studies are provided next.

Intercorrelations Between Similar and Dissimilar Measures for Mentally Retarded and Nonretarded Children

Silverstein et al. (1979) reported that for institutionalized mentally retarded children, similar nonverbal imitation measures are highly intercorrelated, (mean $r = .94$), as are similar vocal (mean $r = .94$) and similar verbal (mean $r = .89$) measures. Bybee and Zigler (1992) reported that similar types of cues (task-relevant to task-relevant, incidental to incidental, and misleading to misleading) are correlated across task-difficulty conditions for mentally retarded children (median $r = .74$) and, to a lesser extent, for children of average intellect (median $r = .37$). Imitation scores on the sticker game correlate across conditions that vary by type of model (peer versus adult, $r = .72$, $p < .001$) as do imitation scores on the preference for faces task, $r = .72$, $p < .001$ (Lustman & Zigler, 1982). Lustman and Zigler (1982) reported that these correlations are similar for mentally retarded children, both institutionalized and noninstitutionalized, and children of average intelligence. Ruble and Nakamura (1973) found a correlation of .60 between glancing scores on similar object assembly tasks administered a month apart.

For dissimilar tasks or types of cues, the results are much less consistent. For children of average intellect, two studies indicated no correlations between dissimilar tasks or types of cues (Bybee & Zigler, 1992; Lustman & Zigler, 1982). For mentally retarded children, three studies reported no correlations between dissimilar imitation scores, while three studies reported significant correlations between dissimilar scores. Of those reporting no correlations, studies found that (a) imitation scores on the sticker game were unrelated to scores on the preference-for-faces task (Lustman & Zigler, 1982) or on a measure of glancing (Gordon & MacLean, 1977); and (b) imitation of relevant cues on one task was unrelated to imitation of irrelevant cues on a second (Strichart, 1974). In contrast, two studies reported significant correlations between the sticker game and discrimination task (Achenbach & Zigler, 1968, Experiment III; Bybee & Zigler, 1992). A final significant positive relation (r = .30 between on-task and off-task imitation scores derived from performance on a single task) was reported by Becker and Glidden (1979).

The large majority of past studies have either not reported correlations between measures, have used only one measure of outerdirectedness, or have employed an across-subjects design so that correlations could not be calculated. Of the studies that did provide correlations, all reported that similar measures of outerdirectedness are correlated with one another (Bybee, LeDuc, & Zigler, 1993; Bybee & Zigler, 1992; Lustman & Zigler, 1982; Silverstein et al., 1979). These studies provide support for the construct validity of similar measures of outerdirectedness and suggest that intercorrelations may be greater for mentally retarded individuals compared with nonretarded individuals.

The best evidence to date suggests that children of average intellect use outerdirectedness in a strategic, circumscribed manner. They increase their reliance on external cues for difficult versus easy tasks (Bybee & Zigler, 1992) and when they are told that the task will be difficult rather than easy (Ruble & Nakamura, 1973; Yando, Seitz, & Zigler, 1978; Zigler & Yando, 1972). Moreover, nonretarded children are selective in their use of external cues, increasing their reliance on task-relevant but not incidental cues on ambiguous versus easy tasks (Bybee & Zigler, 1992). Indeed, many of these children regularly avoid utilizing external cues, preferring instead to solve problems independently, and rely on outerdirected approaches only as a last resort. These children are said to be innerdirected.

For many children with mental retardation, outerdirectedness appears to be a relatively inflexible problem-solving style unaffected by type of cue or difficulty of the task. Mentally retarded children do not increase their reliance on external cues for ambiguous versus easy tasks (Bybee & Zigler, 1992), and they do not become more outerdirected when they are told the task will be difficult rather than easy (Yando, Seitz, & Zigler, 1989).

What does seem to affect outerdirectedness among mentally retarded children is a feeling of personal inadequacy. When mentally retarded children are given a difficult versus easy task, they are more outerdirected on a subsequent task (Bybee & Zigler, 1992; MacMillan & Wright, 1974; Turnure & Zigler, 1964). They are also more outerdirected when they perceive themselves to be less versus more personally competent (this from a study where false feedback on a preceding task was given, Strichart, 1974). Finally, mentally retarded children are more outerdirected in the presence of competent versus incompetent models (Strichart, 1974). Thus, the greater the feelings of personal incompetence, the greater the outerdirectedness. Even here, however, outerdirectedness may not necessarily increase problem-solving success, as changes in outerdirectedness are more calibrated to the difficulty of the preceding task than of the problem at hand (Bybee & Zigler, 1992).

3. *Outerdirectedness interferes with successful task completion for mentally retarded individuals.* Bybee and Zigler (1992) found that those mentally retarded children who are outerdirected are less successful in problem solving than those who are innerdirected. Only 25 percent of the outerdirected sample compared with 79 percent of the innerdirected sample correctly solved both experimental tasks. Differences in the problem-solving success of inner- versus outerdirected nonretarded children did not reach significance.

When presented with misleading external cues, mentally retarded children have consistently shown poorer task performance than nonretarded children (Drotar, 1972; Sanders, Zigler, & Butterfield, 1968; Turnure & Zigler, 1964), even though there were no differences (Drotar, 1972; Turnure & Zigler, 1964) or much less pronounced differences (Sanders, Zigler, & Butterfield, 1968) between the groups in the absence of external cues. Task-relevant external cues helped mentally retarded children more than nonretarded children. Turnure and Zigler (1964) found that the performance of mentally retarded children relative to nonretarded children was enhanced when helpful external cues were present, but two subsequent studies (Drotar, 1972; Sanders, Zigler, & Butterfield, 1968) reported no differences across groups when helpful external cues were offered.

4. *Outerdirectedness is related to worse classroom performance and socioemotional competence among mentally retarded individuals.* The vast majority of past studies have examined outerdirectedness in experimental

situations. Researchers have speculated that outside the laboratory, outerdirectedness may provide a covert means of gaining information, permitting observers to obtain cues to action without exposing ignorance or drawing embarrassing and unwanted attention (Bybee & Zigler, 1998). New evidence, reviewed in a previous section, indicates that in "real life," outerdirectedness is related to worse academic, communication, daily living, and socialization skills among mentally retarded individuals. Tellingly, among mentally retarded children, outerdirectedness was never significantly related to a single positive outcome in classroom or in daily life (as assessed by three measures of outerdirectedness, the six indices of classroom behavior on the T-CRS, and the twelve indices of adaptive behavior from the Vineland as reported by Bybee, Quiles, & Zigler, 1998).

5. *With development, nonretarded individuals become less outerdirected, but mentally retarded individuals* increase *their dependence on misleading cues.* With increases in CA, problem-solving abilities generally improve, and external cues become less important to successful task solution. Evidence that reliance on misleading cues decreases most sharply with development, followed by decreases in incidental cues, and finally by a more modest decline (or even increase) in the use of task-relevant cues would be consistent with the interpretation that selectivity increases with development. Findings reviewed in the history-of-failure section (see effects of development) indicate that nonretarded individuals rely less on all types of cues – helpful as well as misleading – with development.

As reviewed in the earlier section, reliance on task-relevant and incidental cues (offered in the sticker game and glancing tasks) declines or shows no change for mentally retarded children. At the same time, their reliance on misleading cues (offered in the discrimination task) *increases* (or shows no change). Older compared with younger mentally retarded individuals may, in fact, be better able to distinguish task-relevant cues from misleading cues and easy tasks from difficult tasks. The result of this greater knowledge, however, may not be less reliance on external cues but more: Older children may be more aware of situations in which they are being threatened or misled, leading them to become less confident of their own solutions to problems and more outerdirected.

6. *With development, nonretarded individuals employ external cues more strategically, but mentally retarded individuals do not.* Beyond changes in overall levels of outerdirectedness, advancements in cognitive abilities may lead to refinements in the use of outerdirectedness. Use of outerdirectedness becomes more selective and strategic with increased MA as children develop the ability to distinguish relevant cues and tasks from

misleading cues and tasks within from those beyond their realm of problem-solving skills.

A study by Hallahan, Kauffman, and Ball (1974) provides clear support for the hypothesis that intellectually average children become increasingly selective in their use of outerdirectedness with development. In a sample of 7-14 year-olds, these researchers reported that with development, children (a) were better able to distinguish relevant from irrelevant cues, and (b) relied more on relevant cues compared with irrelevant cues. Support also comes from Yando, Seitz, and Zigler (1978). In this study, four-year-olds relied equally on task-relevant and task-irrelevant cues, but children from three older age groups relied significantly more on task-relevant than task-irrelevant cues.

7. *With development, outerdirectedness becomes more strongly correlated with maladaptive behaviors in the classroom and in daily life.* Findings (reviewed in the personal competence section) consistently suggest that at higher age levels, outerdirectedness shows generally more maladaptive relationships with indices of socioemotional and academic competence in mentally retarded and nonretarded samples.

8. *Imitation may promote positive social interactions with the model or experimenter, if one is present.* Researchers have suggested that imitation may be used as a method of communication between parent and infant, and may be used by older children to sustain social interactions and strengthen social bonds (Kuczynski, Zahn-Waxler, & Radke-Yarrow, 1987). Consistent with the old adage that imitation is the sincerest form of flattery, others have noted the high prestige value that being imitated by one's peers accords (Strichart & Gottlieb, 1975). In addition, children react favorably to being imitated, although not in conditions where they feel that they are being deliberately imitated as a form of ingratiation (Brannigan & Duchnowski, 1976; Thelen et al., 1983). Similarly, experimenters are more attracted to those children, both mentally retarded and normal, who rely more heavily on task-relevant cues (Bybee, LeDuc, & Zigler, 1993). Experimenters are less attracted to students who utilize misleading cues less.

New Directions

The introduction of a new questionnaire measure (see Chapter 9) to assess outerdirectedness is already having a number of effects on the field. The advent of a questionnaire measure makes it less costly and less time-consuming to examine outerdirectedness. Moreover, the development of the questionnaire measure has implications for the type of research under way. Studies conducted in the past with experimental measures typically focused on the effects of experimental manipulations – of the type of model, the type of cue, setting conditions, and so on – on levels of outerdirectedness. Studies conducted with the teacher report questionnaire have examined socioemotional and academic correlates of outerdirectedness – expectancy of success, academic achievement, maladjustment, etc. Together, these studies breathe new life into outerdirectedness research as they focus attention on issues involving the larger picture outside the laboratory. Researchers using questionnaire measures, for example, have to date examined correlations between history of real-life failures and outerdirectedness. Studies have also examined scholastic and socioemotional correlates of outerdirectedness. Badly needed examinations of the social precursors and social benefits of outerdirectedness are underway. Yet in the press to utilize the teacher measure, it is important not to lose sight of the role the experimental measures may continue to play, particularly in examining social determinants and sequelae of outerdirectedness that have been largely ignored in the past.

One particularly interesting frontier of research opened by the development of a questionnaire measure of outerdirectedness is that it may be used (with slight modification) to assess imitation of actual peers, siblings, parents, and teachers. The experimental measures are limited in that they only assess reliance on cues provided by the experimenter (who is typically a strange adult). Future studies may examine, for example, whether students who utilize cues provided by teachers are better adjusted than students who utilize cues provided by peers. Studies might examine whether utilization of staff members' cues helps institutionalized children adapt to institutional life, interact with their caregivers, or avoid being singled out for disciplinary actions. The questionnaire measure of outerdirectedness will make possible a whole new venue for research.

References

Achenbach, T., & Zigler, E. (1968). Cue-learning and problem-solving strategies in normal and retarded children. *Child Development, 3,* 827–848.

Anderson, F.J., & Willis, F.N. (1976). Glancing at others in preschool children in relation to dominance. *Psychological Record, 26,* 467–472.

Balla, D., Butterfield, E.C., & Zigler, E. (1974). Effects of institutionalization on retarded children: A longitudinal cross-institutional investigation. *American Journal of Mental Deficiency, 78,* 530–549.

Balla, D., Styfco, S.J., & Zigler, E. (1971). Use of the opposition concept and outerdirectedness in intellectually-average, familial retarded, and organically retarded children. *American Journal of Mental Deficiency, 77,* 663–680.

Bandura, A. (1977). *Social learning theory.* Englewood Cliffs, NJ: Prentice Hall.

Baumrind, D. (1971). Current patterns of parental authority. *Developmental Psychology Monographs, 4,* 1–103.

Becker, S., & Glidden, L.M. (1979). Imitation in EMR boys: Model competency and age. *American Journal of Mental Deficiency, 83,* 360–366.

Brannigan, G.G., & Duchnowski, A.J. (1976). Outer-directedness in the decision making of high and low approval motivated children. *Journal of Genetic Psychology, 138,* 85–90.

Bybee, J., Ennis, P., & Zigler, E. (1989). Effects of institutionalization on the self-concept and outerdirectedness of mentally retarded individuals. *Exceptionality, 1,* 215–226.

Bybee, J., LeDuc, D., & Zigler, E. (1998). Social perceptions and outerdirectedness in normal and mentally retarded children. Manuscript in preparation.

Bybee, J., McGrath, K., & Quiles, Z. (1998). Imitation and wariness in abused, neglected, and nonmaltreated children. Manuscript in preparation, Suffolk University.

Bybee, J., Quiles, Z., & Zigler, E. (1998). Imitation in daily living: Costs and benefits among students with and without mental retardation. Manuscript in preparation, Suffolk University.

Bybee, J., & Zigler, E. (1992). Is outerdirectedness employed in a harmful or beneficial manner by normal and mentally retarded children? *American Journal of Mental Retardation, 96,* 512–521.

    (1998). Outerdirectedness in individuals with and without mental retardation: A review. In J. Burack, R. Hodapp, & E. Zigler (eds.), *Handbook of mental retardation and development* (pp. 434–461). New York: Cambridge University Press.

Cohen, M. E., & Heller, T. (1975). Information producing responses in normal and retarded children. *Journal of Experimental Child Psychology, 20,* 296–306.

Drotar, D. (1972). Outerdirectedness and the puzzle performance of nonretarded and retarded children. *American Journal of Mental Deficiency, 77,* 230–236.

Gordon, D. A., & MacLean, W. E. (1977). Developmental analysis of outerdirectedness in institutionalized EMR children. *American Journal of Mental Deficiency, 81,* 508–511.

Greenberg, S. (1979). The effects of differential reinforcement on generalized imitation. *Journal of Experimental Child Psychology, 27,* 233–249.

Gresham, F. (1982). Misguided mainstreaming: The case for social skills training for handicapped children. *Exceptional Children, 48,* 422–433.

Gruen, G., & Zigler, E. (1968). Expectancy of success and the probability learning of middle-class, lower-class, and retarded children. *Journal of Abnormal Psychology, 73,* 343–352.

Hallahan, D.P., Kauffman, J.M., & Ball, D.W. (1974). Developmental trends in recall of central and incidental auditory material. *Journal of Experimental Child Psychology, 17,* 409–421.

Harnick, F.S. (1978). The relationship between ability level and task difficulty in producing imitation in infants. *Child Development, 49,* 209–212.

Harter, S., & Zigler, E. (1968). Effectiveness of adult and peer reinforcement on the performance of institutionalized and noninstitutionalized retardates. *Journal of Abnormal Psychology, 73,* 144–149.

Hunter, F., & Youiss, J. (1982). Changes in functions of three relations during adolescence. *Developmental Psychology, 18,* 806–811.

Kuczynski, L., Zahn-Waxler, C., & Radke-Yarrow, M. (1987). Development and content of imitation in the second and third years of life: A socialization perspective. *Developmental Psychology, 23,* 276–282.

Kuhn, D. (1972). Mechanisms of change in the development of cognitive structures. *Child Development, 43,* 833–844.

LaFrance, M., & Henley, N.M. (1994). On oppressing hypotheses: Or differences in nonverbal sensitivity revisited. In H.L. Radtke & H.J. Stam (eds.), *Power/gender: Social relations in theory and practice* (pp. 287–311). London: Sage.

Leahy, R. L., Balla, D., & Zigler, E. (1982). Role-taking, self-image, and imitativeness of mentally retarded and nonretarded individuals. *American Journal of Mental Deficiency, 86,* 372–379.

Lustman, N., & Zigler, E. (1982). Imitation by institutionalized and noninstitutionalized mentally retarded and nonretarded children. *American Journal of Mental Deficiency, 87,* 252–258.

Maccoby, E. E., & Jacklin, C.N. (1974). *The psychology of sex differences.* Stanford, CA: Stanford University Press.

MacMillan, D. L., & Cauffiel, S. R. (1973). Outerdirectedness as a function of success and failure in educationally handicapped boys. *Journal of Learning Disabilities, 10,* 48–59.

MacMillan, D. L., & Wright, D. L. (1974). Outerdirectedness in children of three ages as a function of experimentally induced success and failure. *Journal of Educational Psychology, 66,* 919–925.

Maguire, M. (1976). Failure effects on outerdirectedness: A failure to replicate. *American Journal of Mental Deficiency, 81,* 256–259.

Marburg, C. C., Houston, B. K., & Holmes, D. S. (1976). Influence of multiple models on the behavior of institutionalized retarded children: Increased generalization to other models and other behaviors. *Journal of Consulting and Clinical Psychology, 44,* 514–519.

Massari, D.J., & Mansfield, R.S. (1973). Field dependence and outer-directedness in the problem-solving of retardates and normal children. *Child Development, 44,* 346–350.

McGrath, K., Quiles, Z., & Bybee, J. (1998). Effects of child abuse versus child neglect on outerdirectedness, attention seeking, and wariness. Manuscript in preparation, Northeastern University.

Nottelmann, E. D., & Hill, K. T. (1977). Test anxiety and off-task behavior in evaluative situations. *Child Development, 48,* 225–231.

Piaget, J. (1962). *Plays, dreams, and imitation in childhood.* New York: Norton.

Ruble, D. N., & Nakamura, C. (1972). Task orientation versus social orientation in young children and their attention to relevant social cues. *Child Development, 43,* 471–480.

——— (1973). Outerdirectedness as a problem solving approach in relation to developmental level and selected task variables. *Child Development, 44,* 519–528.

Sanders, B., Zigler, E., & Butterfield, E. C. (1968). Outer-directedness in the discrimination learning of normal and mentally retarded children. *Journal of Abnormal Psychology, 73,* 368–375.

Silverstein, A. B., Aguilar, B. F., Jacobs, L. J., Levy, J., & Rubenstein, D. M. (1979). Imitative behavior by Down's syndrome persons. *American Journal of Mental Deficiency, 83,* 409–411.

Strichart, S. S. (1974). Effects of competence and nurturance on imitation of nonretarded peers by retarded adolescents. *American Journal of Mental Deficiency, 78,* 665–673.

Strichart, S. S., & Gottlieb, J. (1975). Imitation of retarded children by their nonretarded peers. *American Journal of Mental Deficiency, 79,* 506–512.

Sussman, A. L. (1988). Individual characteristics mediating the link between failure and outerdirectedness. Master's thesis, Yale University.

Sussman, A. L., Bennett-Gates, D., & Zigler, E. (1998). Outerdirectedness and coping strategies: Children's responses to failure. Manuscript in preparation, Yale University.

Thelen, M. H., Miller, D. J., Fehrenbach, P. A., & Frautschi, N. M. (1983). Reactions to being imitated: Effects of perceived motivation. *Merrill-Palmer Quarterly, 29,* 159–167.

Turner, J. D. (1998). Personality and motivational characteristics of middle SES, low SES, and children with mental retardation. Master's thesis, Yale University.

Turnure, J. E. (1970). Reactions to physical and social distracters by moderately retarded institutionalized children. *Journal of Special Education, 4,* 283–294.

——— (1973). Outerdirectedness in EMR boys and girls. *American Journal of Mental Deficiency, 78,* 163–170.

Turnure, J. E., Larsen, S. N., & Thurlow, M. L. (1976). Outerdirectedness in retarded children as a function of sex of the experimenter and sex of subject. *American Journal of Mental Deficiency, 80,* 460–468.

Turnure, J. E., & Zigler, E. (1964). Outer-directedness in the problem-solving of normal and retarded children. *Journal of Abnormal and Social Psychology, 69,* 427–436.

Yando, R., Seitz, V., & Zigler, E. (1978). *Imitation: A developmental perspective.* Hillsdale, NJ: Erlbaum.

(1989). Imitation, recall, and imitativeness in organic and familial retarded children. *Research in Developmental Disabilities, 10,* 383–397.

Yando, R., & Zigler, E. (1971). Outerdirectedness in the problem-solving of institutionalized and noninstitutionalized normal and retarded children. *Developmental Psychology, 4,* 277–288.

Zigler, E., Abelson, W. D., & Seitz, V. (1973). Motivational factors in the performance of economically disadvantaged children on the Peabody Picture Vocabulary Test. *Child Development, 44,* 294–303.

Zigler, E., & Hodapp, R. M. (1986). *Understanding mental retardation.* New York: Cambridge University Press.

Zigler, E., & Kanzer, P. (1962). The effectiveness of two classes of verbal reinforcers on the performance of middle- and lower-class children. *Journal of Personality, 30,* 157–163.

Zigler, E., & Yando, R. (1972). Outerdirectedness and imitative behavior of institutionalized and noninstitutionalized younger and older children. *Child Development, 43,* 413–425.

9   Assessing Personality Traits of Individuals with Mental Retardation

Edward Zigler
Dianne Bennett-Gates
Robert Hodapp

For decades, Zigler has argued that individuals with mental retardation, like those of average or above average intellect, are more than cognitive systems. Nevertheless, the essential feature of mental retardation is cognitive functioning at a level below that found for individuals of average intellect. Despite attempts to include aspects of adaptive functioning into the definition of mental retardation (Luckasson et al., 1992), an emphasis on cognition has dominated the field. This skewed mind-set has given rise to the assumption that the behaviors of individuals with mental retardation are the inexorable product of a faulty cognitive system. For evidence on this point, one need only turn to the review by Zigler and Balla (1982) of the myriad cognitive defect theories that have been advanced over the last half-century.

Despite the lengthy history of attempts to understand the behavior of persons with retardation solely in terms of their cognitive apparatus, mentally retarded individuals remain whole people complete with daily experiences, personal histories, and adaptive efforts that affect their motivational and/or personality structures. These structures are often more important in determining task performance and overall behavior than are cognitive deficiencies. For example, motivational deterrents can help to explain the frequently found MA-deficit phenomenon in which individuals with mental retardation perform at a level beneath that predicted by their intellectual resources (Haywood, 1987). In this chapter, we will briefly review prior research into personality and motivation factors among persons with retardation, and we will describe the development of a new instrument devised to measure aspects of personality and motivation. Finally, we will present research conducted to establish the psychometric properties of this new measure, which has potential for applications in the work of clinicians, educators, and researchers.

206

Research into Motivational Factors

A relatively small number of workers have investigated the role motivational factors play in the behavior of individuals with mental retardation. (See Switzky, 1997, for an excellent review of this body of work, as well as the chapter by Harvey Switzky in this book.) We are among the researchers who have explored personality traits thought to be particularly salient in determining the behavior of individuals with mental retardation.

Five aspects of personality and motivation have been examined in detail: (a) positive-reaction tendency (Chapter 5), or the heightened motivation of individuals with mental retardation to both interact with and be dependent on a supportive adult (Balla et al., 1974; Zigler, 1961; Zigler & Balla, 1972); (b) negative-reaction tendency (Chapter 5), or the initial wariness shown by individuals with mental retardation when interacting with strange adults (Harter & Zigler, 1968; Shallenberger & Zigler, 1961; Zigler, Balla, & Butterfield, 1968); (c) expectancy of success (Chapter 6), defined as the degree to which one expects to succeed or fail when presented with a new task (Cromwell, 1963; MacMillan & Keogh, 1971; MacMillan & Knopf, 1971); (d) outerdirectedness (Chapter 8), which is the tendency of retarded persons to look to others for the solutions of difficult or ambiguous problems (MacMillan & Wright, 1974); and (e) effectance motivation (Chapter 7), or the pleasure derived from tackling and solving difficult problems (White, 1959). Over time, broad findings have emerged from this research: Individuals with mental retardation have been found to have lower levels of expectancy of success and effectance motivation than those of normal intellect and higher levels of the other three traits.

The Need for a Combined Measure

One reason why the relationship between personality-motivational factors and behavioral performance has not been examined more thoroughly has to do with measurement difficulties. To date, there has been no questionnaire that assesses the personality traits common in individuals with mental retardation. Until recently, the Yale group has been obliged to use individual experimental tasks to assess separately each of the motivational factors noted earlier. The time required for this kind of administration, and the problem of order effects, has meant that studies were necessarily limited to the investigation of only one or two of the personality-motivational factors of interest. A further problem with existing experimental measures is that of validity – do they measure what they purport to measure? Although face validity has been demonstrated, it has become clear that existing instruments are not pure measures of the constructs they were designed to operationalize.

The purpose of our research was to develop and analyze the psychometric properties of a single instrument that would give us a better picture of personality functioning in individuals with mental retardation. Accordingly, we conducted three studies to establish the factor structure, reliability, and validity of a measure of personality traits common in individuals with mental retardation – the EZ-Yale Personality Questionnaire (EZPQ). Once the instrument was found to have acceptable psychometric properties, a fourth study used scores from the EZPQ to compare the personality functioning of individuals with and without mental retardation.

Description of the Instrument

Our measure, the EZPQ, is composed of thirty-seven items designed to tap the five personality-motivational constructs that have been studied among individuals with mental retardation. The items were randomly distributed such that questions tapping the same construct did not immediately follow one another. To minimize the potential for response bias, we intermixed items. Thus, items involving the effectance motivation and expectancy of success constructs (which are related to success in school and appropriate adaptation) were mixed with items addressing constructs related to maladaptive behavior and academic difficulties: positive-reaction tendency, negative-reaction tendency, and outerdirectedness. Although most questions were worded so that agreement indicated higher levels of the construct, as an additional precaution against response bias, some of the questions were negatively worded such that disagreement indicated higher levels of the construct.

Teachers familiar with the students' behavior rated each statement using a 1 to 5 scale, with 1 signifying that the item was very much untrue of a given individual, and 5 that the item was very much true. In order to accommodate the age range of the sample, two versions of the instrument – one rating a "child" and the other rating an "individual" – were used.

To score each scale, the responses for negatively worded items were reversed such that 1, for example, became 5. In this way, higher scale scores represent a higher degree of each construct. As there were unequal numbers of items on the scales, mean scale scores were used in the analyses and summed to provide a total score. To allow for the positive or negative valence of the scales, the mean scores for scales measuring constructs that

Table 9.1. *Mean CA, MA, and IQ for study samples*

Sample	N	CA Mean (SD)	MA Mean (SD)	IQ Mean (SD)
Study 1	661	13.1(3.9)	7.8(2.1)	59.6(10.9)
Factor structure	(349 male)			
Studies 2 & 3	60	11.2(4.1)	6.5(2.4)	58.1(12.4)
Reliability and validity	(36 male)			
Study 4				
Comparative analyses				
Nonretarded	114	7.9(3.3)	8.5(2.6)	107.6(11.9)
	(71 male)			
Retarded	114	14.5(3.9)	8.3(2.8)	57.3(11.1)
	(71 male)			

may undermine academic and adaptive functioning (positive-reaction tendency, negative-reaction tendency, and outerdirectedness) were reversed before calculating the total score. Thus, total scores across the five basic constructs can range from 5 to 25, with a higher total score on the EZPQ indicating better functioning; totals including the two additional constructs (creativity/curiosity and obedience) obtained from the factor analysis can range from 7 to 35. Background information about the participants as to gender, age, and IQ were recorded on the cover sheet accompanying the EZPQ. The characteristics of the participants in each of the four studies are presented in Table 9.1.

Factor Structure and Item Analyses of the EZPQ

The purpose of the first study was to determine the item characteristics and factor structure of the EZPQ. In preliminary work, 115 items were generated by a group of four experts in the field of mental retardation to reflect positive-reaction tendency, negative-reaction tendency, expectancy of success, effectance motivation, and outerdirectedness. By consensus, this pool of items was narrowed to a 70-item questionnaire that was completed by the respondents. Using both item and factor analyses, we deleted items that were adjudged to be inconsistent, redundant, or inappropriate. This process left a 37-item measure as the final version of the EZPQ.

Sample. The primary sample for the item and factor analyses of the instrument consisted of 349 male and 312 female students from three Eastern states (New Jersey, Pennsylvania, and Connecticut). They ranged in age from 5.2 to 20.1 years. All had been identified by their schools as mentally retarded and were attending special education classes. The sample was obtained by asking special education teachers in the fifty-three participating schools to complete questionnaires for students in their classes who met the inclusion criteria of retarded intellectual functioning (IQ ranging between 45 and 75), no identified organic etiology, and no secondary diagnoses such as hearing impairment or psychopathology. Although the students in the sample were drawn from a variety of ethnic and social backgrounds, the majority attended schools where 50–60 percent of the students participated in subsidized meal programs.

Statistical Analyses. Several analyses were conducted to eliminate items that were adding "noise" and to refine the EZPQ into a more concise instrument. Items were deleted from the questionnaire if they did not meet established criteria for acceptable psychometric properties, specifically: (a) discrimination index of less than or equal to .30; (b) correlation with scores on the item's scale below .55; (c) correlation with more than one scale equal or greater than .55.

We examined the factor structure of the EZPQ through exploratory factor analytic procedures, following the recommendations of Cattell (1966), Comrey (1988), and DeVellis (1991). DeVellis (1991) argued that hypothesized factors confirmed on their own through this approach offer more reassurance of validity than results from confirmatory procedures in which the analysis attempts to fit an a priori structure. Principal component factor analyses with squared multiple correlations as communality estimates were conducted using a varimax rotation. The number of factors to extract was determined on the basis of examination of scree plots, eigenvalues greater than 1, and factor loadings above .40. Items that failed to load on any one factor equal to or greater than .40, as well as items loading on more than one factor at a level equal to or greater than .35, were eliminated. In all, thirty-three items from the initial version of the EZPQ were deleted to form the final version of the questionnaire.

Findings. The remaining thirty-seven items and their associated scales are shown in Table 9.2 in conjunction with the item analysis results. These results are well within acceptable limits and indicate satisfactory item characteristics in all cases. The mean of the item-to-overall score correlations corrected for redundancy was .45 (range = .33 to .70).

Psychometric properties for the EZPQ are summarized in Table 9.3. To examine whether each scale measured a distinct component of personality-motivational functioning that was not measured by the other scales, we calculated the correlation of scores on each scale with the overall score (Table 9.3). We also calculated the intercorrelations of the scale scores (Table 9.4) and the correlations of each item with each scale (Table 9.5). In all cases, we obtained the greatest item-to-scale correlation coefficients with the scale of which the item is a part.

Interpreting the Findings. The intercorrelations among the scale scores revealed several significant relationships. Individuals who demonstrated either a dependency on adults or a wariness of strangers had less confidence in the success of their efforts and found less satisfaction in task completion. We also found significant negative relationships between outer-directedness and the two factors of creativity/curiosity and expectancy of success. Obedient individuals showed a higher degree of effectance motivation, expectancy of success, positive-reaction tendency, and outer-directedness. Those who tended to look to others for solutions in problem-solving situations were rated by their teachers as being more obedient, less likely to expect success from their efforts, and less likely to be creative or curious. Creativity/curiosity showed a significant positive relationship with both expectancy of success and effectance motivation.

In addition, we discovered that our initial examination of Bartlet's sphericity test of the item response correlation matrix (7583, $p < .0001$) and the Kaiser–Meyer–Olkin measure of sampling adequacy (KMO = .84) supported the undertaking of a factor analysis. A varimax rotation of a principal axis factor analysis revealed a seven-factor solution using conventional criterion. Although we were able to confirm positive-reaction tendency, negative-reaction tendency, and expectancy of success in the factor analyses, some of the items on the outerdirectedness and effectance motivation scales formed two additional, distinct constructs. Some of the items we originally construed to reflect outerdirectedness ultimately loaded onto a separate factor characterized by obedience, while some items on the effectance motivation scale formed a factor indicative of curiosity/creativity. All thirty-seven items, however, loaded only on their "own" factor, with none exceeding a .35 loading on any of the other factors. Overall, the seven-factor solution was able to account for 75.4 percent of the variance (see Table 9.3). The loadings are presented in Table 9.5 in the order in which they were recovered.

Table 9.2. Item analysis results for the EZ-Yale Personality Questionnaire

Item	Scale[a]	Mean	Discrimination	
			SD	Index
1. Child works earnestly, doesn't take it lightly	EM	2.25	1.12	.67
2. Child tends to keep thoughts, feelings or products to him/herself	NR	2.65	1.01	-.15
3. Child accepts imposed limits	OB	3.48	.91	.33
4. Child spends more time alone	NR	3.56	1.32	-.16
5. Child imitates others' work	OD	3.81	1.21	.34
6. Child is confident	ES	2.41	.86	.43
7. Child is too familiar with strangers	PR	3.73	1.23	-.22
8. Child is disobedient, doesn't mind well^R	OB	3.45	.85	.43
9. Child shows curiosity about many things	CC	2.69	.69	.36
10. Child is a follower	OD	3.73	1.03	.38
11. Child tends to withdraw and isolate him/herself when supposed to be in a group	NR	2.39	.97	-.17
12. Child seeks physical contact with others	PR	3.46	1.40	-.26
13. Child does what others say regardless of the consequences	OD	3.91	1.33	.39
14. Child works for the pleasure the work gives him/her	EM	2.74	1.16	.52
15. Child is easily discouraged^R	ES	2.16	1.28	.37
16. Child uses material in imaginative ways	CC	2.78	.81	.33
17. Child does something just because social custom dictates	OD	3.81	1.19	.36
18. Child isolates him/herself	NR	2.29	1.31	-.17
19. Child is constantly seeking attention and praise	PR	3.27	1.04	-.40
20. Child is apt to pass up something he/she wants to do when others feel it isn't worth doing	OD	3.75	1.22	.35
21. Child carries out requests responsibly	EM	2.48	1.28	.57
22. Child wants adult help even when it's not really needed	PR	3.63	1.36	-.42
23. Child could be more friendly	NR	2.71	1.30	-.16
24. Child does not listen to rules^R	OB	3.29	.94	.43
25. Child is sure things will work out well when he/she has trouble solving a problem at school	ES	2.67	.89	.44

Item		Scale[a]	Mean	Discrimination SD	Index
26.	Child works hard even when no reward is available	EM	2.34	1.25	.70
27.	Child is creative	CC	2.84	.73	.36
28.	Child usually does as told	OB	3.52	1.03	.51
29.	Child is a self-starter	EM	2.82	1.31	.53
30.	Child is sure things will work out well when he/she has new work to do at school	ES	2.38	.92	.42
31.	Child usually doesn't trust others	NR	2.44	.97	−.13
32.	Child likes to be given a lot of direction	OD	3.91	.76	.38
33.	Child sticks with a goal or task until it is complete	EM	2.24	1.32	.65
34.	Child seems to prefer adults to children	PR	3.65	1.17	−.45
35.	Child expects to succeed at most things	ES	2.73	1.28	.51
36.	Child finishes school work quickly	EM	2.81	1.03	.48
37.	Child observes what others are doing to guide his/her own actions	OD	3.81	.99	.42

[a]EM = Effectance Motivation, OB = Obedience, NR = Negative-Reaction Tendency, PR = Positive-Reaction Tendency, CC = Creativity/Curiosity, ES = Expectancy of Success, OD = Outerdirectedness.
[R]Item scoring reversed.

Table 9.3. *Psychometric properties for the EZ-Yale Personality Questionnaire*

Index	Overall instrument	Scale Score						
		EM	OB	NR	PR	CC	ES	OD
Mean[a]	21.39	3.24	3.57	2.44	3.38	2.76	2.79	3.12
SD	2.76	1.01	1.27	.72	1.14	.95	.79	.81
R_{xx}[b]	.89	.82	.93	.60	.68	—	.84	.74
r_{t1t2}[c]	.87	.84	.92	.65	.72	.94	.88	.81
alpha[d]	.78	.91	.86	.83	.76	.79	.81	.83
Mean r_{it}[e]	.80	.86	.85	.78	.76	.75	.83	.80
Percent of variance explained	75.4	28.5	13.8	9.5	8.8	5.2	4.4	4.3

[a]EM = Effectance Motivation, OB = Obedience, NR = Negative-Reaction Tendency, PR = Positive-Reaction Tendency, CC = Creativity/Curiosity, ES = Expectancy of Success, OD = Outerdirectedness.
[b]Spearman–Brown corrected split-half reliability coefficient. Not calculated for CC, which only had three items.
[c]Test-retest reliability.
[d]Cronbach's alpha homogeneity coefficient.
[e]Mean of the item-to-overall score or item-to-scale score correlations.

Table 9.4. *Correlations between the seven scales*

Scale	EM	OB	NR	PR	CC	ES	OD
EM	—						
OB	.43***	—					
NR	−.22**	−.26**	—				
PR	−.47***	.52***	−.04	—			
CC	.44***	.03	−.18*	−.05	—		
ES	.52***	.28***	−.22**	−.35**	.46**	—	
OD	−.13*	.22**	−.02	.01	−.31***	−.27***	—

[a]EM = Effectance Motivation, OB = Obedience, NR = Negative-Reaction Tendency, PR = Positive-Reaction Tendency, CC = Creativity/Curiosity, ES = Expectancy of Success, OD = Outerdirectedness.
   *$p < .01$
  **$p < .005$
 ***$p < .001$

Table 9.5. *Scale specificity coefficients and factor loadings*

Inventory item no.	EM r	F1	OB r	F2	NR r	F3	PR r	F4	CC r	F5	ES r	F6	OD r	F7
EM 1	82	85	48		-17		-38		35		49		-18	
14	76	60	42		-32		-37		47		53		-24	
21	77	55	62		-33		-38		34		47		-11	
26	82	67	59		-24		-46		38		51		-25	
29	79	59	39		-33		-36		52		61		-32	
33	83	76	48		-25		-43		46		56		-22	
36	79	76	31		-19		-36		35		49		-21	
OB 3	48		85	80	-21		-37		09		34		01	
8	41		83	76	-24		-44		13		29		09	
24	53		88	74	-31		-48		21		40		14	
28	50		87	81	-25		-39		14		33		02	
NR 2	-20		20		63	53	05		-18		-15		23	
4	-26		-23		73	79	16		-16		-24		08	
11	-32		-25		78	82	18		-27		-27		14	
18	-31		-18		84	83	17		-25		-37		11	
23	-27		-25		78	60	18		-29		-26		08	
31	-25		-35		68	47	18		-14		-37		14	
PR 7	-34		30		03		72	69	-22		-26		36	
12	-23		29		07		68	67	-09		-17		31	
19	-45		40		19		74	67	-20		-36		28	
22	-38		39		18		72	55	-33		-30		37	
34	-29		33		30		65	48	-21		-27		25	
CC 9	39		11		-29		-19		75	70	35		-37	
16	49		22		-22		-30		90	85	53		-38	
27	46		13		-20		-28		89	81	45		-38	
ES 6	45		24		-37		-25		41		72	60	-35	
15	43		37		-33		-31		35		78	53	-41	
25	36		32		-25		-36		46		86	73	-41	
30	42		42		-28		-51		45		82	62	-35	
35	51		29		-25		-30		41		77	61	-26	
OD 5	-23		03		11		35		-37		-31		79	60
10	-29		05		25		29		-44		-45		74	62
13	-33		18		14		36		-41		-34		76	65
17	-27		17		17		21		-26		-17		67	68
20	-29		02		16		28		-39		-29		64	54
32	-25		09		20		25		-40		-32		85	69
37	-29		12		19		29		-38		-35		72	70

[a]EM = Effective Motivation, OB – Obedience, NR = Negative-Reaction Tendency, PR = Positive-Reaction Tendency, CC – Creativity/Curiosity, ES = Expectancy of Success, OD = Outerdirectedness.
Decimal points have been omitted.
Cut-off values for N = 661 are .12 $p < .001$; .09 $p < .01$; .07 $p < .05$.

Reliability of the EZPQ

In this second study, we ascertained the reliability of the EZPQ and its seven scales by analyzing internal consistency, split-half reliability, and test-retest reliability of the instrument.

Sample. Data from the entire primary sample of 661 individuals with mental retardation were used to determine the internal consistency and the split-half reliability for the EZPQ. To evaluate the test-retest reliability of the instrument, we used a second sample (see Table 9.1), which consisted of thirty-six males and twenty-four females who were initially assessed as part of the primary sample. These individuals were in special education programs in nearby urban schools and were recruited on the basis of being representative of the age group, intellectual level, and SES of the primary sample.

Statistical Analyses. Cronbach's alpha, which we used to estimate the internal consistency, yielded satisfactory homogeneity coefficients. For the calculation of split-half reliability, we randomly divided the EZPQ into two parts, with the condition that each part had approximately equal numbers of items for each of the scales. Because some scales had an odd number of items, we could not construct a completely equal distribution of scale items in each of the split-halves. Furthermore, because the creativity/curiosity subscale consisted of three items only, we did not include it in the split-half analysis. In order to establish the stability of the EZPQ over time, we also performed a test-retest analysis. The scores obtained in the initial administration of the EZPQ for the item and factor analyses were correlated with scores from a second administration of the instrument after a three-month interval.

Findings. The alphas (see Table 9.3), which ranged from .76 to .91, indicate a high degree of internal consistency across all seven scales, and uniformly exceed acceptable standards for instruments of this nature and length. Our calculation of split-half reliability using the Spearman–Brown formula yielded a correlation coefficient of $r = .84, p < .001$. The temporal stability of the overall instrument was at a similarly high level, with a test-retest correlation coefficient of $r = .81$ using total scores. The correlations associated with the individual scales ranged from .65 (negative-reaction tendency) to .97 (creativity/curiosity) (see Table 9.3). Thus, the reliability of the measure, as determined by the split-half and test-retest methods, was well within acceptable levels.

Concurrent Validity of the EZPQ

In this third study, we examined the concurrent validity of the EZPQ by correlating scores on the individual scales with existing experimental measures of each construct.

Sample and Procedure. To establish the concurrent validity of the EZPQ, we used the sixty individuals who participated in the second study as our sample. Characteristics of the sample are summarized in Table 9.1. We administered a series of well-established measures of the five personality constructs tapped by the EZPQ to the sixty participants. In a quiet room at their schools, we tested the students individually in 1½–2 hour sessions. The order in which the tasks were presented was randomly varied across participants to minimize any potential order effect. At the end of the session, we thanked the students for their involvement and gave them a small prize. The research session was scheduled to coincide with data collection for the test-retest reliability study three months after the initial administration of the EZPQ. Teachers completed a second EZPQ on the same day their students were tested.

Description of Measures. *Sticker Game.* In this measure of outerdirectedness, the experimenter makes a picture on colored construction paper with various geometrical shaped stickers, labels it, and then asks the participant to make a picture and name it. The procedure is repeated for a total of three designs. Performance is scored for the degree of similarity in the name, form, sticker color, and background of the subject's designs and those of the experimenter. For details of the scoring procedures and reliability, see Yando and Zigler (1971).

Probability-Learning Task. This experimental measure of expectancy of success consists of a three-knobbed apparatus that dispenses marbles after one of the knobs is pushed. Reinforcement is given in response to only one of the knobs, and only 66 percent of the time. The degree to which the participant attempts to receive 100 percent reinforcement by pushing other (nonreinforced) knobs determines the expectancy of success. (See Luthar & Zigler, 1988, for details of procedures, scoring, etc.)

Marble-in-the-Hole Game. This task is used to assess both positive- and negative-reaction tendencies. It is a monotonous, two-part game. In part 1, the participant drops marbles of one color into one of two holes on the top of the box and marbles of another color into the other hole; the side in which the marble colors are dropped is reversed in part 2. The experimenter verbally reinforces the child at designated intervals. Measures are the total length of time that the child plays the game (need for adult attention or positive-reaction tendency) and the increase in playing time from part 1 to part 2 (wariness or negative-reaction tendency). For a more extensive description of the measure, see Zigler and Balla (1972).

Puzzle Preference, Maze, Pictorial Curiosity, and Peg Sorting. With these tasks, we measure different aspects of effectance motivation. In the measure of preference for challenging tasks (puzzle preference), we ask the participant which of three partially completed puzzles, varying in difficulty, he or she would like to put together. In the maze, we measure response variation by examining similarity in the participant's solution to five identical mazes. The child's interest in novel, as opposed to familiar, stimuli is reflected in the picture curiosity task. Finally, we look at mastery for sake of competence by means of a peg task in which the child arranges five different shapes, each of which is in five different colors, on five pegs. The participant is free to sort entirely by shape, color, or in a vertical pattern. Flavell (1982) and Harter and Zigler (1974) provide more detailed descriptions of the equipment, procedures, and scoring of these tasks.

Interpretation of Findings. In Table 9.6, we present the correlations between the experimental measures and each of the scales. In most cases, the highest correlations obtained in the validity study were between a given scale and the experimental measure used to assess the construct. The exceptions were two of the measures that have generally been used to estimate effectance motivation through preference for a challenge (puzzle preference) and novelty (picture curiosity). We found that the correlations with the effectance motivation scale and puzzle preference and pictorial curiosity were lower than the correlations with the curiosity/creativity scale. The other two measures associated with effectance motivation – peg sorting and mazes – yielded higher correlations. For the marble-in-the-hole task, we discovered that total time spent playing was highly correlated with positive-reaction tendency; there was a smaller, but significant, correlation between difference in time 1 and time 2 and scores on the negative-reaction tendency scale. The correlation between the probability-learning task and the scale measuring expectancy of success was also significant, as was the r between the scores on the sticker game and the outerdirectedness scale. In sum, the correlations between the experimental measures and the scales on

Table 9.6. *Correlations between experimental measures and the seven scales*

| Scale | Experimental Measure[a] | | | | | | | |
	SP OD	PL ES	MT PR	MD NR	PP EM	MZ EM	PS EM	PC EM
EM	−.29	.37	−.41	−.13	.44	.52	.56	.39
OB	.22	.31	.38	−.19	.18	.13	.09	.10
NR	.08	−.09	−.07	.39	−.13	−.20	−.05	−.11
PR	.17	−.19	.61	−.05	−.23	−.16	−.12	−.08
CC	−.15	.36	−.10	−.06	.68	.52	.41	.76
ES	−.12	.73	−.07	−.11	.24	.19	.34	.27
OD	.71	−.08	.21	.09	−.39	−.22	−.16	−.43

[a] SP = Sticker Picture; PL = Probability Learning; MT = Total Time for Marble-in-the-Hole; MD = Difference between time 2 and time 1 for Marble-in-the-Hole; PP = Puzzle Preference; MZ = Mazes; PS = Peg Sorting; PC = Picture Curiosity; EM = Effectance Motivation; OB = Obedience; NR = Negative-Reaction Tendency; PR = Positive-Reaction Tendency; CC = Creativity/Curiosity; ES = Expectancy of Success; OD = Outerdirectedness.
Cut-off values for N = 60 are .25, $p < .05$; .32, $p < .01$; .34, $p < .005$; .39, $p < .001$.

the EZPQ were all within acceptable limits to establish the validity of the questionnaire.

Construct Validity of EZPQ

According to the developmental formulation of mental retardation, the personality-motivational functioning of individuals with low intelligence reflects in part the chronic failure they experience in attempting to meet the challenges of life – at home, in school, and in social situations. In keeping with this formulation, we expected that the scores on the EZPQ would readily discriminate between retarded and nonretarded groups. To be specific, individuals with mental retardation should receive higher scores on positive-reaction tendency, negative-reaction tendency, and outerdirectedness, and lower scores on expectancy of success and effectance motivation than individuals without mental retardation. To test the discriminative value of the EZPQ, and thereby establish its construct validity, we compared the total EZPQ scores and the seven scale scores between the two groups.

Sample. We drew the retarded group in this study (see Table 9.1) from the primary sample. To minimize demographic differences, we recruited the individuals in the MA-matched nonretarded group (also described in Table

9.1) from the same schools as the retarded students. The bases we used for inclusion in the nonretarded group were an IQ score (obtained from administration of the Kaufman–Brief Intelligence Test; Kaufman & Kaufman, 1990) above 85 and no identified physical disabilities or psychopathology.

Statistical Analyses. On our initial examination of the data, we found no gender differences. Thus we performed a one-way MANOVA (retarded vs. nonretarded) on the total and scale scores of the participants in the third sample. We then investigated significant findings through univariate analyses. A discriminant function analysis was performed in order to further evaluate the accuracy of the EZPQ in differentiating between the personality-motivational functioning of individuals with and without mental retardation.

Interpretation of Findings. Our one-way MANOVA for the seven scales indicated a multivariate effect attributable to group ($F_{7,220} = 29.38$, $p <$ .001) using Wilks lambda. We did not include the total score in the MANOVA because it was mathematically derived from the scales. Subsequent univariate analyses revealed significant differences in the scores of retarded and nonretarded individuals on six of the scales; negative-reaction tendency did not reach significance. Overall, the individuals with mental retardation demonstrated significantly higher levels of outerdirectedness and positive-reaction tendency. In contrast, nonretarded individuals obtained significantly higher scores on the scales measuring creativity/curiosity, expectancy of success, obedience, and effectance motivation. The results are summarized in Table 9.7.

Total scores for the function that emerged from the discriminant analysis (eigenvalue = 2.317) accounted for 89 percent of the variance and was highly significant ($p < .0001$). We found that the overall percentage of cases correctly classified as retarded or nonretarded was 92.3 percent, which indicated that the total score on the EZPQ discriminated between the two groups with a high degree of accuracy. The "hit" rates were 88.9 percent for nonretarded individuals and 95.7 percent for individuals with mental retardation.

Discussion and Conclusion

Given the encouraging results of the four studies described in this chapter, we believe that our investigations satisfactorily establish the psychometric properties of the EZPQ. Moreover, we have concluded that the measure has

Table 9.7. *Summary of MANOVA on the seven scales*

Scale	MR		NonMR		F
	Mean	SD	Mean	SD	(df = 1,226)
EM	3.12	(.95)	3.94	(.81)	14.85*
OB	3.49	(1.18)	4.03	(.78)	18.47*
NR	2.48	(.83)	2.11	(.89)	5.67 ns
PR	3.11	(.84)	2.21	(.78)	19.60*
CC	3.13	(.95)	4.37	(.66)	27.29**
ES	2.89	(.77)	3.87	(.87)	16.62*
OD	3.15	(.76)	2.36	(.38)	18.86*
Overall score	21.89	(2.58)	27.53	(1.73)	8.31**

 * $p < .01$
** $p < .001$
[a]EM = Effectance Motivation, OB = Obedience, NR = Negative-Reaction Tendency, PR = Positive-Reaction Tendency, CC = Creativity/Curiosity, ES = Expectancy of Success, OD = Outerdirectedness.
In determining the total score, reciprocals of PR, NR, and OD were used so that a higher score would indicate better functioning.

considerable promise for future use in examining personality-motivational functioning in individuals with mental retardation. Based on the samples employed, we found that the thirty-seven-item, seven-scale instrument showed good internal reliability, temporal stability, and concurrent validity. The measure was also quite successful in distinguishing between individuals with and without mental retardation.

The scales identified in the factor analyses of EZPQ scores both confirm and refine the original five hypothesized constructs of outerdirectedness, expectancy of success, effectance motivation, positive-reaction tendency, and negative-reaction tendency. The two additional constructs that were found – obedience and curiosity/creativity – which represent refinements in the conceptualization of outerdirectedness and effectance motivation, may explain some of the noise previously detected in the established measures of these traits. As the term is usually understood, "obedience" carries either an explicit or tacit understanding that specific directions will be followed in a given situation; individuals do not have an option in generating their own behavior in a situation requiring obedience to a set of directions. This construct differs from outerdirectedness, in which individuals have the opportunity to determine their own behavior by choosing to rely on environmental cues or self-generated solutions. The lower degree of obedience reflected in lower scores for individuals with mental retardation may be attributed to either misunderstanding directions or being presented with tasks beyond their abilities. Effectance motivation has been conceptualized as the joy of undertaking a difficult task and seeing it through to completion.

The revision to which we are directed by our recent factor analyses is that fulfillment in mastering a task is not limited to novel and difficult situations. Satisfaction may also be gleaned from the successful completion of familiar and mundane tasks in which tried and true solutions are used. The desire to experience novel situations and try inventive solutions, while positively related to effectance motivation, was found to be distinct from the sense of accomplishment at a task's completion.

The relationships we discovered among the five hypothesized factors were generally supportive of the developmental formulation of mental retardation. Whereas outerdirectedness is attributed to a history of chronic failure, expectancy of success, and hence effectance motivation, are thought to arise from more positive experiences, such as the pleasure of being able to generate viable solutions in problem-solving situations. Through our recent investigations, we have been able to document the predicted relationships between outerdirectedness and both effectance motivation and expectancy of success.

Among the seven individual factors identified in the EZPQ, we discovered that negative-reaction tendency, although internally consistent, demonstrated the least temporal stability and experimental validity. Moreover, negative-reaction tendency alone failed to discriminate between the retarded and nonretarded samples. As a construct, negative-reaction tendency has been ascribed to the social deprivation encountered in institutional settings. With the widespread implementation of mainstreaming, the majority of individuals with mental retardation now experience more inclusion. Thus, the wariness of strangers that characterizes negative-reaction tendency may not have developed in the sample of noninstitutionalized individuals used in our comparative analyses.

The differences we obtained in the functioning of individuals with and without mental retardation across the other four originally hypothesized personality constructs (effectance motivation, expectancy of success, positive-reaction tendency, and outerdirectedness) were all in the direction predicted by the developmental model. We found that individuals with mental retardation were indeed more likely to look for external cues in solving problems and to be more dependent on adults than their nonretarded peers. Further, we found that individuals with mental retardation were less likely to expect success when undertaking tasks, experienced less satisfaction in the mastery of tasks, were less likely to be curious about new situations, showed less creativity in their approaches to tasks, and were less likely to follow specific directions. Total scores from the EZPQ, in addition to the separate scores, also accurately predicted whether an individual was functioning in the range of retarded or nonretarded intelligence.

Future Considerations

The next steps we have planned in the development of the EZPQ will include broadening the standardization sample and efforts to ascertain and delineate the measure's utility for researchers, educators, and therapists. We would also like to broaden the range of persons with retardation for whom the EZPQ might be utilized. The samples we used in the studies described in this chapter were limited to individuals without an identified organic etiology underlying their mental retardation. In the future, we would like to examine the factor structure of the EZPQ using samples of individuals with biological bases for their impairments. Because some of the constructs tapped by the measure have been found to show a developmental progression (e.g., outerdirectedness), age norms should be established. Our future psychometric research should be focused as well on ameliorating the current sampling limitations and on developing a parent version of the instrument.

In addition to the instrument's likely utility in applied settings, the advantage of being able to assess functioning on several dimensions of personality in any given study, the ease of administration, and the psychometric properties of the EZPQ should facilitate research as well. Potential research uses include studies of the development of personality characteristics and their relationship to behavioral performance. In applied settings, we believe that the EZPQ can eventually be used to screen for maladaptive behaviors, so that clinicians and educators will be able to consider a variety of interventions more meaningfully. The measure can also be used pre- and postintervention to assess attainment of behavioral objectives. Once the measure is refined, we hope that the EZPQ will yield a better understanding of the relationship between personality and both adaptive and cognitive functioning in individuals with mental retardation, and that it will become a useful guide in treatment regimens.

References

Balla, D., Butterfield, E. C., & Zigler, E. (1974). Effects of institutionalization on retarded children: A longitudinal, cross-institutional investigation. *American Journal of Mental Deficiency, 78,* 530–549.

Cattell, R.B. (1966). The scree test for the number of factors. *Multivariate Behavioral Research, 1*, 245–276.

Comrey, A.L. (1988). Factor analytic methods of scale development in personality and clinical psychology. *Journal of Consulting and Clinical Psychology, 56,* 754–761.

Cromwell, R. (1963). A social learning approach to mental retardation. In N.R. Ellis (ed.), *Handbook of mental deficiency.* New York: McGraw-Hill.

DeVellis, R.F. (1991). *Scale development: Theory and applications.* Newbury Park, CA: SAGE Publications.

Flavell, J. (1982). Structures, stages, and sequences in cognitive development. In W.A. Collins (ed.), *The Concept of Development: The Minnesota Symposia on Child Psychology.* Vol. 15. Hillsdale, NJ: Erlbaum.

Harter, S., & Zigler, E. (1968). Effectiveness of adult and peer reinforcement on performance of institutionalized and noninstitutionalized retardates. *Journal of Abnormal Psychology, 73,* 144–149.

(1974). The assessment of effectance motivation in normal and retarded children. *Developmental Psychology, 10,* 169–180.

Haywood, H.C. (1987). The mental age deficit: Explanation and treatment. *Upsala Journal of Medical Science, Supplement 44,* 191–203.

Kaufman, A., & Kaufman, N. (1990). *K:BIT Kaufman Brief Intelligence Test.* Circle Pines, MN: American Guidance Service.

Luckasson, R., Calter, D., Polloway, E., Reiss, S., Schalock, R., Snell, M., Spotalnik, D., & Stark, J. (1992). *Mental retardation: Definition, classification, and systems of support* (9th ed.). Annapolis Junction, MD: American Association on Mental Retardation.

Luthar, S., & Zigler, E. (1988). Motivational factors, school atmosphere, and SES: Determinants of children's probability task performance. *Journal of Applied Developmental Psychology, 9,* 477–494.

MacMillan, D., & Keogh, B. (1971). Normal and retarded children's expectancy for failure. *Developmental Psychology, 4,* 343–348.

MacMillan, D., & Knopf, E. (1971). Effect of instructional set on perceptions of event outcomes by EMR and nonretarded children. *American Journal of Mental Deficiency, 76,* 185–189.

MacMillan, D., & Wright, D. (1974). Outerdirectedness in children of three ages as a function of experimentally induced success and failure. *Journal of Educational Psychology, 68,* 136–148.

Schallenberger, P., & Zigler, E. (1961). Rigidity, negative reaction tendencies and cosatiation effects in normal and feebleminded children. *Journal of Abnormal and Social Psychology, 63,* 20–26.

Switzky, H.N. (1997). Motivational systems in persons with mental retardation. In W.E. MacLean, Jr. (ed.), *Handbook of mental deficiency: Psychological theory and research* (pp. 343–377). Hillsdale, NJ: Erlbaum.

White, R. (1959). Motivation reconsidered: The concept of competence. *Psychological Review, 88,* 297–333.

Yando, R., & Zigler, E. (1971). Outerdirectedness in the problem-solving of institutionalized and noninstitutionalized normal and retarded children. *Developmental Psychology, 4,* 277–282.

Zigler, E. (1961). Social deprivation and rigidity in the performance of feebleminded children. *Journal of Abnormal and Social Psychology, 62,* 413–421.

Zigler, E., & Balla, D. (1972). Developmental course of responsiveness to social reinforcement in normal children and institutionalized retarded children. *Developmental Psychology, 6,* 66–73.

(1982). *Mental retardation: The developmental-difference controversy.* Hillsdale, NJ: Erlbaum.

Zigler, E., Balla, D., & Butterfield, E.C. (1968). A longitudinal investigation of the relationship between preinstitutional social deprivation and social motivation in institutionalized retardates. *Journal of Personality and Social Psychology, 10,* 437–445.

10   Parenting, Etiology, and Personality-Motivational Functioning in Children with Mental Retardation

Robert M. Hodapp
Deborah J. Fidler

Over the past four decades, personality-motivational functioning has become an important research topic concerning children with mental retardation. Led by Edward Zigler (1984) and his colleagues, we now know that children with mental retardation differ from nonretarded children in a number of ways. These children are more dependent, wary, and outerdirected, and they look to others for solutions to difficult problems, show lower levels of self-efficacy, and expect to fail more often (see Zigler & Hodapp, 1986, for a review). As a result, children with mental retardation show less-optimal levels of performance than their abilities would suggest.

In considering studies of personality-motivational functioning in persons with mental retardation, one is struck by the comprehensiveness of this body of work. Studies have been performed with children and adults who reside at home, in group homes, and in institutions. Studies have employed a wide variety of laboratory measures, each constructed specifically to tap a particular motivational-personality construct. More recently, research on personality-motivational functioning has gained a more "real-world" focus, as new studies more closely link to intervention (Bybee & Zigler, 1992) and use nonlaboratory measures (for example, the easy-to-use questionnaire designed by Zigler, Bennett-Gates, & Hodapp; see Chapter 9). Taken together, these studies – which by now number into the hundreds – have examined constructs including success, failure, positive- and negative-reaction tendencies, imitation, outerdirectedness, and self-image. As noted by Weisz (1982), Zigler's personality-motivational research constitutes a "lasting legacy" to the field of mental retardation.

But two issues have as yet received scant attention in the personality-motivational literature. The first concerns the very reasons why such differences occur. Although the supposed – and seemingly obvious – reason involves the greater degrees of intellectual failure experienced by persons with mental retardation, recent studies call into question such a single, straightforward causal mechanism. Although failure may be one

226

cause of motivational differences in persons with mental retardation, other factors may also play a role.

A second unstudied issue concerns parent-child interaction. To date, few studies relate personality-motivational functioning to parent-child interaction per se. What is it that parents actually do that contributes to later dependency, or outerdirectedness, or any of the other personality-motivational differences found by Zigler and his colleagues? Conversely, might certain parental behaviors change the child's personality-motivational structure, and might these behaviors be included in interventions with parents, educators, or other adult interactors?

This chapter explores issues of causality and of mother-child interactions on the personality-motivational functioning of children with mental retardation. We begin by examining why personality-motivational functioning differs between children with and without mental retardation. We first examine Zigler's (1971) traditional causal explanation, then suggest two additional causes. After discussing all three possible causes, we suggest possible alternative interaction strategies that may prove useful to parents, teachers, and other people in the child's surrounding personal environment.

Why Do Children with Mental Retardation Differ from Nonretarded Children in Their Personality-Motivational Structures?

Like anyone who has ever pondered why human behavior occurs, personality-motivational researchers have historically ascribed behavior to many causes. In addition to the general genetic background, temperament, and other organismic features, one must of course add the child's upbringing and experiences. As a complex human behavior, personality-motivational functioning also seems to be multiply determined. In the discussion that follows, we focus on three possible – but not mutually exclusive – causes for the personality-motivational differences found in children with retardation: increased intellectual failure, differences in mother-child interactions, and direct and indirect effects of genetic mental retardation disorders.

Failure Due to Intellectual Deficiencies

In considering why children with mental retardation differ from nonretarded children in their motivational structures, Zigler and his colleagues have proposed several environmental causes. In the earliest studies, positive- and negative-reaction tendencies – dependency and wariness – were thought to be caused by the lack of social interactions with parents and other adult figures. Much of this work was performed within institutional settings, where oftentimes children did indeed suffer from the lack of warm, affectionate, and long-lasting ties to surrounding adults (see Zigler, 1971, for a review).

More recently, however, few children are institutionalized, and the research focus has shifted to other environmental factors. Most salient here has been failure. In many publications, Zigler and his colleagues propose that children with mental retardation fail more often than do nonretarded children. "The retarded child has also experienced frequent failure, which can lead to lower or non-existent goal setting, learned helplessness, negative self-image, and an unwillingness to try" (Zigler, 1971). Taken together, these lead to the vexing "I can't do it" attitudes of many children with mental retardation as they are faced with performing complex intellectual tasks (Zigler, 1984).

Although it may seem surprising, little direct evidence exists that children with mental retardation fail more often in many naturally occurring environments. Only a few studies document more failure at home, at school, or with peers or siblings. Indeed, connections between failure and changed personality-motivational structures have only occasionally been studied by special educators or interactional researchers.

By indirect evidence, however, such failure experiences do seem to lead to learned helplessness and setting lower-level goals. In several naturalistic and experimental studies, children with mental retardation received relatively frequent negative feedback when in a classroom (Raber & Weisz, 1981), and negative feedback more adversely affected performance on concept-formation problems in children with versus without mental retardation (Weisz, 1981). Similarly, Bybee and Zigler (1992) found that when difficult problems are presented first during a testing session, children with mental retardation become more imitative, whereas the ordering of problems has much less effect on typically developing children.

Certain findings, then, imply that children with mental retardation fail more often, and seem more adversely affected by such failure. Most of this evidence, however, involves more laboratory-type experiments, and all such studies have been performed on older children with many different types of mental retardation.

Maternal Directiveness

A second, possibly complementary, explanation for personality-motivational differences concerns parental interactions. In short, mothers of children with mental retardation may be "trying too hard" to foster their child's intellectual development. Such an overly didactic, intrusive style of interaction may hinder the development of the child's own motivation to succeed.

In reviewing this line of work, one needs to understand the idea of interaction within the field of developmental psychology and mental retardation. Following from Bell's (1968; also Bell & Harper, 1974) influential writings, developmental psychologists of the 1970s and 1980s began to examine the interactions between mothers and their children – the ways that children and their parents mutually influence one another. Most of this work involved mother-infant interactions.

By the late 1970s and 1980s, researchers extended mother-child interactional research to dyads in which the child has mental retardation. As this work progressed, a curious pattern of findings emerged. On one hand, mother-child interactions differed little in the two groups. Once children in each group were matched on overall levels of abilities, mothers of children with mental retardation behaved almost identically to mothers of non-retarded children. In their linguistic input, for example, these mothers shortened their sentences (as measured by the MLU, or Mean Length of Utterance), repeated key words, talked in a higher pitch voice, and engaged in the "motherese" common to mothers of nonretarded children. As Rondal (1977) noted in his study of mothers of young children with Down syndrome, "the maternal linguistic environment of Down syndrome children between MLU 1 and 3 is an appropriate one" (p. 242). By "appropriate," Rondal meant that mothers of children with mental retardation provide almost identical linguistic environments to those provided by mothers of nonretarded children who are at the same levels of language.

But in contrast to the MLU findings, mothers of children with mental retardation did differ from mothers of nonretarded children in other ways. Specifically, these mothers seemed much more directive and didactic. They took more – and longer – interactive turns (Tannock, 1988), more often "clashed" – or spoke at the same time as – their children (Victze et al., 1978), and did not allow their children to initiate interactions (Jones, 1980).

Many of these stylistic differences may relate to differing maternal perceptions in the two sets of mothers. In contrast to mothers of children with retardation, mothers of typically developing young children possess a variety of interactive goals. These mothers attempt to achieve emotional closeness with their children, teach their children about the world, and socialize their children about manners, how to resolve conflict, and other social issues. Mother-infant games and other interactions may embed such goals within their structure. A game like peek-a-boo therefore involves emotional closeness as well as object permanence skills, and a game like roll-the-ball fosters the child's concepts of causality and social turn-taking (Hodapp & Goldfield, 1983). Across many different everyday interactions, mothers of typically developing children possess diverse expectations for their infants.

In contrast to the diverse goals of mothers of nonretarded children, mothers of children with mental retardation may almost single-mindedly focus on alleviating their child's perceived problems. Furthermore, different perceived problems may be salient to mothers of children with different types of disabilities. Compared with mothers of children with cerebral palsy, for example, mothers of children with Down syndrome are extremely worried about communication milestones, such issues as whether the child will learn to read or to say the "ABCs." Conversely, mothers of children with cerebral palsy, a disorder in which motor problems are the major concern, are less concerned about communicative milestones (Hodapp et al., 1992).

Such concerns may in turn show up in how mothers interact with their children with mental retardation. Compared with mothers of typically developing children, mothers of children with retardation may feel more compelled to teach their children in order to alleviate their children's current or future intellectual disabilities (Hodapp, 1988). To mothers of children with mental retardation, "play" per se may not be enough. As one mother in Jones' (1980) study noted, "It's sit him on your knee and talk to him, that's the main object. Play with him, speak to the child, teach him something" (p. 221; see also Cardoso-Martins & Mervis, 1984).

In addition to a more intrusive, didactic style of interaction, mothers of children with retardation may also more often demand higher-level behaviors. In one study, Mahoney, Fors, and Wood (1991) compared maternal behaviors in dyads with two groups of children: children with Down syndrome (CA = 30 months, MA = 17 months) and nonretarded children (MA and CA = 17 months). On average, mothers of children with Down syndrome requested behaviors at the 15-month level, whereas mothers of nonretarded children averaged requests at the 10-month level. Mothers of children with Down syndrome were thus "keeping on the pressure," attempting to force their children to perform at their highest possible levels.

But such intrusive, demanding behaviors may not be effective in speeding along their infants' development. Kasari and her colleagues recently examined the effects of different linguistic input on the early language development of young children with Down syndrome (see Kasari & Bauminger, 1997, for a review). In one study, mothers and their children were observed once when the children were between 13 and 41 months, and again 13 months later (Harris, Kasari, & Sigman, 1996). The most important maternal behaviors involved following the child's lead. Thus, mothers who commented on what the child was focused on – thereby maintaining the child's focus of attention – had children who showed increased levels of receptive language 13 months later. In contrast, mothers who changed their child's focus of attention had children who advanced less from the first to the second session.

Several lessons arise from these studies. The first is that children with mental retardation may have difficulties in handling too much stimulation. When mothers force children to change attention from one topic to another, the children may be unable to learn. Conversely, when mothers stick for a longer period of time to a single topic, children's learning may improve. Furthermore, children in other disabled groups may also benefit from a maternal style that focuses on fewer interactive topics. Thus, it appears that children who are deaf and acquiring American Sign Language learn better when the mother is signing about the child's topic of interest; blind children, too, may do better when mothers follow the objects and actions in which their infants are currently engaged (see Hodapp, in press, for a review). For young children with many disabilities, then, it may be important to keep to a single topic for longer periods of time.

The other, more motivationally related lesson involves self-efficacy. Partly due to their concern with their child's development, many mothers of children with mental retardation may be overly invested in fostering their child's development. Unfortunately, these children may benefit less from direct teaching, demands, and redirecting their attention. Mothers who are intrusive may not allow their children with mental retardation to explore the environment, to try out new and creative games, or to learn about the world in their own way, at their own pace. Although we return to these topics later, for now suffice it to say that young children with mental retardation seem to develop faster when mothers foster self-efficacy as opposed to passive learning.

Effects of Different Etiologies of Mental Retardation

Until now, we have considered failure and mother-child interaction as if the child's type of mental retardation did not matter. And, indeed, in most research on personality-motivational behavior, etiology has played little role. In the work of Zigler and his colleagues, for instance, only a few studies have distinguished between familial and organic retardation (e.g.,

Yando, Seitz, & Zigler, 1989); none has compared different etiologies. But it may be that children with different types of mental retardation show different learning and motivational-personality styles; children with different types of retardation may also elicit different behaviors from surrounding adults. Both their own and others' behaviors, then, may contribute to personality-motivational differences in these children.

In thinking about the effects on personality-motivation of different types of mental retardation, we here limit our discussion to the various genetic causes. Granted, even though 750 different genetic etiologies of mental retardation have now been identified (Opitz, 1996), genetic etiologies comprise only a portion of the many pre-, peri-, and post-natal organic causes of mental retardation. And although exact figures are hard to find, all forms of organic mental retardation probably account for only about 50 percent (or possibly slightly less) of all individuals with mental retardation (Zigler & Hodapp, 1986).

Even more problematic are the few behavioral studies of most etiologies of mental retardation. Only Down syndrome has been the subject of much behavioral work; indeed, it is estimated that Down syndrome has been the subject of as many behavioral studies as all other types of mental retardation combined (Dykens, 1996; Hodapp, 1996). In contrast, most etiologies of mental retardation have not been the subject of even a few behavioral studies (Hodapp & Dykens, 1994). But this situation may be changing. Specifically, over the past decade sophisticated behavioral research has begun on children with fragile X syndrome (Dykens, Hodapp, & Leckman, 1994), Prader–Willi syndrome (Dykens & Cassidy, 1996), and Williams syndrome (Pober & Dykens, 1996). The review that follows, then, is based predominantly on behavioral work in Down syndrome, with behavioral findings from other syndromes provided when available.

Direct Effects of Genetic Etiology. Although all children with mental retardation share a cognitive impairment of some sort, children with certain genetic disorders may differ behaviorally from other children with mental retardation. This phenomenon, called the "direct effects" of a specific genetic disorder (Hodapp, 1997), has recently been examined in several different disorders, across many different domains of functioning.

One such area involves differences in profiles of intellectual strengths and weaknesses, particularly the distinction between sequential processing, simultaneous processing, and achievement (Das, Kirby, & Jarman, 1975; Kaufman & Kaufman, 1983). Sequential processing involves the step-by-step, serial processing of information; the ability to repeat a series of digits (i.e., a "digit span" task) is one example of sequential processing. Simultaneous processing, in contrast, involves gestalt, holistic processing, as one might perform when recognizing a face or a picture. Achievement involves all of a child's learned information, including culturally related facts as well as the ability to read, write, or solve math problems.

In examining children with different types of mental retardation, we have found that boys with fragile X syndrome perform poorly on tasks of sequential processing as opposed to simultaneous processing or achievement (Dykens, Hodapp, & Leckman, 1987). This sequential processing deficit is also noted in children with Prader–Willi syndrome (Dykens et al., 1992). In contrast, children with Down syndrome show no such distinction between their abilities in sequential versus simultaneous processing (Hodapp, et al., 1992; Pueschel et al., 1986). Thus, individuals with certain types of mental retardation show characteristic strengths and weaknesses that may not be found in most children with mental retardation.

So too might different etiologies lead to differences in motivational and personality styles. The most intriguing findings here relate to children with Down syndrome – indeed, few studies exist on children with any other disorder. The main personality-motivational factors examined in such studies involve these children's reaction to failure, their sociability, and their personality.

Like many children with mental retardation, children with Down syndrome show lower levels of task persistence than do nonretarded children, possibly due to their inability to accomplish many academic and intellectual tasks. But in a series of studies, Pitcairn and Wishart (1994) showed that children with Down syndrome have developed an interesting "escape strategy." Given a series of impossible tasks (such as putting square pegs into round holes), children with Down syndrome did not show frustration or anger. Instead, these children often looked to the examiner, and established eye contact, usually followed by a vocalization. These children then, according to Pitcairn and Wishart (1994), "performed an 'act,' often involving hand-clapping, or banging on the table. The word 'act' is used deliberately here, as mothers often reported that the behaviors seen were party pieces" (p. 488). In essence, children with Down syndrome were attempting to charm their way out of a difficult situation. While such behavior may be endearing to surrounding adults, avoidance would seem to constitute a poor problem-solving strategy.

A second line of work involves "sociability." Although researchers have long attempted – with mixed success – to understand the social behaviors of children with Down syndrome (Kasari & Bauminger, 1997), recent studies conclude that these children may indeed be more sociable than children with other types of mental retardation. For example, in naturalistic play interactions with their mothers and other adult interactors, children with Down syndrome look longer at the adult than do other children (Kasari et al., 1990). Furthermore, when children with Down syndrome smile, they most often do so while looking to the adult (as opposed, for example, to children with autism, who smile as often, but rarely at the same time as they look to the adult interactor). Thus, children with Down syndrome appear "social" to others – they are looking directly at the adult interactor, and smiling as they look. Such behaviors may communicate a willingness for social interaction and elicit positive reactions from others.

A third direct effect concerns the possibility that individuals with Down syndrome may more often share a certain personality. Although many workers reject the possibility of a "Down syndrome personality," some evidence exists for its presence. In one study, researchers used the many earlier studies on Down syndrome to construct a scale of the Down syndrome personality (Wishart & Johnston, 1990). They then gave this scale to parents, teachers, and other professionals who possessed varying levels of experience in working with these children. In contrast to the many professionals – who generally did not feel that there was such a thing as a Down syndrome personality – the children's parents agreed with most of the scale's items. Given possible scores ranging from 23 for the least stereotypical to 115 for the most stereotypical, mothers averaged 97 in the scores that they gave to their own children with Down syndrome. When rating their own children – the individual with Down syndrome whom they saw every day – these mothers agreed that the syndrome is characterized by a particular personality type.

In other ways, too, children with Down syndrome are perceived as having a particular personality. In a recent study, Hornby (1995) asked fathers to describe their 7- to 14-year-old children with Down syndrome. Although these fathers provided a variety of adjectives and stories, the single characteristic that they mentioned most often concerned the child's personality. A full 46 percent of these fathers spontaneously noted that their child had a bright disposition; nearly one-third referred to their child as being lovable, and nearly a quarter remarked that their child was sociable or friendly.

Before discussing indirect effects, two remaining issues must be addressed concerning direct effects. First, not every individual with a particular genetic disorder will show that disorder's characteristic behaviors. This phenomenon is called "consistency" (Pennington, O'Connor, & Sudhalter,

1991) and refers to the idea that a specific genetic disorder's effects on behaviors involve "the heightened probability [that] people with a given syndrome will exhibit certain behavioral sequelae relative to those without the syndrome" (Dykens, 1995, p. 68). This "heightened probability" – but not 100 percent certainty – is seen even in the physical sequelae of specific genetic disorders. For example, although epicanthal folds around the eyes – the feature that caused Langdon Down to refer to "mongolism" – may be Down syndrome's most predominant physical feature, only 57 percent of newborns with Down syndrome display this attribute (although higher percentages show epicanthal folds later in life; Pueschel, 1983). Such within-group variation must be taken into account when examining the direct effects of mental retardation.

Second, not every genetic etiology need be unique in any aspect of behavior. To return to an earlier example, both boys with fragile X syndrome and children with Prader–Willi syndrome show deficits in sequential processing compared with simultaneous processing and achievement. This deficit is therefore not unique in that most individuals with either syndrome show this pattern. The deficit in sequential processing does, however, still differ compared with findings from individuals with mental retardation in general (Sparrow, Balla, & Cicchetti, 1984); in addition, no deficit in sequential processing is seen in children with Down syndrome. Thus, although any single behavior may not be unique to a particular syndrome or occur in every single person with a syndrome, that behavior may still be of interest as a direct effect of a genetic disorder of mental retardation.

Indirect Effects of Genetic Disorders. So far, we have discussed the direct effects of genetic disorders of mental retardation. But if children with different genetic disorders show characteristic behaviors, might not individuals surrounding the child also be affected indirectly? Might not there be a ripple effect of the child's behaviors on the child's surrounding environment, and might these elicited behaviors also relate to the child's personality-motivational functioning?

The reasoning here comes from Sandra Scarr's (1993) views of environmental effects. According to Scarr, environments can work in any of three ways. They can be active and the child passive. A good example of this might be the death of a parent, or a young child's family move – in both cases, the child is relatively powerless to change the environment. In contrast, a second view sees children as actively choosing and structuring their environments. Particularly as they get older, children (like adults) choose their friends, their favorite activities, and in other ways shape their own environments.

But it is the third type of environment that may be most interesting when considering genetic etiologies of mental retardation (Hodapp, 1997). This type of environment has been called "evocative." That is, children evoke reactions from others. Children who are happy or good-natured elicit happy, good-natured reactions from others. Children who are cranky or colicky do not. This sense of evoking reactions from others may be a main mechanism by which adult-child interactions must be understood, particularly as regards the personality-motivational aspects of these interactions.

So far, data on the evocative nature of indirect effects are limited, although some intriguing findings are emerging. In examining family stress, for example, two findings are of interest. First, although not shown in every study, many studies find that families of children with Down syndrome experience less stress than families of children with other disabilities. For example, when compared with children with autism and children with unidentified mental retardation, parents of children with Down syndrome exhibit significantly lower amounts of stress (Holroyd & McArthur, 1976; Seltzer, Krauss, & Tsunematsu, 1993; Kasari & Sigman, 1997). Similarly, in a study that classified families of children with mental retardation into varying types, 66 percent of the "cohesive-harmonious" families – the most intact family type – consisted of families of children with Down syndrome (Mink, Nihira, & Myers, 1993). Mothers of children with Down syndrome even report experiencing greater support from friends and the greater community (Erikson & Upshure, 1989).

This advantage to families of children with Down syndrome also seems to occur across a range of ages and compared with a variety of contrast groups. The studies referred to here, for example, examined families of individuals with mental retardation who ranged from below 2 years (Erikson & Upshure, 1989) through 25 years of age (Seltzer et al., 1993). In addition, some studies compared individuals with Down syndrome with other retarded groups, and some to groups of children with autism. In one study (Thomas & Olsen, 1993), researchers began by considering families of adolescents with Down syndrome as "problem families," akin to two groups of families of adolescents with emotional disturbance. As the study progressed, however, these researchers ultimately combined their "normal" and Down syndrome families into a single control group, concluding that families of children with Down syndrome were really not problem families after all. At present, we cannot determine whether this "Down syndrome advantage" is related to aspects of the children themselves, or to the advantages Down syndrome parents experience by having many support groups and much information. Whatever the reasons, families of individuals with Down syndrome appear to be coping better.

A second, related issue concerns family reactions to certain child behaviors. Across several studies examining families of children with different genetic disorders of mental retardation, the amount of the child's maladaptive behavior most relates to familial stress. In studies of children with Prader–Willi syndrome, for example, the child's degree of maladaptive behavior strongly related to levels of family stress; the higher the child's scores on Achenbach's Child Behavior Checklist, the more stress experienced by families (Hodapp, Dykens, & Masino, 1997). And in line with the idea that several genetic etiologies might show identical indirect effects, similar findings linking child maladaptive behaviors to family stress have been shown in families of children with 5p-(cri-du-chat)syndrome (Hodapp, Wijma, & Masino, in press), and with Smith–Magenis syndrome (Hodapp, Fidler, & Smith, 1998). Although the exact direction of causality remains unclear, it seems likely that parents experience greater stress levels when their children show more maladaptive behaviors.

It may even be the case that parents and families react to other aspects of the child beyond personality and a lack of maladaptive behaviors. Indeed, one interesting feature of several disorders relates to their characteristic facial features. Such facial features are shown in several disorders, including Down syndrome, Williams syndrome, and fragile X syndrome. In order to understand the effects on parents of the child's facial features, we first briefly describe some recent findings from this branch of social psychology, particularly research on the "babyface overgeneralization."

Psychologists and folklore have long intuited that one's facial appearance provides information about an individual. In a series of studies, Zebrowitz (1997) extensively researched one aspect of this perceptual preparedness: the adaptive responses adults show to babies and their appearances. As proof that humans perceive and respond differently to the appearances of babies versus adults, Zebrowitz described uniform adult reactions when interacting with infants. These behaviors include the extended mutual gaze between adults and babies and an "eyebrow flash" in adults, such that adults come eyeball-to-eyeball with a baby on a first encounter. Zebrowitz attributes these warm, familiar reactions to the ability of infants to "disarm adults." In effect, the infant's appearance communicates to the adult that the baby is developmentally immature, and is dependent on the adult for survival. The involuntary nurturing and protective responses to offspring may also be evolutionarily adaptive, and help the young of the species to develop into adults. There is even evidence that an infant's appearance may help inhibit adult aggression toward irritating behaviors such as crying, wetting, and vomiting (McCabe, 1988).

Given its probable evolutionary importance, such "babyface reactions" may be "overgeneralized to individuals whose appearance merely resembles" a baby in some way (Zebrowitz, 1997, p. 56). As a result, humans are left with an acute ability to detect and respond not only to babies, but to things that appear babylike. When this over-responsiveness is manifested in reactions to adults who retain babylike facial proportions, Zebrowitz terms this the "babyface overgeneralization."

Across numerous studies, people react in specific ways to adult faces that retain babylike features, or babyfaces (Berry & McArthur, 1985, 1986; Zebrowitz & Montepare, 1992; Zebrowitz, Olson, & Hoffman, 1993). Observers attribute higher ratings of warmth, weakness, and naivete to pictures of adult faces with babyish eyes than to adult faces with typical eye proportions. Pictures of babyfaces are also rated as more likely to believe a far-fetched story, less likely to cheat on an exam, and less able to lift heavy boxes (McArthur & Apatow, 1983–4). Even when given outlines of two heads – one drawn with adult proportions and one with more babylike proportions – observers viewed the latter as less alert, less strong, and less intelligent. These are all perceptions of dependency that foster warm, protective responses.

What characterizes a babyfaced appearance? From Zebrowitz's studies, the following appear to be considered babylike – and to elicit protective responses – from most adults:

- larger eyes relative to the face
- fine, high eyebrows and fair eye- and hair-coloring
- a small, concave nose with a sunken bridge
- redder lips that are proportionately smaller than adults'
- larger forehead and shorter chin, resulting in lower vertical placement of features on the face
- fuller cheeks and rounder chin, resulting in a rounder face (Berry & McArthur, 1986).

Though the babyface overgeneralization has its most pronounced effects in faces with the entire configuration of babyish features, the effect is still found for varying combinations of individual features (Zebrowitz, 1997).

If features and proportions of the prototypical Down syndrome face coincide with the prototypical babyface, then individuals with Down syndrome may be included in the babyface overgeneralization. In this sense, a positive indirect effect on parents and families may be partially mediated by the child with Down syndrome's facial appearance. Evidence of similarity is found in a study of 199 individuals with Down syndrome, ages 6 to 61 years. In that study, Allanson, O'Hara, Farkas, and Nair (1993) compared the prototypical features of the Down syndrome face with age- and sex-matched normal standards. Their findings show many similarities between the Down syndrome faces and the babyfaces described by Zebrowitz. Down syndrome faces characteristically show:

- striking negative nasal protrusion (similar to Zebrowitz's "sunken bridge")
- reduced ear length (i.e., "smaller features")
- reduced mouth width (i.e., "smaller mouth")
- head length shorter than width (i.e., "rounder face")
- lower facial width (i.e., "lower placement of features on the face")

These results suggest that individuals with Down syndrome have babyface features, and as a result are included in the babyface overgeneralization. Consequently, they may be eliciting more protective and positive reactions from others, as do their typically developing babyfaced peers. In effect, parents may be reacting to the behaviors and to the appearance of their children, and such reactions may differ based on the child's type of mental retardation. Indeed, individuals with certain syndromes – most notably Down syndrome and Williams syndrome – seem to appear more "babylike" to adults, whereas others (fragile X syndrome) do not. Although at present these ideas must remain speculative, it does seem as if facial appearance joins with the child's behavior to influence the amount and type of parents' interactive efforts.

When considering personality-motivational differences in children with mental retardation, then, several complementary causes must be considered: failure, maternal interactions, and direct and indirect effects of genetic disorders of mental retardation. As identified by Zigler and his colleagues, it may indeed be the case that children with mental retardation fail more often. Such failures may especially occur in the school setting, when academic and intellectual abilities most come to the fore. Before the school years, however, mothers of children with mental retardation may be overly didactic and intrusive, not allowing their children to develop their own, intrinsic pleasure in solving difficult tasks. Added to the general findings of more intrusive maternal styles may be the child's specific type of mental retardation. Different genetic etiologies may more often display specific intellectual strengths and weaknesses, different degrees of sociability, and different personality types; each of these behavioral characteristics may help or hinder children's abilities to learn. Indirectly, parents may react to such personalities – and even to the child's facial appearance – in ways that also relate to the development of more versus less effective strategies to solve problems.

Changing Personality-Motivational Functioning: The Parent's Role

Research on failure, mother-child interaction, and direct and indirect effects of genetic etiology leads to both general and specific advice about parents' roles in fostering their children's personality-motivational development. As we noted earlier, many issues apply to children with all types of mental retardation – increased amounts of failure and more intrusive maternal interactive styles are probably experienced by many children with mental retardation. Other concerns – including learning styles and reactions from surrounding individuals – are probably more specific to the child's particular type of mental retardation. We examine each in turn.

General Suggestions

As Zigler and his colleagues have shown repeatedly, children with mental retardation less often choose difficult problems, and show less satisfaction in solving such problems (Harter & Zigler, 1974). Given that mothers more often teach and intrude on their children and that the school environment may provide more negative feedback as opposed to positive feedback, it seems almost predetermined that children with mental retardation will feel less of a desire themselves to solve difficult problems.

The most important general suggestion, then, involves different ways to foster the child's own, internally generated solutions to difficult problems. These internal solutions can be fostered in both how problems are presented and in how parents think about their child's problem-solving. In accordance with Bybee and Zigler's (1992) "easy-to-hard" principle, it might be best if children with mental retardation are given easy problems first, and more difficult problems only later on. But even the word "problems" needs to be examined, particularly in the context of interactive sessions involving mothers playing with their children. In the Mahoney et al. (1990) study of mother-child interactions, mothers repeatedly asked their children to solve problems close to the child's level of cognitive abilities (15 months compared with the children's 17-month MA). As a result, these mothers may have overly taxed their infants. In short, it may be better to start easy, and to gradually make the problems more difficult for the child with mental retardation.

More important than even the easy-to-hard principle, however, might be the idea of following the child's lead. In the various studies that show mothers of children with mental retardation to be more didactic and intrusive, mothers are both putting their children in a passive role and making their children switch their focus. Mothers in these interactions, for example, are showing how one object works, then another, or asking for the child to do one thing, then another. For their part, children are forced to watch passively as they are denied the opportunity to control the nature and topic of these interactions.

Across a variety of studies with many types of children with mental retardation, the lesson seems to be to follow the child's interactive focus. Indeed, many researchers have begun to discuss issues of "shared attention," the idea that parents and their young children are sharing a single, long-lasting topic of conversation (Kasari & Bauminger, 1997). Keeping within this shared focus may be critically important for children with mental retardation. Mothers may help their children to perform an activity or comment on an ongoing activity, but children seem to develop faster when parents do not quickly shift the child's attention from one object or demand to another. The best interactions seem to be those in which the mother follows and elaborates on the child's lead.

One way to follow the child's lead is to imitate the child's behaviors or to comment on what the child is looking at or doing. These ideas are implemented in TRIP, the Transactional Intervention Program instituted by Gerald Mahoney (1988). According to Mahoney, the TRIP program has two goals. The first attempts to make parents and their infants equal or near-equal in their turn-taking. Instead of the parents' taking more and longer turns, TRIP attempts to teach parents to allow their child to more often take the interactive turn. Second, TRIP hones in on the interactional focus. Again, the goal is to allow mothers and their children to control the conversational topic for approximately equal amounts of the time. Such control would seem to be highly beneficial for promoting the child's own feelings of self-efficacy in solving difficult problems.

Specific, Etiology-Related Suggestions

In addition to these more general suggestions, it also appears that children's personality-motivational development may be enhanced when etiologically specific interventions are considered. These interventions relate to profiles of intellectual abilities, as well as existing personality-motivational characteristics.

Interventions Based on Intellectual Strengths-Weaknesses of Different Etiological Groups. In line with the direct effects of different genetic disorders of mental retardation, children with different genetic disorders may be more likely to possess different learning styles. For intervention to be most effective, mothers and interventionists might consider playing to the child's strengths, to present information in ways that are most likely to be of benefit to the child.

As noted earlier, children with fragile X syndrome and with Prader–Willi syndrome show relative weaknesses in sequential processing as opposed to simultaneous processing. Given this pattern, for these children it may be best to present information in a more "simultaneous" manner. Thus, in fragile X syndrome (and possibly in Prader–Willi syndrome as well), it may be best to present pictures, models, and diagrams. So far in fragile X syndrome, several workers have suggested using common logos – for example, STOP signs – to teach reading (Braden, 1989). Conversely, given these children's sequential deficits, long sequences of commands may not prove as beneficial; it may thus be counterproductive to teach children in a style of "first we will do this, then that, then that" (Dykens & Hodapp, 1997; Dykens, Hodapp, & Leckman, 1994).

In Down syndrome, most effective interventions may center around avoiding these children's particular deficits in auditory processing and capitalizing on their strengths in visual processing (Pueschel et al., 1986). As a result of the visual processing strength, Sue Buckley (1995) has emphasized training in early reading for these children. Although it seems too early to evaluate her findings, Buckley and her colleagues' preliminary reports suggest that up to half of the children with Down syndrome can accomplish at least some productive reading skills. In addition, these children's accomplishments in early reading may spill over into gains in two other areas thought to be particularly problematic in this syndrome – syntax and articulation (Buckley, Bird, & Byrne, 1996).

Across each syndrome, the main issue is that children will become more motivated to learn when information is presented in ways that are easiest for the child. In essence, just as for normal children, success breeds success for children with mental retardation. If one wants to foster children who independently choose and enjoy solving difficult problems, one must present problems in ways that take advantage of children's existing profiles of intellectual strengths and weaknesses.

Interventions Based on Existing Personality-Motivational Characteristics. Just as it may help to take into account the profiles of children's intellectual abilities, so too may interventions capitalize on children's existing personalities and problem-solving strategies. For example, parents and interventionists may utilize knowledge about the child with Down syndrome's propensity to escape from intellectual tasks. Instead of being affected by these interesting, entertaining displays from children who are also more often physically cute and babyfaced, parents and other adults can nicely but firmly insist that the child continue to work on a particular intellectual problem.

But in a more positive sense, parents and interventionists can use the child with Down syndrome's interest in people within intervention itself. This interest can be used either as a reinforcement for hard work or as an intrinsic part of any academic or intellectual problem. Just as most of us enjoy learning about people – and acquire unrelated facts about the world as we do so – so too can the child with Down syndrome learn more about reading, math, language, or other subjects through "people-oriented" problems. Such an orientation toward people is not always seen in several other genetic syndromes of mental retardation; for most children with other, "less sociable" disorders (such as fragile X syndrome), different intervention strategies may be appropriate (see Dykens & Hodapp, 1997; also Chapter 11, this book).

Conclusion

Despite its long and successful history, research on personality-motivational functioning has several gaps. As this chapter shows, the issue remains unsettled as to why children with mental retardation are more dependent and less often choose or enjoy solving difficult problems. As Zigler suggests, increased amounts of intellectual failure may account for these children's different personality-motivational structures, although other factors may also be involved. Specifically, it would seem that maternal over-directiveness and the direct and indirect effects of different genetic disorders of mental retardation may all influence personality-motivational functioning.

Taken together, failure, more intrusive maternal interactive styles, and direct and indirect effects of genetic retardation disorders all lead to a variety of suggestions for intervention. Some of these suggestions may apply to all children with mental retardation; most salient here are the presentation of tasks in an easy-to-hard order and following the child's focus of conversation or activity. Others will be specific to children with only one or a few different types of disabilities; such recommendations pertain to different intellectual profiles as well as to personality characteristics of different disorders of mental retardation. By combining both general and specific suggestions, however, more fine-grained, tailored interventions would seem possible. Although much work remains to be done, the large amount of personality-motivational work performed so far leads directly to a host of important intervention implications. Granted, though children with mental retardation may always suffer from intellectual deficits, we can still intervene to allow them to perform at their highest possible levels.

References

Allanson, J.E., O'Hara, P., Farkas, L.G., & Nair, R.C. (1993). Anthropometric craniofacial pattern profiles in Down syndrome. *American Journal of Medical Genetics, 47,* 748–752.

Bell, R.Q. (1968). A reinterpretation of direction of effects in studies of socialization. *Psychological Review, 75,* 81–95.

Bell, R.Q., & Harper, L.V. (1977). *Child effects on adults.* Hillsdale, NJ: Erlbaum.

Berry, D.S., & McArthur, L.Z. (1985). Some components and consequences of a babyface. *Journal of Personality and Social Psychology, 48,* 312–323.

    (1986). Perceiving character in faces: The impact of age-related craniofacial changes on social perception. *Psychological Bulletin, 100,* 3–18.

Braden, M.L. (1989). *Logo reading system* (available from 100 E. St. Vrain Street, Colorado Springs, CO 80903).

Buckley, S. (1995). Teaching children with Down syndrome to read and write. In L. Nadel & D. Rosenthal (eds.), *Down syndrome: Living and learning in the community* (pp. 158–169). New York: Wiley-Liss.

Buckley, S., Bird, G., & Byrne, A. (1996). The practical and theoretical significance of teaching literacy skills to children with Down's syndrome. In J.A. Rondal, J. Perera, L. Nadel, & A. Comblain (eds.), *Down's syndrome: Psychological, psychobiological, and socio-educational perspectives* (pp. 119–128). London: Whurr Publishers.

Bybee, J.A., & Zigler, E. (1992). Is outerdirectedness employed in a harmful or beneficial manner by students with and without mental retardation? *American Journal on Mental Retardation, 96,* 512–521.

Cardoso-Martins, C., & Mervis, C. (1984). Maternal speech to prelinguistic children with Down Syndrome. *American Journal of Mental Deficiency, 89,* 451–458.

Das, J.P., Kirby, J., & Jarman, R.F. (1975). Simultaneous and successive abilities: An alternative model for cognitive abilities. *Psychological Bulletin, 82,* 87–103.

Dykens, E.M. (1995). Measuring behavioral phenotypes: Provocations from the "new genetics." *American Journal on Mental Retardation, 99,* 522–532.

   (1996). DNA meets DSM: The growing importance of genetic syndromes in dual diagnosis. *Mental Retardation, 34,* 125–127.

Dykens, E.M., & Cassidy, S.B. (1996). Prader–Willi syndrome: Genetic, behavioral, and treatment issues. *Child and Adolescent Psychiatry Clinics, 5,* 913–927.

Dykens, E.M., & Clarke, D.J. (1997). Correlates of maladaptive behavior in persons with 5p- (cri-du-chat) syndrome. *Developmental Medicine and Child Neurology, 39,* 752–756.

Dykens, E.M., & Hodapp, R.M. (1997). Treatment approaches in genetic mental retardation syndromes. *Professional Psychology: Research and Practice, 28,* 263–270.

Dykens, E.M., Hodapp, R.M., & Leckman, J.F. (1987). Strengths and weaknesses in the intellectual functioning of males with fragile X syndrome. *American Journal of Mental Deficiency, 92,* 234–236.

   (1994). *Behavior and development in fragile X syndrome.* Newbury Park, CA: Sage.

Dykens, E.M., Hodapp, R.M., Walsh, K., & Nash, L. (1992). Profiles, correlates, and trajectories of intelligence in individuals with Prader–Willi Syndrome. *Journal of the American Academy of Child and Adolescent Psychiatry, 31,* 1125–1130.

Erikson, M., & Upshure, C.C. (1989). Caretaking burden and social support: Comparison of mothers of infants with and without disabilities. *American Journal on Mental Retardation, 94,* 250–258.

Harris, S., Kasari, C., & Sigman, M. (1996). Joint attention and language gains in children with Down syndrome. *American Journal on Mental Retardation, 100,* 608–619.

Harter, S., & Zigler, E. (1974). The assessment of effectance motivation in normal and retarded children. *Developmental Psychology, 10,* 169–180.

Hodapp, R.M., (1988). The role of maternal emotions and perceptions in interactions with young handicapped children. In K. Marfo (ed.), *Early intervention in transition* (pp. 32–46). New York: Praeger.

   (1996). Down syndrome: Developmental, psychiatric, and management issues. *Child and Adolescent Psychiatric Clinics of North America, 5,* 881–894.

   (1997). Direct and indirect behavioral effects of different genetic disorders of mental retardation. *American Journal on Mental Retardation, 102,* 67–79.

   (in press). *Developmental and disabilities: Intellectual, sensory, and motor impairments.* New York: Cambridge University Press.

Hodapp, R.M., & Dykens, E.M. (1991). Toward an etiology-specific strategy of early intervention with handicapped children. In K. Marfo (ed.), *Early intervention in transition: Current perspectives on programs for handicapped children* (pp. 41–60). New York: Praeger.

  (1994). Mental retardation's two cultures of behavioral research. *American Journal on Mental Retardation, 98,* 675–687.

Hodapp, R.M., Dykens, E.M., Evans, D.W., & Merighi, J.R. (1992). Maternal emotional reactions to young children with different types of handicaps. *Journal of Developmental and Behavioral Pediatrics, 13,* 118–123.

Hodapp, R.M., Dykens, E.M., & Masino, L.L. (1997). Families of children with Prader–Willi Syndrome: Stress-support and relations to child characteristics. *Journal of Autism and Developmental Disorders, 27,* 11–24.

Hodapp, R.M., Fidler, D.J., & Smith, A.C.M. (1998). Stress and coping in families of children with Smith Magenis syndrome. *Journal of Intellectual Disability Research, 42,* 331–340.

Hodapp, R.M., & Goldfield, E.C. (1983). Self and other regulation in the infancy period. *Developmental Review, 5,* 274–288.

Hodapp, R.M., Leckman, J.F., Dykens, E.M., Sparrow, S., Zelinsky, D., & Ort, S. (1992). K-ABC profiles in children with fragile X syndrome, Down syndrome, and nonspecific mental retardation. *American Journal on Mental Retardation, 97,* 39–46.

Hodapp, R.M., Wijma, C.A., & Masino, L.L. (in press). Families of children with 5p- (cri-du-chat) syndrome: Familial stress and sibling reactions. *Developmental Medicine and Child Neurology.*

Holroyd, J., & MacArthur, D. (1976). Mental retardation and stress on parents: A contrast between Down's syndrome and childhood autism. *American Journal of Mental Deficiency, 80,* 431–436.

Hornby, G. (1995). Fathers' views of the effects on their families of children with Down syndrome. *Journal of Child and Family Studies, 4,* 103–117.

Jones, O. (1980). Prelinguistic communication skills in Down's Syndrome and normal infants. In T. Field, S. Goldberg, D. Stern, & A. Sostek (eds.), *High-risk infants and children: Adult and peer interaction* (pp. 205–225). New York: Academic Press.

Kasari, C., & Bauminger, N. (1997). Social and emotional development in children with mental retardation. In J.A. Burack, R.M. Hodapp, & E. Zigler (eds.), *Handbook of mental retardation and development* (pp. 411–433). New York: Cambridge University Press.

Kasari, C., & Sigman, M. (1997). Linking parental perceptions to interactions in young children with autism. *Journal of Autism and Developmental Disorders, 27,* 39–57.

Kasari, C., Sigman, M., Mundy, P., & Yirmiya, N. (1990). Affective sharing in the context of joint attention interactions. *Journal of Autism and Developmental Disabilities, 20,* 87–100.

Kaufman, A.S., & Kaufman, N.L. (1983). *Kaufman Assessment Battery for Children.* Circle Pines, MN: American Guidance Service.

Mahoney, G. (1988). Enhancing the developmental competence of handicapped infants. In K. Marfo (ed.), *Early intervention in transition: Current perspectives on programs for handicapped children* (pp. 203–219). New York: Praeger.

Mahoney, G., Fors, S., & Wood, S. (1990). Maternal directive behavior revisited. *American Journal on Mental Retardation, 94,* 398–406.

McArthur, Leslie Z., & Apatow, K. (1983–4). Impressions of baby-faced adults. *Social Cognition, 2,* 315–342.

McCabe, V. (1988). Facial proportions, perceived age, and caregiving. In Thomas R. Alley (ed.), *Social and applied aspects of perceiving faces. Resources for ecological psychology.* Hillsdale, NJ: Erlbaum.

Mink, T., Nihira, K., & Meyers, C.E. (1983).Taxonomy of family life styles. I. Home with TMR children. *American Journal of Mental Deficiency, 87,* 484–497.

Opitz, J.M. (1996). *Historiography of the causal analysis of mental retardation.* Speech to the 29th Gatlinburg Conference on Research and Theory in Mental Retardation, Gatlinburg, TN.

Pennington, B., O'Connor, R., & Sudhalter, V. (1991). Toward a neuropsychology of fragile X syndrome. In R.J. Hagerman & A.C. Silverman (eds.), *Fragile X syndrome: Diagnosis, treatment, and research* (pp. 173–201). Baltimore: Johns Hopkins University Press.

Pitcairn, T.K., & Wishart, J.G. (1994). Reactions of young children with Down syndrome to an impossible task. *British Journal of Developmental Psychology, 12,* 485–489.

Pober, B.R., & Dykens, E.M. (1996). Williams syndrome: An overview of medical, cognitive, and behavioral features. *Child and Adolescent Psychiatric Clinics of North America, 5,* 929–943.

Pueschel, S. (1983). The child with Down syndrome. In M. Levine, W. Carey, A. Crocker, & R. Gross (eds.), *Developmental-behavioral pediatrics* (pp. 353–362). Philadelphia: Saunders.

Pueschel, S.R., Gallagher, P.L., Zartler, A.S., & Pezzullo, J.C. (1986). Cognitive and learning processes in children with Down syndrome. *Research in Developmental Disabilities, 8,* 21–37.

Raber, S.M., & Weisz, J.R. (1981). Teacher feedback to mentally retarded and non-retarded children. *American Journal of Mental Deficiency, 86,* 148–156.

Rondal, J. (1977). Maternal speech in normal and Down syndrome children. In P. Mittler (ed.), *Research to practice in mental retardation, Vol. 3, Education and training* (pp. 239–243). Baltimore: University Park Press.

Scarr, S. (1993). Developmental theories for the 1990s: Development and individual differences. *Child Development, 63,* 1–19.

Seltzer, M.M., Krauss, M.W., & Tsunematsu, N. (1993). Adults with Down Syndrome and their aging mothers: Diagnostic group differences. *American Journal on Mental Retardation, 97,* 496–508.

Sparrow, S.S., Balla, D.A., & Cicchetti, D.V. (1984). *Vineland Adaptive Behavior Scales.* Circle Pines, MN: American Guidance Service.

Tannock, R. (1988). Mothers' directiveness in their interactions with children with and without Down Syndrome. *American Journal on Mental Retardation, 93,* 154–165.

Thomas, V., & Olsen, D.H. (1993). Problem families and the circumplex model: Observational assessment using the clinical rating scale (CRS). *Journal of Marital and Family Therapy, 19,* 159–175.

Vietze, P., Abernathy, S., Ashe, M., & Faulstich, G. (1978). Contingency interaction between mothers and their developmentally delayed infants. In G.P. Sackett (ed.), *Observing behavior* (VOL. 1, pp. 115–132). Baltimore: University Park Press.

Weisz, J.R. (1981). Learned helplessness in black and white children identified by their schools as retarded and non-retarded: Performance deterioration in response to failure. *Developmental Psychology, 17,* 499–508.

(1982). Learned helplessness and the retarded child. In E. Zigler & D. Balla (eds.), *Mental retardation: The developmental-difference controversy* (pp. 137–168). Hillsdale, NJ: Erlbaum.

Wishart, J.G., & Johnston, F.H. (1990). The effects of experience on attribution of a stereotyped personality to children with Down's syndrome. *Journal of Mental Deficiency Research, 34,* 409–420.

Yando, R., Seitz, V., & Zigler, E. (1989). Imitation, recall, and imitativeness in children with low intelligence of organic and familial etiology. *Research in Developmental Disabilities, 10,* 383–397.

Zebrowitz, L.A. (1997). *Reading faces: Window to the soul?* Boulder, CO: Westview Press.

Zebrowitz, L.A., & Montepare, J.M. (1992). Impressions of babyfaced individuals across the life span. *Developmental Psychology, 28,* 1143–1152.

Zebrowitz, L.A., Olson, K., & Hoffman, K. (1993). Stability of babyfaceness and attractiveness across the life span. *Journal of Personality and Social Psychology, 64,* 453–466.

Zigler, E. (1971). The retarded child as a whole person. In H.E. Adams & W.K. Boardman (eds.), *Advances in experimental clinical psychology* (pp. 47–121). Oxford, England: Pergamon.

(1984). A developmental theory on mental retardation. In B. Blatt & R. Morris (eds.), *Perspectives in special education: Personal orientations* (pp. 173–209). Santa Monica, CA: Scott, Foresman.

Zigler, E., & Hodapp, R.M. (1986). *Understanding mental retardation.* New York: Cambridge University Press.

11   Personality-Motivation: New Ties to Psychopathology, Etiology, and Intervention

Elisabeth M. Dykens

People with mental retardation have distinctive personality and behavioral features, yet workers only began to appreciate these behavioral issues relatively recently. In the 1960s and 1970s, Edward Zigler launched a series of studies on the personality of children with mental retardation, a line of work that tested his innovative concept of children with mental retardation as "whole" people (Zigler, 1971). At the same time, other researchers were planting seeds for an entire new field of study on psychopathology in people with mental retardation.

Sparked in large part by the Kennedy-era's renewed interests in mental retardation, research on both personality and psychopathology has prospered over the last decades. Yet despite their shared historical roots, these lines of work grew up in relative isolation of one another. On the personality front, although researchers examined the interplay between personality and cognition and social deprivation, they did not link these findings to psychiatric illness or maladaptive behavior (although see Zigler & Burack, 1989). Similarly, workers in psychopathology focused on prevalence and treatment issues, yet they did not generally relate psychiatric or behavioral problems to specific personality styles.

But personality problems have long been considered a risk factor for psychopathology in people without mental retardation. Characteristic personality traits or problems are associated with many psychiatric disorders (APA; DSM-IV), and full-blown personality disorders are increasingly recognized in the nonretarded population. Further, people with mental retardation are at increased risk for many behavioral and psychiatric disorders (e.g., Borthwick-Duffy, 1994; Menolascino & Fleisher, 1993). Indeed, for some disorders such as psychosis, people with mental retardation have a two- to three-fold increase in frequency relative to the general population. Exact reasons for the increased risks of psychopathology remain unknown, yet are likely associated with compromised cognitive, adaptive, social, neurological, and personality functioning (e.g., Matson,

1985; Matson & Sevin, 1994). Indeed, as we show in this chapter, the personality styles outlined by Zigler and his colleagues may emerge as one of several risk factors in the development of psychopathology. With good reason, then, the time is ripe to better integrate personality styles with psychopathology in people with mental retardation.

This chapter begins by specifying several probable clinical correlates of Zigler's personality formulations, or how these constructs might extend into the psychopathology arena. We then develop a new rationale for expanding previous work on personality styles that moves away from environmental social deprivation as the underpinnings of Zigler's personality styles. Instead, we build on recent advances in genetics and propose that genetic etiology of mental retardation is a new, relatively unexplored pathway to distinctive personality styles, including the styles proposed by Zigler three decades ago. Studies have yet to explore Zigler's five core constructs within specific genetic or other etiological groups; instead, work in this area has relied on heterogeneous subject groups. Yet, based on findings to date, people with certain syndromes are especially prone to distinctive personality styles and psychopathologies, and these genetic groups thus hold considerable promise for personality research. We end the chapter by describing guidelines for treatment and intervention that target areas of dysfunction in each of Zigler's personality constructs.

Clinical Manifestations of Personality Constructs

Although a review of Zigler's five personality styles is offered elsewhere in this book, we describe here how these styles might be associated with specific behavioral or psychiatric vulnerabilities (Table 11.1). One style, initially described as "positive-reaction tendency," refers to children's heightened need to interact with or be dependent on warm, supportive adults – a trait especially characteristic of children living in depriving environments. At the same time, these and other children often show a wary, slow-to-warm style with others, labeled "negative-reaction tendency." If well-modulated and not too extreme, these styles seem adaptive – certainly children, delayed or not, should seek attention from supportive adults and be wary of strangers.

Yet what happens to children in whom these tendencies are exaggerated, extreme, or poorly modulated? In broad terms, we might label these youngsters as showing inappropriate social skills and poor or odd social relating. These social difficulties may be manifest in children who are overly familiar with others, socially disinhibited, and perhaps superficial as well. Often,

Table 11.1. *Adaptive and maladaptive components of five personality styles*

Personality style	Adaptive components	Maladaptive components
Positive-reaction tendency	Seeks attention from supportive adults Appropriately dependent	Superficial social interactions Dependent personality disorder Social disinhibition Anxiety disorders
Negative-reaction tendency	Wary of strangers Shy or slow to warm	Withdrawn, avoidant, detached, Avoidant personality disorder, social phobia, Pervasive developmental disorder, autistic-spectrum disorders
Outerdirectedness	Help-seeking Getting support for difficult or novel tasks	Impulsive problem-solving style Depending on others for solutions Mistrusting self Low self-esteem Problems attending long enough to solve problems Attention deficit hyperactivity disorder
Expectancy of success and effectance motivation	Adequate esteem Pleasure in problem-solving Willingness to approach tasks	Low self-esteem, feeling ineffectual Sadness, depression Affective disorders Masked depression, acting out Disruptive behavior disorders

this type of social disinhibition in people is related to their heightened levels of generalized anxiety. Alternatively, these children might be labeled as shy, withdrawn, avoidant, detached, and perhaps as showing avoidant disorders, social phobias, or autistic spectrum disorders (see Table 11.1).

Other personality constructs also have both an adaptive and maladaptive component. Up to a certain point, for example, it is appropriate for children to be "outerdirected" – that is, to turn to others for solutions to difficult problems, especially when learning novel concepts. Yet in children with a more entrenched or extreme outerdirected style, we might expect to see a range of clinical issues, such as problems attending to complex stimuli, adopting an impulsive problem-solving style, mistrusting one's own judgments, low self-esteem, and increased dependency on others for solutions. These problems may be more likely in children who have difficulties sustaining their attention or motor activity long enough to tackle a complex problem, including those with attention deficit hyperactivity disorder (ADHD).

Similarly, children show adaptive personality and problem-solving styles when they have high or well-developed "expectations for success," and when they take pleasure from solving difficult problems ("effectance motivation"). Yet in youngsters with inadequate or poorly developed expectations for success, we might expect a wide range of problems. These include low self-esteem, sadness, lack of pleasure in activities, and feeling ineffectual or worthless. These symptoms may or may not be associated with vegetative signs (e.g., changes in sleep, appetite, activity level) and full-blown mood disorders.

In short, each of the five personality styles initially proposed by Zigler and his colleagues has an adaptive and a maladaptive component. Risks of problems and psychopathology are high when these styles are deeply entrenched, extreme (i.e., too high or too low), or poorly modulated or developed. Although the proposed ties between personality constructs and psychopathology are preliminary to more systematic study, they provide a first step toward linking together two fields of work – personality and psychopathology. Such ties also pave the way to work that examines the relationships between personality and etiology of mental retardation.

Personality and Etiology: From Environment to Genes

One commonality of Zigler's five different personality styles is that they were born of an era when children with mental retardation were often institutionalized, and treated very differently than they are today. These youngsters were at high risk for environmental, social-emotional depriva-tion and for failure, and these observations formed the cornerstones of Zigler's personality formulations. Not surprisingly, then, many of these children – often from large state schools or other residential programs – were eager to interact with a team of supportive researchers (positive-reaction tendency), or else were wary of them, perhaps because of disrup-tions in care or multiple care providers (negative-reaction tendency).

Today, however, it is unusual for young children with mental retardation to be placed in large institutions. Instead, residential and educational oppor-tunities are based on principles of "least restrictive environments," main-streaming, and inclusion. Relative to the 1950s and 1960s, then, social deprivation may be less of an issue for children living at home or other homelike settings, and who also receive community-based educational and other support services.

Further, recent years have brought renewed commitment from workers in the mental retardation field to certain principles such as self-deter-mination, choice, personal rights, and full community inclusion. On face value, these principles call into question the assumption that children with mental retardation are more apt than their nonretarded peers to encounter failure experiences (low expectancy of success) and thus to turn to others for solutions (outerdirectedness). Theoretically, then, unlike years ago, people with mental retardation are themselves now deciding how and where to live, work, and recreate. They routinely attend and participate in their Individualized Educational Program (IEP) and school-to-work transi-tion meetings, and they are encouraged to actively help plan their own futures, called "personal-centered planning."

With these trends increasingly in place, might we see a decline in the five personality styles based on social-emotional deprivation and failure? We offer two answers to this question. First, we propose that even with radical philosophical changes in the field, people with mental retardation still encounter failure. One could argue that failure is a necessary part of learning, and that people with mental retardation are far from exempt from this rule. Indeed, because people with mental retardation are defined by cognitive and adaptive delays or deficits, they seem at increased risk for failure. Studies have yet to demonstrate how often people with mental retardation actually fail, and how failure relates to their feeling efficacious or not. Work that addresses these questions seems especially important as people with mental retardation strive to meet the complex demands of an increasingly inclusive world.

In light of the renewed push toward inclusion and self-determination, then, studies are needed that reexamine the extent to which people with mental retardation fail. In doing so, failure needs to be defined both by objective standards and by how people with mental retardation themselves perceive and judge their successes and failures.

Second, though social deprivation (and perhaps failure) may be on the decline for many people with mental retardation, we propose that new evidence for the five personality styles is found in people with distinctive genetic etiologies. In this section of the chapter, we develop the argument that genetic mental retardation syndromes are an important, albeit relatively unexplored, means of studying personality in people with mental retardation. In doing so, we move away from a personality model based on environmental factors such as social deprivation or failure to a model that includes genetic predispositions to distinctive personality styles.

Similar to behavioral research in general, work in personality and psychopathology has relied on mixed or heterogenous groups of people with mental retardation (Dykens, 1995, 1996; Hodapp, 1997; Hodapp & Dykens, 1994) including early work on personality (e.g., Yando & Zigler, 1971). Although some work (e.g., Balla, Styfco, & Zigler, 1971; Zigler, 1962) classified people into two broadly defined groups – those with different types of organic etiologies and those with cultural-familial mental retardation – for the most part, studies paid little attention to etiology. As a result, we know more about personality and psychopathology in the general population of people with mental retardation than we do in people with distinctive genetic or other etiologies.

Recent advances in molecular genetics provide new opportunities to study the behavioral features, or so-called behavioral phenotypes, of people with clearly defined genetic mental retardation syndromes. Data from behavioral phenotype studies help refine treatment and intervention (Dykens & Hodapp, 1997) as well as provide important clues to gene-brain relationships and function (Dykens, 1995; Dykens & Hodapp, in press). Although less common than mixed-group approaches, behavioral phenotypic studies to date find that many syndromes show distinctive cognitive, adaptive, personality, and maladaptive features.

Indeed, one could argue that because people with a given syndrome have a shared genetic anomaly, they are more apt to show similar personality and behavioral predispositions relative to mixed or heterogenous groups of mentally retarded subjects. Our working definition of a behavioral phenotype reflects this idea. Specifically, we view phenotypes as the "increased probability or likelihood that people with a given syndrome will show certain behavioral or developmental sequelae relative to those without the syndrome" (Dykens, 1995, p. 523).

If phenotypes are probabilistic, then it follows that not every individual with a specific syndrome will show that syndrome's characteristic behavior. Further, if the individual does show a characteristic behavior, he or she may not show it to the same extent as others at the same point in development. Thus, individual differences exist within syndromes, and identifying the genetic and psychosocial sources of within-syndrome variability is a particularly exciting aspect of phenotypic work. Equally exciting and compelling, however, are the ways in which people with syndromes are alike in their behaviors or behavioral predispositions.

We now describe some remarkable similarities in the personality and behavior in people with several different genetic syndromes: Williams syndrome, fragile X syndrome, Smith–Magenis syndrome, and Prader–Willi syndrome. We briefly review these syndromes, using them as case examples that show some intriguing and particularly promising relationships to Zigler's five personality styles. The syndrome review is not meant to be exhaustive, but instead to highlight disorders that show the benefits of an etiology-specific approach for furthering our understanding of personality.

Syndrome Review

Williams Syndrome and Positive-Reaction Tendency

Williams syndrome affects about 1 in 20,000 people, and is caused in most cases by a deletion on one of the chromosome 7s that includes the gene for elastin (Ewart et al., 1993). Persons with Williams syndrome often show hyperacusis, cardiovascular disease, hypercalcemia, and characteristic facial features described as elfin-like, cute, and appealing (see Pober & Dykens, 1996, for a review). We propose that many of the cognitive and behavioral features of Williams syndrome are consistent with the "positive-reaction tendency," including the maladaptive correlates of this style outlined in Table 11.1.

Williams syndrome is perhaps best known for its cognitive-linguistic profile. Many people with Williams syndrome show remarkable strengths in expressive language and linguistic functioning, especially in syntax and semantics; story-telling and narrative enrichment strategies involving affective prosody and a sense of drama; and a reliance on stereotypic, adult social phrases, sometimes referred to as "cocktail party speech" (e.g., Reilly, Klima, & Bellugi, 1990; Udwin & Yule, 1990). Although compelling, these strengths are not seen in all persons with Williams syndrome, and the representativeness of this profile is open to debate (Karmiloff-Smith et al., 1997).

In contrast to linguistic strengths, most people with Williams syndrome have difficulties with nonverbal, perceptual-spatial skills. Problems with fine-motor and paper-and-pencil tasks have been noted, especially integrating details into a whole (Bihrle et al., 1989). Yet certain visual-spatial skills may be well-preserved even within this area of global deficit. In particular, persons with Williams syndrome generally do well on facial perception and recognition tasks, and they often look intently at the faces of both strangers and familiar people (Bellugi, Wang, & Jernigan, 1994). Not surprisingly, people with Williams syndrome appear "acutely attentive to the emotional states of others" (Bellugi et al., 1994, p. 35) and "responsive to any and all facial cues" (p. 46).

Facial recognition skills and heightened interests in the emotions of others are likely associated with a set of distinctive personality features often seen in Williams syndrome. Many researchers have been impressed by a "classic" Williams syndrome personality, typically described as pleasant, unusually friendly, affectionate, engaging, outgoing, and interpersonally sensitive and charming (e.g., Dilts, Morris, & Leonard, 1990). These features, coupled with a cute and appealing face, likely facilitate positive interactions with others.

Yet as children with Williams syndrome develop, they are apt to show increased behavioral and emotional difficulties, including problems relating to peers. Sociability remains, but it may reflect a form of disinhibition that is characteristic of people who are overly anxious or aroused. Indeed, excessive anxiety is a prominent finding in virtually all studies to date on the emotional concerns of persons with Williams syndrome (e.g., Einfeld, Tonge, & Florio, 1997). In addition, many persons with Williams syndrome show overactivity, restlessness, and a short attention span (e.g., Dilts et al., 1990). Increased risks of anxiety disorders and attention deficit hyperactivity disorder are thus strongly suggested in Williams syndrome.

Of the five personality constructs initially proposed by Zigler, then, we predict that people with Williams syndrome show marked predispositions for positive-reaction tendency. To the extent that individuals with Williams syndrome also turn to others for solutions, or show impulsivity or attention deficits, they may also show high levels of outerdirectedness. Though studies have yet to test this hypothesis, we also predict that these styles will be high relative to heterogeneous groups with mental retardation. As apparent in the overview of Williams syndrome, these personality styles have an adaptive element, especially for social interaction. Yet the maladaptive features of these styles are also strikingly present, especially in risks for anxiety and attention deficit disorders. As described at the end of the chapter, both the adaptive and maladaptive elements of positive-reaction tendency and outerdirectedness shed light on treatment and intervention.

Fragile X Syndrome and Negative-Reaction Tendency

Fragile X syndrome, the most common, known inherited cause of mental retardation, represents a newly identified type of human disease, caused by an amplification (or excessive repetition) of a three-nucleotide sequence that makes up DNA (Caskey et al., 1992). Fragile X syndrome results in a wide range of learning and behavioral problems (see Dykens, Hodapp, & Leckman, 1994, for a review). Males are more often and more severely affected than females, showing moderate mental retardation. About two-thirds of the females who carry and transmit the fragile X gene have mild delays or learning difficulties, and both males and females show predispositions to problems with social relationships. We hypothesize that many of the behavioral features seen in people with fragile X syndrome are strikingly similar to "negative-reaction tendency."

Early studies focused on males with fragile X syndrome, often diagnosing these males with autism. These studies emphasized symptoms common to both fragile X syndrome and autism, including stereotypies, perseveration, tactile defensiveness, poor social relating, and self-injury (Dykens & Volkmar, 1997). In contrast, recent work finds that only a relatively small percentage of affected males have full-blown autistic disorder (e.g., Fisch, 1992). Instead of autism per se, the majority of these males show a spectrum of social relatedness problems, including social anxiety, shyness, and mutual gaze aversion (Bregman, Leckman, & Ort, 1988; Cohen et al., 1989). Many males become less shy or withdrawn as their familiarity with others increases, and this slow-to-warm stance contrasts with the persistent aloofness and social indifference typical of autism (Dykens & Volkmar, 1997). Some males with fragile X syndrome meet criteria for anxiety disorder (Bregman et al., 1989) or for pervasive developmental disorder–not otherwise specified (Reiss & Freund, 1990).

Many females with fragile X syndrome have similar vulnerabilities, showing a range of social dysfunction involving shyness, gaze aversion, social anxieties, and withdrawal. As adults, some females meet diagnostic criteria for schizotypal and avoidant personality disorders (Freund et al., 1992). Depressive features are also commonly seen, even compared with non-fragile X women with developmentally delayed offspring (Reiss et al., 1988).

In addition to problems with social relatedness, many males and females show attention deficits and hyperactivity (Bregman et al., 1988; Lachiewicz, 1992). Adult ADHD or problems sustaining attention have also been found in cognitively unaffected males and females who carry the fragile X gene (Dorn, Mazzocco, & Hagerman, 1994; Mazzocco et al., 1992). Though both males and females thus show problems with social relationships and attention, these difficulties seem to be more severe in males.

Behavioral findings in both males and females with fragile X syndrome thus bear a striking resemblance to features of negative-reaction tendency. Though others with mental retardation may also show this predilection, people with fragile X syndrome seem especially prone to shyness, wariness, and social anxiety. Fragile X syndrome may thus prove to be an especially fruitful avenue for future studies on the correlates and development of negative-reaction tendency.

Smith–Magenis Syndrome and Outerdirectedness

Affecting about 1 in 25,000 births, Smith–Magenis syndrome is caused by an interstitial deletion of chromosome 17 (p11.2) (Smith et al., 1986). Many genes are now mapped to this region, though none explains the syndrome's complex physical and behavioral phenotype. Physically, many people show short hands and stature, visual problems, a hoarse voice, and craniofacial abnormalities (see Smith, Dykens, & Greenberg, 1997, for a review). Behaviorally, findings to date suggest that people with Smith–Magenis syndrome may be particularly vulnerable to outerdirectedness.

People with Smith–Magenis syndrome often show a wide range of severe behavior problems. These include impulsivity, aggression, temper tantrums, attention deficits, attention seeking, hyperactivity, and significant sleep disturbance (see Smith, Dykens, & Greenberg, 1997, for a review). Although many of these difficulties are also seen in others with mental retardation, they appear to be more frequent or severe in people with Smith–Magenis syndrome (Dykens & Smith, 1997). Self-injurious behaviors such as head-banging and self-biting are also common, observed in 75 percent of a sample of thirty-five children aged 4 to 18 years (Dykens & Smith, 1997). A smaller percentage of children (30 percent) show more unusual self-injurious behaviors: finger- and toe-nail yanking and inserting objects into bodily orifices. Many children with Smith–Magenis syndrome also show stereotypies, including a characteristic upper-body squeeze, or self-hug (Finucane et al., 1994), often cast as an endearing feature of the syndrome.

In a recent study of thirty-five children with Smith–Magenis syndrome, attention seeking and demanding attention from others were seen in 100 percent of the sample; moreover, these problems were rated as the most severe relative to all other difficulties. Indeed, parents and teachers note that relative to their siblings or peers, these youngsters often need considerable input, direction, and reassurance from adults, and that they are quick to turn to adults for interaction or help. This demanding style may be associated with attention deficits and hyperactivity, seen in the majority of children with this syndrome. These children may have difficulties sustaining attention long enough to solve problems, and are thus quick to turn to supportive adults for prompts, help, support, and encouragement. In these ways, then, Smith–Magenis syndrome may prove to be a particularly helpful group for future studies on outerdirectedness. This is especially true for studies that aim to sort out how an outerdirected personality style might be associated with a wide variety of behavioral problems.

Prader–Willi Syndrome and Expectancy of Success and Effectance Motivation

In this section, we use hyperphagia, or overeating, in Prader–Willi syndrome to exemplify issues of low expectancy of success and effectance motivation. The ties between personality (expectancy of success) and genetic etiology are less direct or clear cut in Prader–Willi syndrome than in previous examples. Yet we selected Prader–Willi syndrome for review because many individuals with this disorder are able to articulate how their struggles and failures with eating and food adversely affect their expectations for success in many aspects of their lives.

Prader–Willi syndrome affects about 1 in 15,000 people, and typically results in mild levels of mental retardation (Dykens et al., 1992). Prader–Willi syndrome is the first known human disease associated with genomic imprinting. In particular, most cases (70 percent) result from a deletion in a specific region of chromosome 15 (15q11–q13) that is derived from the father. The majority of remaining cases are associated with maternal uniparental disomy, or when both copies of chromosome 15 are derived from the mother (Nichols et al., 1989). Either way, Prader–Willi syndrome is associated with a lack of paternally derived information to the Prader–Willi critical region. When missing information in this same region of chromosome 15 comes from the mother, it results in a completely different and more severe developmental disorder, Angelman's syndrome (Williams et al., 1995).

Babies with Prader–Willi syndrome show hypotonia and feeding/sucking difficulties, and children between 2 and 6 years of age develop hyperphagia, marked interests in food, and food-seeking behaviors (Holm et al., 1993). Food-related behaviors are life-long, often wax and wane over time, and are as likely to be seen in persons with high as low IQs (Dykens & Cassidy, 1995).

Contrary to popular belief, hyperphagia in people with Prader–Willi syndrome is not due to a weak character or to a lack of willpower around food. Rather, hyperphagia likely stems from altered function of the hypothalamus, the part of the brain that controls appetite and feelings of satiety (Swaab et al., 1995). Though hyperphagia's exact cause is unknown, people with Prader–Willi syndrome do not have normal feelings of fullness or satiety, and if left to their own devices, will eat voraciously. While persons with the syndrome may be quite knowledgeable about food or calories, such knowledge does not reliably translate into safe dietary practice. It is common for people with Prader–Willi syndrome to steal food, forage through garbage, and eat unpalatable items. Without persistent dietary intervention, then, Prader–Willi syndrome is life-threatening, with most deaths related to complications of obesity.

While obsessive thoughts about food are invariably seen, a remarkably high proportion of persons also show non-food related obsessions and compulsive behaviors (Dykens, Leckman, & Cassidy, 1996). In addition to persistent skin-picking, these non-food symptoms include hoarding, needing to tell or ask, and concerns with symmetry, exactness, ordering, arranging, and sameness in daily routine. Such symptoms are associated with increased risks of obsessive-compulsive disorder in both children and adults with Prader–Willi syndrome. In addition, many persons with Prader–Willi syndrome show high rates of stubbornness, temper tantrums, and emotional lability, even compared with others with mental retardation (Dykens & Kasari, in press). Increased risks of depression and impulse control problems have also been suggested.

Unlike hyperphagia, however, many of these non-food behaviors are amenable to pharmacological or behavioral intervention. Thus, pharmacological trials, milieu treatment, and behavioral modification techniques have all been successfully used to treat non-food obsessive-compulsive symptoms, depression, tantrums, and to some extent, skin-picking as well. Yet to date, no medications – including appetite suppressants – or behavioral techniques have proven consistently effective in treating hyperphagia, especially on a long-term basis. Hyperphagia and risks of obesity are thus typically treated with life-long external supports: a reduced calorie diet, regular exercise, close supervision around food and money, and locking the refrigerator and other food sources. Clinically, we find that many people with Prader–Willi syndrome know exactly what they need to do to maintain a safe diet, yet are frustrated and disappointed in themselves when they are not able to independently do so. For many, meeting with defeat with a single symptom – hyperphagia – may spill over into other areas of life, and contribute to poor esteem, sadness, a defeatist attitude, a lack of pleasure in problem-solving ("effectance motivation"), and perhaps acting-out behavior as well. Based on these clinical observations, studies are now underway that assess the impact of hyperphagia on self-esteem and expectations for success in people with this syndrome.

Summary of Etiology and Personality Styles

As shown in the review of various genetic syndromes, some disorders are more vulnerable to certain personality styles than others. Thus, positive-reaction tendency seems salient in Williams syndrome, negative-reaction tendency in fragile X syndrome, outerdirectedness in Smith–Magenis syndrome, and low expectations for success in Prader–Willi syndrome.

Although not exhaustive, the review shows how specific etiologies can be used as a springboard to further understandings of personality in people with mental retardation. Many syndromes, including the ones in the review, are useful in that they provide researchers with a sample that is enriched or primed for specific personality styles. We thus recommend that future personality research more rigorously examine etiology. Studies are needed that identify syndromes that show distinctive personality styles, that relate personality styles to genetic or psychosocial variables, and that examine personality similarities and differences across syndromes. Controlled studies are also needed that assess the differential role of etiology versus mental retardation or developmental delay on personality styles and functioning. With the success of the Human Genome Project, new genetic causes of mental retardation are rapidly being discovered and delineated, with over 750 causes already identified (Opitz, 1996). We can thus anticipate that genetic etiology will continue to be a promising avenue for future personality research.

Intervention and Treatment Implications

Many people with mental retardation and co-occurring psychopathology are helped by a variety of behavioral, psychotherapeutic, and pharmacologic interventions (see Bregman, 1991, for a review). Although it is beyond the scope of this chapter to review the efficacy of these treatments, here we briefly describe some general guidelines that address the maladaptive components of Zigler's five personality styles. In general, these suggestions aim to increase expectancy of success and effectance motivation, and to keep positive- and negative-reaction tendencies and outerdirectedness at adaptive instead of maladaptive levels. Recommendations apply equally well to people with or without genetic disorders, as members of both groups may show maladaptive personality styles that are helped by environmental interventions. Guidelines include behavioral and psychotherapeutic techniques, as well as ideas for home, school, and work. Any individual with mental retardation and co-occurring maladaptive personality styles or psychopathology should be carefully evaluated by qualified mental health professionals, with an eye toward individualized behavioral, pharmacological, or other treatments. Recommendations below are thus general guidelines that have yet to be empirically validated.

Positive-Reaction Tendency

Several themes are of importance in designing treatments or interventions for people high in positive-reaction tendency (see Table 11.2). First, if the individual presents an outgoing, disinhibited, or engaging style, as in people with Williams syndrome, clinicians will want to be sure that these features don't mask underlying sadness, worry, or anxiety. To the extent that anxiety is present, it should be carefully evaluated and treated using typical clinical treatments (e.g., medication consultation, symptom recognition, relaxation training, cognitive restructuring, role play, self-talk).

Second, though all people with mental retardation are at some risk for exploitation, given their social disinhibition and needs for approval, people with strong positive-reaction tendencies seem at high risk for exploitation and abuse. Clinicians, teachers, parents, and other care providers may thus want to teach these individuals about danger (e.g., being wary of strangers, good touch/bad touch), and they may also want to more carefully assess these individuals' needs for supervision.

Third, people with high positive-reaction tendencies are likely to need help channeling their sociability or appropriately expressing their interests

Table 11.2. *Intervention implications for personality styles*

Positive-reaction tendency
Ensure that engaging or superficial style doesn't mask sadness or anxiety
Assess increased risk of exploitation and sexual abuse
Teach certain social skills (e.g., making friends, wariness)
Use the team or buddy system at work or school
Emphasize people-oriented jobs
Assess feasibility of group therapy
Be aware of strong or immediate therapeutic transference
Be aware of heightened sensitivities to loss

Negative-reaction tendency
Allow the person to set the pace and tone for social interaction
Appreciate slow-to-warm style, and gauge interactions accordingly
Assess need for teaching early social communication skills (e.g., joint reference)
Emphasize individualized tasks as opposed to team approaches
Minimize changes in teachers, therapists, care providers, and living settings
Reduce flow of people through classroom or work site

Outerdirectedness
Introduce easily mastered material before novel or challenging problems
Use successive approximation to move toward increased independence
Reward problem-solving efforts
Establish clear expectations for how and when to ask for help
Use teacher aides, job coaches, and so on for the group, instead of as an individual's "shadow"
Minimize visual and auditory distractors at school or work
Use behavioral techniques (timeouts, contingencies) to decrease impulsivity

Expectancy of success and effectance motivation
Reduce behavioral problems that impede success (behavioral, pharmacotherapies)
Avoid blaming people for their behaviors
Reward efforts aimed at increasing success and mastery, regardless of outcome
Aim to manage rather than eliminate certain behaviors
Develop reasonable expectations for behavioral successes
Take into account how person him/herself perceives success or failure
Foster pleasure and fun through hobbies, interests, play, and leisure-time activities
Use hobbies or interests as motivators for learning at school or work

in others. Social skills training is thus recommended, with an emphasis on how to make and keep friends, maintain interpersonal boundaries, seek appropriate support from others, and be wary of strangers. Given their tendencies to approach others, with proper training and support many people with this style may ultimately do well in group therapies, in people-oriented jobs, and in team or buddy approaches to tasks at school or work. If superficiality or overfamiliarity are issues, clinicians should also be aware of strong or immediate therapeutic transference. Many individuals with this style may also overreact to loss (e.g., friend moves away, death) or changes in relationships (e.g., new teacher, therapist), and may benefit from extra support during these times.

Negative-Reaction Tendency

In contrast, a different set of intervention guidelines is suggested for people with strong negative-reaction tendencies (see Table 11.2). Many wary, slow-to-warm individuals do best in social situations where they are allowed to set the pace and tone for interactions with others. Some of these individuals, including those with fragile X syndrome, may react adversely if they are taught certain social skills that don't take their slow-to-warm style into account. To the extent that withdrawal and autistic-like features are involved, individuals with this style may need interventions that target specific aspects of early social development and communication – for example, joint attention, referencing, gaze, eye contact. Different interventions are suggested if negative-reaction tendency is associated with social phobias or extreme shyness. In these cases, interventions might include relaxation training, role modeling, assertiveness training, contingency management, and systematic desensitization.

People with strong negative-reaction tendencies may respond well to individualized approaches to learning and tasks as opposed to the team or buddy systems recommended for people with high positive-reaction tendency. If group activities or team approaches are used, they should be with the same group of peers. Similarly, given their slow-to-warm stance, youngsters with a negative-reaction style may do better with a relatively stable set of teachers, therapists, and care providers. Further, people with this style may be less anxious if the flow of people through the classroom or work-site is kept to a minimum.

Outerdirectedness

Several general themes arise in considering treatment guidelines for people with maladaptive levels of outerdirectedness (see Table 11.2). One theme targets their turning to others for solutions to problems. Children in the classroom setting may be less outerdirected when they are first given easy-to-master tasks, followed by more challenging or novel tasks (Bybee & Zigler, 1992). Similarly, behavioral techniques such as successive approximation may work well as building blocks or steps toward increased independence. Other techniques might include rewarding people for independent problem-solving efforts and establishing clear expectations for when and how children can ask for help.

Individuals with high outerdirectedness, including those with Smith–Magenis syndrome, may be more apt than others to become overly dependent on supports such as teacher aides, job coaches, bus monitors, and others who are individually assigned to them via their IEPs or school-to-work transition plans. Dependencies may be curtailed by casting these support personnel as helpers for everyone, instead of as individual shadows for the target person.

Remaining themes pertain to possible clinical correlates of high outer-directedness. To the extent that this style also involves impulsivity or attention deficits, then multimodal approaches may be helpful that draw from pharmacology, behavioral modification, and managing environmental stimuli. Some of these approaches might include minimizing visual and auditory distractors at school or work; using time out, contingency management, and role playing; and setting consistent behavioral limits and expectations at home, school, or work. To the extent that outerdirectedness is associated with low self-esteem or feeling self-defeated, other interventions may prove helpful, as discussed next.

Expectancy of Success and Effectance Motivation

A variety of strategies are available to improve expectancy of success and effectance motivation, and most fall into two broad categories: reducing obstacles to success, and improving self-esteem, self-efficacy, and pleasure (see Table 11.2). Maladaptive behavior and psychopathology are now cast as major impediments to optimal success and adjustment in people with mental retardation. These problems impede adaptive functioning, and are the biggest culprits in causing people to need more restrictive levels of care (e.g., Borthwick-Duffy, 1994).

Fortunately, many maladaptive behaviors shown by people with mental retardation (e.g., tantrums, inattention, aggression) are amenable to modification through behavioral, pharmacological, or other interventions (see Bregman, 1991, for a review). To the extent that people can gain control over these behaviors, as well as replace them with more prosocial or adaptive behaviors, we would predict that these individuals will have the basic building blocks for good, solid expectations of success, and to derive some pleasure from problem-solving. To the extent that people are distressed or troubled by these behaviors, or have difficulty managing them, we would expect them to have low expectations for success in these and perhaps other areas as well.

Interventionists thus need to identify both environments or settings that impede expectations for success, as well as obstacles related to the maladaptive behaviors of the people they serve. On the environmental level, workers need to ensure that people with mental retardation live, learn, work, and play in settings that are conducive to mastery and success. On an individual level, interventions aimed at reducing problem behaviors vary widely. These include behavioral techniques (e.g., time out, contingency management), pharmacotherapy, avoiding a blameful stance, and aiming to manage instead of eliminate certain enduring, hard-to-treat behaviors, such as hyperphagia in Prader–Willi syndrome.

In addition to removing obstacles, interventions that actively promote feelings of mastery, success, and pleasure in people with mental retardation are needed. Some sense of success and mastery comes from gaining control over problem behaviors or areas, or solving difficult problems. Yet pleasure is also derived from things that have little to do with reducing negative factors, and more to do with promoting positive factors – hobbies, interests, fun, and pleasurable activities. Indeed, how people with mental retardation develop appropriate recreation and leisure options is now a popular area of research in the adaptive behavior and quality of life literature. On a more applied level, recreation and leisure goals are now key components of IEPs and adult transition plans.

Other, more intensive interventions are necessary if low expectations for success are symptomatic of a clinical picture involving significant sadness or depression, or full-blown affective disorders such as major depressive or dysthymic disorders. Here, treatment is likely to include a pharmacology evaluation, as well as cognitive-behavioral techniques.

Conclusion

This chapter addressed three salient issues related to personality and psychopathology in people with mental retardation. First, we hypothesized about possible ties between Zigler's personality constructs and maladaptive behavior or psychopathology. As we strive to better understand the interplay between these two fields, workers need to reassess to what extent social deprivation and failure remain causal factors of personality dysfunction in light of dramatic changes in the field today. Second, we proposed that genetic etiology is a particularly promising new avenue for future personality research. We presented behavioral data from several different syndromes (Williams, fragile X, Smith–Magenis, and Prader–Willi syndromes), each with a distinctive personality style that is remarkably reminiscent of the personality constructs that Zigler introduced over thirty years ago. Third, we offered several guidelines for interventions aimed at ameliorating personality dysfunction. In doing so, we expand Zigler's "whole person" personality concept to include the mental health and successful long-term adjustment of people with mental retardation.

References

American Psychiatric Association. (1994). *Diagnostic and statistical manual of mental disorders* (4th ed.). Washington, DC: American Psychiatric Association.

Balla, D., Styfco, S., & Zigler, E. (1971). Use of the opposition concept and outerdirectedness in intellectually average, familial retarded, and organically retarded children. *American Journal of Mental Deficiency, 75,* 863–880.

Bellugi, U., Wang, P., & Jernigan, T.L. (1994). Williams syndrome: An unusual neuropsychological profile. In S.H. Browman & J. Grafram (eds.), *Atypical cognitive deficits in developmental disorders* (pp. 23–56). Hillsdale, NJ: Erlbaum.

Bihrle, A.M., Bellugi, U., Delis, D., & Marks, S. (1989). Seeing either the forest or the trees: Dissociation in visuospatial processing. *Brain Cognition, 11,* 37–49.

Borthwick-Duffy, S.A. (1994). Epidemiology and prevalence of psychopathology in people with mental retardation. *Journal of Consulting and Clinical Psychology, 62,* 17–27.

Bregman, J.D. (1991). Current developments in the understanding of mental retardation. Part II: Psychopathology. *Journal of the American Academy of Child and Adolescent Psychiatry, 30,* 861–872.

Bregman, J.D., Leckman, J.F., & Ort, S.I. (1988). Fragile X syndrome: Genetic predisposition to psychopathology. *Journal of Autism and Developmental Disorders, 18,* 343–354.

Caskey, C.T., Pizzuti, A., Fu, Y.H., Fenwick, R.G., & Nelson, D.L. (1992). Triplet repeat mutations in human disease. *Science, 256,* 784–789.

Cohen, I.L., Vietze, P.M., Sudhalter, V., Jenkins, E.C., & Brown, W.T. (1989). Parent-child dyadic gaze patterns in fragile X males and in non-fragile X males with autistic disorder. *Journal of Child Psychology and Psychiatry, 30,* 845–856.

Dilts, C.V., Morris, C.A., & Leonard, C.O. (1990). Hypothesis for development of a behavioral phenotype in Williams syndrome. *American Journal of Medical Genetics, 36,* 126–131.

Dorn, M.B., Mazzocco, M.M., & Hagerman, R.J. (1994). Behavioral and psychiatric disorders in adult male carriers of fragile X. *Journal of the American Academy of Child and Adolescent Psychiatry, 33,* 256–264.

Dykens, E.M. (1995). Measuring behavioral phenotypes: Provocations from the "new genetics." *American Journal on Mental Retardation, 99,* 522–532.

(1996). DNA meets DSM: Genetic syndromes' growing importance in dual diagnosis. *Mental Retardation, 34,* 125–127.

Dykens, E.M., & Cassidy, S.B. (1995). Correlates of maladaptive behavior in children and adults with Prader–Willi syndrome. *American Journal of Medical Genetics (Neuropsychiatric Genetics), 60,* 546–549.

Dykens, E.M., & Hodapp, R.M. (1997). Treatment issues in genetic mental retardation syndromes. *Professional Psychology: Research and Practice, 28,* 263–270.

(in press). Behavioural phenotypes: Toward new understandings of people with developmental disabilities. In N. Bouras (ed.), *Psychiatric and behavioural disorders in developmental disabilities* (2nd ed.). Cambridge, England: Cambridge University Press.

Dykens, E.M., Hodapp, R.M., & Leckman, J.F. (1994). *Behavior and development in fragile X syndrome.* Thousand Oaks, CA: Sage.

Dykens, E.M., Hodapp, R.M., Walsh, K., & Nash, L.J. (1992). Profiles, correlates and trajectories of intelligence in Prader–Willi syndrome. *Journal of the American Academy of Child and Adolescent Psychiatry, 31,* 1125–1130.

Dykens, E.M., & Kasari, C. (in press). Maladaptive behavior in children with Prader–Willi syndrome, Down syndrome, and nonspecific mental retardation. *American Journal on Mental Retardation.*

Dykens, E.M., Leckman, J.F., & Cassidy, S.B. (1996). Obsessions and compulsions in Prader–Willi syndrome. *Journal of Child Psychology and Psychiatry, 37,* 995–1002.

Dykens, E.M., & Smith, A.C.M. (1997). *Distinction and correlates of maladaptive behavior in children and adolescents with Smith–Magenis syndrome.* Submitted for publication.

Dykens, E.M., & Volkmar, F.R. (1997). Medical conditions associated with autism. In D.J. Cohen & F.R. Volkmar (eds.), *Handbook of Autism and Pervasive Developmental Disorders* (2nd ed., pp. 388–406). New York: Wiley.

Einfeld, S.L., Tonge, B.J., & Florio, T. (1997). Behavioral and emotional disturbance in individuals with Williams syndrome. *American Journal on Mental Retardation, 102,* 45–53.

Ewart, A.K., Morris, C.A., Atkinson, D., Jin, W., Sternes, K., Spallone, P., Stock, A., Leppart, M., & Keating, M. (1993). Hemizygosity at the elastin locus in a developmental disorder, Williams syndrome. *Nature Genetics, 5,* 11–16.

Finucane, B.M., Konar, D., Haas-Givler, B., Kurtz, M.D., & Scott, C.I. (1994). The upper body spasmodic squeeze: A characteristic behavior in Smith–Magenis syndrome. *Developmental Medicine and Child Neurology, 36,* 78–83.

Fisch, G.S. (1992). Is autism associated with the fragile X syndrome? *American Journal of Medical Genetics, 43,* 47–55.

Freund, L., Reiss, A.L., Hagerman, R.J., & Vinogradov, S. (1992). Chromosome fragility and psychopathology in obligate female carriers of the fragile X chromosome. *Archives of General Psychiatry, 49,* 54–60.

Hodapp, R.M. (1997). Direct and indirect behavioral effects of different genetic disorders of mental retardation. *American Journal on Mental Retardation, 102,* 67–79.

Hodapp, R.M., & Dykens, E.M. (1994). Mental retardation's two cultures of behavioral research. *American Journal on Mental Retardation, 98,* 675–687.

Holm, V.A., Cassidy, S.B., Butler, M.G., Hanchet, J.M., Greenswag, L.R., Whitman, B.Y., & Greenberg, F. (1993). Prader–Willi syndrome: Consensus diagnostic criteria. *Pediatrics, 91,* 398–402.

Karmiloff-Smith, A., Grant, J., Berthoud, I., Davies, M., Howlin, P., & Udwin, O. (1997). Language and Williams syndrome: How intact is "intact"? *Child Development, 68,* 246–262.

Lachiewicz, A.M. (1992). Abnormal behavior of young girls with fragile X syndrome. *American Journal of Medical Genetics, 43,* 72–77.

Matson, J.L. (1985). Biosocial theory of pathology: A three factor model. *Applied Research in Mental Retardation, 6,* 199–227.

Matson, J.L., & Sevin, J.A. (1994). Theories of dual diagnosis in mental retardation. *Journal of Consulting and Clinical Psychology, 62,* 6–16.

Mazzocco, M.M., Hagerman, R.J., Cronister-Silverman, A., & Pennington, B.F. (1992). Specific frontal lobe deficits among women with the fragile X gene. *Journal of the American Academy of Child and Adolescent Psychiatry, 31,* 1141–1148.

Menolascino, F.J., & Fleischer, M.H. (1993). Mental health care in persons with mental retardation: Past, present, and future. In R. Fletcher & A. Dosen (eds.), *Mental health aspect of mental retardation* (pp. 18–44). New York: Lexington Books.

Nichols, R.D., Knoll, J.H., Butler, M.G., Karam, S., & Lalande, M. (1989). Genetic imprinting suggested by maternal heterodisomy in nondeletion Prader–Willi syndrome. *Nature, 16,* 281–284.

Opitz, J.M. (1996, March). *Historiography of the causal analysis of mental retardation.* Speech to the 29th annual Gatlinburg Conference on Research and Theory on Mental Retardation and Developmental Disabilities. Gatlinburg, TN.

Pober, B.R., & Dykens, E.M. (1996). Williams syndrome: An overview of medical, cognitive and behavioral features. *Child and Adolescent Psychiatric Clinics of North America, 5,* 929–944.

Reilly, J., Klima, E.S., & Bellugi, U. (1990). Once more with feeling: Affect and language in atypical populations. *Development and Psychopathology, 2,* 367–391.

Reiss, A.L., & Freund, L. (1990). Fragile X syndrome, DSM-III-R and autism. *Journal of the American Academy of Child and Adolescent Psychiatry, 29,* 885–891.

Reiss, A.L., Hagerman, R.J., Vinogradov, S., Abrams, M., & King, R.J. (1988). Psychiatric disability in female carriers of the fragile X chromosome. *Archives of General Psychiatry, 45,* 697–705.

Smith, A.C.M., Dykens, E.M., & Greenberg, F. (1997). *The behavioral phenotype of Smith–Magenis syndrome.* Submitted for publication.

Smith, A.C.M., McGavran, L., Robinson, J., Waldstein, G., Macfarlane, J., Zonona, J., Reiss, J., Kahr, M., Allen, L., & Magenis, E. (1986). Interstitial deletion of 17(p11.2,p11.2) in nine patients. *American Journal of Medical Genetics, 24,* 393–414.

Swaab, D.F., Purba, J.S., & Hofman, M.A. (1995). Alterations in the hypothalamic paraventricular nucleus and its oxytocin neurons (putative satiety cells) in Prader–Willi syndrome: A study of five cases. *Journal of Clinical Endocrinology and Metabolism, 80,* 573–579.

Udwin, O., & Yule, W. (1990). Expressive language of children with Williams syndrome. *American Journal of Medical Genetics, 6,* 108–114.

Williams, C.A., Zori, R.T., Hendrickson, J., Stalker, H., Marum, T., Whidden, E., & Driscoll, D.J. (1995). Angelman syndrome. *Current Problems in Pediatrics, 25,* 216-231.

Yando, R., & Zigler, E. (1971). Outerdirectedness in the problem-solving of institutionalized and non-institutionalized normal and retarded children. *Developmental Psychology, 4,* 277–288.

Zigler, E. (1971). The retarded child as a whole person. In H.E. Adams & W.K. Boardman (eds.), *Advances in experimental clinical psychology* (pp. 47–121). New York: Pergamon.

Zigler, E., & Burack, J.A. (1989). Personality development in the dually diagnosed individual. *Research in Developmental Disabilities, 10,* 225–240.

Index